A READER'S GUIDE *to* WRITERS' LONDON

For Catriona

For my mother and father

And for Peter and Hetty

A READER'S GUIDE *to* WRITERS' LONDON

Ian Cunningham

First published in 2001 by Prion Books Ltd.,
Imperial Works,
Perren Street, London NW5 3ED
www.prionbooks.com

ISBN-1-85375-425-0

Special Photography by Mark Turner
Jacket design by Bob Eames
Book design by Bookwork
Printed in China by Everbest Printing Company

CONTENTS

INTRODUCTION

Great was my joy with London at my feet –
All London mine, five shillings in my hand
And not expected back till after tea!
John Betjeman, *Summoned by Bells*

'London is illimitable,' wrote Ford Madox Ford in *The Soul of London*. He was speaking metaphorically, of course, but the sheer size and diversity of the city can be daunting for anyone who wants to write about it. For a start, how do you define London? Until the reign of Queen Victoria, the capital consisted of Westminster, as the seat of government, the City, as the centre of commerce, and not much else; outlying districts such as Clapham and Putney and Bow were villages where you went to escape London. Today, the term London is used to cover an amorphous mass of land which was never meant to be a coherent whole. Depending where you are, 'London' can mean the riverside tranquillity of Richmond, the self-conscious solemnity of Belgravia and Westminster, or the windswept open spaces of Wanstead and Blackheath. It was all very different two hundred years ago, when Thomas De Quincey could walk along Oxford Street and see open countryside less than a mile to the north. Dickens, who began his career in the 1830s, was perhaps the last writer truly to have the measure of London, before it grew too big and too complicated to take in. Yet even in his own lifetime, London was expanding at a prodigious rate, and it's worth remembering that many of his novels, such as *The Pickwick Papers*, *David Copperfield* and *Little Dorrit* are set not in their own time, but in the London of Dickens's childhood – a largely pre-industrial London which had already ceased to exist. Since Dickens's death, writers have tended to cultivate their own patch of London, rather than grapple with the metropolis as a whole. The ghost of John Betjeman is still a benign presence in Highgate; Patrick Hamilton's characters can still be seen any weekday lunchtime in the pubs of Fitzrovia and Earls Court; and, at the time of writing, Iain Sinclair reigns supreme in the East between Stoke Newington and the river.

Like most large cities, London treats both newcomers and long-term residents with supreme indifference. Like an aging, cynical courtesan, she is long past caring whether she makes a good impression. Instead, she relies on her writers to do the job for her. No-one who's read Trollope can enter Westminster Abbey without remembering Septimus Harding's lonely afternoon there in *The Warden*. If you're a fan of Graham Greene's *The End of the Affair* you'll never walk across Clapham Common again without thinking of Maurice and Sarah, separated by 'less than five hundred yards of flat grass'. And if your childhood reading included Dodie Smith's *The 101 Dalmations*, I would challenge you to walk around the Outer Circle on a summer evening without thinking of Pongo and Missis on their way to the Twilight Barking on Primrose Hill.

Selecting such scenes and matching them to the spot where they happened is only half of the remit of this guide. The other is to match their creators with the places where they themselves went for entertainment and inspiration. Many of these writers would be roused to fury if they knew some of their most private moments would be posthumously exposed to public gaze, though diarists such as Samuel Pepys, James Boswell and Joe Orton ultimately have only themselves to blame. Their Bacchanalian exploits around the metropolis – ranging from getting paralytically drunk on Coronation Day and waking to find himself 'wet with my spewing' (Pepys), to *al fresco* sex on Westminster Bridge (Boswell), to an erotic encounter on a number 19 bus (Orton) – enliven the pages of their journals and, hopefully, of this book. The task of compiling it has been made infinitely easier by the plethora of outstanding literary biographies which have appeared over the last decade and a half, of which Peter Ackroyd's lives of Blake, Dickens and TS Eliot, Andrew Motion's of Keats and Richard Holmes's of Coleridge are just a few examples. I hope these authors will not object to my cherry picking some of their juiciest anecdotes in the pages that follow.

Other acknowledgements are more personal. I am grateful to Fiona Hunter for invaluable library assistance; Nick Higgins and Chris Bell for a series of long-term loans from their own collection; Marc Werner for unstinting advice and practical help; all at Prion Books, especially Alex Kent and Andrew Goodfellow for their encouragement; and, above all, my wife Catriona for her patience during the year it has taken to research and write this book. On hearing that her daughter was about to marry a writer, my late mother-in-law, Hetty, expressed the hope that I might one day produce a blockbuster; I hope this guide to other people's literary achievements will serve as a step in the right direction.

Ian Cunningham
London

CHAPTER 1

CENTRAL LONDON

An American writer in London: Henry James (1843–1916) dominated the literary scene on both sides of the Atlantic for nearly 40 years.

MAYFAIR

For Henry James London was 'not agreeable, or cheerful, or easy, or exempt from reproach', but 'only magnificent... the complete compendium of the world'. Yet his first reaction to Mayfair and its main thoroughfare, Piccadilly, was not favourable. Newly arrived in the capital in the winter of 1869, the callow, homesick 26-year-old James surveyed the city from his drab lodgings at 7 Half Moon Street and found it 'hideous, vicious, cruel and, above all, overwhelming... It appeared to me that I would rather remain dinnerless than sally forth into the infernal town, where the natural fate of an obscure stranger was to be trampled to death in Piccadilly and have his carcass thrown into the Thames.'

He overcame his fears sufficiently to venture into one of the local chop houses, the Albany, opposite the famous bachelor chambers of the same name. There, diners faced each other on hard wooden benches packed so close together 'as fairly to threaten with knife and fork each others' more prominent features'. The scene reminded him of the paintings of Hogarth, the books of Boswell, Smollett and Dickens, and the old copies of *Punch* which he had devoured at home in New England. He knew he could write here.

Eight years later, in the winter of 1877, he returned to stay, moving into rooms at 3 Bolton Street with a sideways view – if he leaned far enough out of the window – of Green Park. It was at Bolton Street that James established the regular working habits that would serve him for the rest of his life. He would write assiduously during the morning and early afternoon, then take long walks in the rain, borrowing books from Mudie's library, and spending the evenings reading by the fire. His social life developed too, aided by the proximity of London's clubland (see St James's). The Athenaeum, in Pall Mall, was a particular godsend. He could walk there after a day spent grappling with *The Portait of a Lady* or *Washington Square*, enjoy a good, cheap dinner and cultivate friendships with like-minded spirits. 'I am getting quite into the current of London life,' he wrote

2

to his parents in Boston after just six weeks. That winter he would accept no fewer than 107 invitations to dine out.

James's arrival in London came at a time when Mayfair's social cachet was still on the rise. Its central position and plentiful shops had already made it a popular location for young authors about town – especially when the large town house called Albany was converted into bachelor chambers in 1802. Over the years its distinguished residents would include Lord Byron, 'Monk' Lewis, Aldous Huxley, Terence Rattigan, Patrick Hamilton and Graham Greene. Hatchard's, the famous bookshop on the other side of Piccadilly, opened here in 1801, deriving much of its custom from Albany and serving as an unofficial literary club. In the early 1890s – shortly before her husband's downfall – Oscar Wilde's wife, Constance, had a brief affair with the manager, Arthur Humphreys. The equally celebrated Heywood Hill book-shop on nearby Curzon Street is where Nancy Mitford worked during the Second World War.

T he Royal Institution, at the northern end of Albemarle Street, was founded in 1799 with the aim of 'diffusing the knowledge and facilitating the general introduction of useful mechanical inventions and improvements, and for teaching by courses of philosophical lectures and experiments the application of science to the common purposes of life'. In 1808 its director, Humphry Davy, persuaded his friend Samuel Taylor Coleridge to deliver a series of lectures on 'The Principles of Poetry' and, in particular, the definition of 'Taste' and the role of the imagination.

Coleridge's first lectures, in the dramatic setting of the Great Lecture Room, were not a success. Suffering from agonizing stomach pains and 'acrid scalding evacuations' – by-products of his addiction to laudanum – his early appearances at the lectern were, not surprisingly, lacklustre. One member of the audience was the Romantic Movement groupie Thomas De Quincey, whose own opium addiction lay only a few years in the future. He described Coleridge's appearance on the dais as 'generally that of a person struggling with pain and overmastering illness. His lips were baked with feverish heat, and often black in colour; and, in spite of

Originally built for the first Viscount Melbourne, Albany has been the ultimate writers' address for over 200 years.

*J*ohn Murray's drawing room, in 1815, showing John Murray II (second left), Sir Walter Scott (with walking stick) and Lord Byron (far right and inset).

Since 1812 the publishers John Murray have been based at 50 Albemarle Street, just off Piccadilly. Just before moving here John Murray II had published Byron's *Childe Harold* and their Fleet Street office was clogged with book-sellers' messengers demanding copies, which had to be handed out through the window.

In Albemarle Street, Murray's large first-floor drawing room became a meeting place for authors to exchange literary gossip. Byron was introduced to Walter Scott here in 1815. After Byron's death in 1824, Murray obtained the manuscript of his memoirs but, due to concern that they would damage Byron's reputation, they were burnt in the drawing room fireplace. Posterity has not thanked Murray for his action, though in the 1970s one of his descendants, John Murray VI, oversaw the publication of Byron's complete *Collected Letters and Journals.*

water which he continued drinking throughout the whole course of the lecture, he often seemed to labour under an almost paralytic inability to raise the upper jaw from the lower.' As the lecture season went on, however, Coleridge's health improved and, with it, the quality of his performances. By the end of the season he was abandoning his prepared text before he even started, and speaking brilliantly, and entirely off the cuff, for two hours.

As public performances, Coleridge's lectures would not be equalled until Dickens's mesmerizing readings from his novels half a century later. Coleridge's deaf, elderly landlady, however, made sure the public adulation didn't go to his head. When the famous artist John Landseer called to see him, she sent him away, explaining to Coleridge afterwards that it was only 'a sort of a Methody preacher at that Unstitution where you goes to spout, sir'.

Occupying a large portion of Albemarle Street is Brown's Hotel, which has accommodated numerous distinguished literary visitors since it opened in 1837. Rudyard Kipling had his wedding breakfast there in 1892, before setting off on a round-the-world honeymoon, and Agatha Christie used the hotel as her London base. Brown's appears, thinly disguised, in a late Miss Marple novel, *At Bertram's Hotel* (1965), whose elderly heroine finds the place an oasis of old-fashioned calm in the heart of Swinging London.

AA Milne used Brown's to host an annual party for his friends. Partially paralysed after a stroke, Milne held his final Brown's gathering in February 1954, travelling to and from Albemarle Street in an ambulance. It was his last public appearance, and he died early in 1956 at his home near the Ashdown Forest, where the *Winnie-the-Pooh* stories were set.

PG Wodehouse endowed Bertie Wooster with a fictional Mayfair address. Berkeley Mansions, in Berkeley Square, is a short walk away from Bertie's club, the Drones, which Richard Usborne, the leading authority on Wodehousiana, has tentatively located at 16 Dover Street. For Bertie, the Drones is a sort of throwback to public school, with no lessons, no masters but continuous games (usually involving fights with bread rolls) and a ready supply of like-minded chums, among them Oofy Prosser, Gussie Fink-Nottle, 'Stilton' Cheesewright and Bingo Little.

For a time, all the best literary detectives also lived in Mayfair. Dorothy L Sayers gave Lord Peter Wimsey a flat in 'a new, perfect and expensive block' at 110a Piccadilly (now the Park Lane Hotel), while Sapper's thuggish hero Bulldog Drummond resided in Half Moon Street. The Drummond stories enthralled the young Ian Fleming, who was born nearby at 27 Green Street in 1908, and he drew on them liberally when he created James Bond. Another ambiguous character is EW Hornung's gentleman jewel thief, Raffles, who lives in one of the bachelor apartments in Albany. The actor and writer David Niven had his first starring role playing Raffles in a 1940 film, and was Ian Fleming's first choice to play Bond. In his autobiography *The Moon's a Balloon*, Niven describes how as a 14-year-old he used to go to Piccadilly Circus to watch the neon signs. In the course of one such expedition, he was relieved of his virginity by an obliging courtesan in Cork Street.

Charles Dickens once had a disturbing experience in Cork Street. Walking along the street one morning in 1854, the novelist suddenly 'found an icy coolness come upon me, accompanied with a general stagnation of the blood, a numbness of the extremities, great bewilderment of mind, and a vague sensation of wonder'. Dickens remained mystified by the episode. With hindsight, however, it was probably a transient ischaemic attack, or mini-stroke – portent of the series of strokes which would kill him 16 years later.

Guests at the timeless Brown's Hotel have included Rudyard Kipling, Mark Twain, Agatha Christie and AA Milne.

Between the 1890s and the 1920s the Café Royal in Regent Street was a favourite meeting place of the *literati*. Oscar Wilde, Max Beerbohm, Walter Sickert and Augustus John were among the famous patrons who whiled away long hours among the distinctive marble tables and red velvet seats of the Domino Room. As a young woman, the future author of *National Velvet*, Enid Bagnold, was seduced under a table in one of the private rooms by one of Wilde's friends, the journalist Frank Harris. In John Wyndham's *The Day of the Triffids* the narrator, William Masen, helps himself to a free brandy at the Regent Palace Hotel, while a mob of blind men, led by a resourceful sighted leader, plunders the more upmarket Café Royal.

Wilde and his lover Lord Alfred Douglas were having lunch at the Café Royal one day in April 1895 when the Marquess of Queensberry appeared. Wilde invited him to join them at their table, and proceeded to entertain and charm him for the rest of the meal. 'I don't wonder you are so fond of him,' Queensberry told his son afterwards. 'He is a wonderful man.' It was only a momentary truce. Queensberry soon took to following Wilde around London and publicly insulting him in the hope of goading him into a reaction. On the morning of Thursday 28 April 1895, he succeeded. Waiting for Wilde at his club, the Albemarle at 13 Albemarle Street, was Queensberry's visiting card, with a scrawled, misspelt message: 'To Oscar Wilde, posing Somdomite.' Wilde wrote to a friend in desperation: 'Bosie's father has left a card at my club with hideous words on it. I don't see anything now but a criminal prosecution. My whole life seems ruined by this man.' Wilde probably had no choice but to sue for libel, but the subsequent trial was to destroy him. As for Queensberry, today he would probably be diagnosed as suffering from

Charles Dickens liked to meet his friends in Burlington Arcade, which links Cork Street and Piccadilly.

6

a personality disorder. Shortly after Wilde's libel action began, the Marquess got into a celebrated street brawl with his other son, Percy, outside Scott's the hatters in Bond Street, in which he gave his son a black eye. Both combatants were arrested and bound over to keep the peace.

On the same day that he was released from prison in 1897, Wilde sent a messenger with a letter to the headquarters of the English Jesuits, at the Church of the Immaculate Conception in Farm Street. In the letter, Wilde asked to be accepted as a penitent on a six-month religious retreat. A few hours later, the messenger returned with a reply. The priests had turned him down: Wilde would have to wait at least a year before he could even be considered. Wilde wept bitterly, though at heart he was probably relieved: at intervals throughout his life he flirted with Catholicism without ever quite bringing himself to embrace it.

Graham Greene and Evelyn Waugh were more committed converts. Both

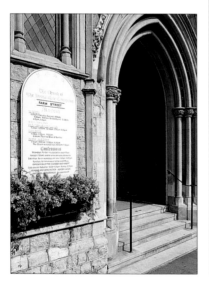

men regularly went to Farm Street for confession and mass. In Waugh's novel *A Handful of Dust* (1934), the Savile Club in Brook Street appears as the Greville, famed for its 'tradition of garrulity'. In *Vile Bodies* (1930) the Shepheard Hotel in Dover Street is based on the Cavendish in Jermyn Street, whose proprietor, Rosa Lewis, is caricatured as Lottie Crump. Rosa Lewis, a former kitchen maid, was furious, calling Waugh 'a little swine' and refusing to allow him in her hotel until 1945.

As for Greene, his 1936 short story 'The Jubilee' involves one Mr Chalfont, 'stony broke but unquestionably Mayfair', who lives in a bedsit in Shepherd Market. Visiting his club in Berkeley Square, he is engaged in conversation by an obviously wealthy woman whom he assumes he must have met somewhere before; in fact she is a prostitute. Greene's screenplay for the film *The Third Man* had nothing to do with London – it's set in post-war Vienna – but the inspiration for the story came to him, quite unexpectedly, while he was using the gents in Brick Street late one night in 1947.

Among his peers, Henry James was the most compassionate and thoughtful of men. However, an 1877 travel essay, 'London at Midsummer', reveals him at his insensitive worst. Discoursing on Green Park and the homeless men who could be seen sleeping there every day, James muses on 'the

The Café Royal in Regent Street. The Domino Room is described in Max Beerbohm's story 'Enoch Soames' : 'There, in that exuberant vista of gilding and crimson velvet set amidst all those opposing mirrors and upholding caryatids, with fumes of tobacco ever rising to the painted and pagan ceiling, with the hum of presumably cynical conversation broken into so sharply now and again by the clatter of dominoes shuffled on marble tables, I drew a deep breath, and "This indeed," said I to myself, "is life!"'

Committed converts to Catholicism Graham Greene and Evelyn Waugh both attended the Church of the Immaculate Conception in Farm Street.

*M*ichael Arlen's *novel* The Green Hat *(1924) starts in rooms above a seedy alley in Shepherd Market (above).*

*H*omeless men in *Green Park. This photograph first appeared in Jack London's* The People of the Abyss *in 1902.*

rough characters who are lying on their faces in the sheep-polluted grass'.

Their velveteen legs and their colossal high-lows, their purple necks and ear-tips, their knotted sticks and little greasy hats, make them look like stage-villains of realistic melodrama … It is their look of having walked over half England, and of being pennilessly hungry and thirsty, that constitutes their romantic attractiveness. The six square feet of brown grass are their present sufficiency; but how long will they sleep, whither will they go next, and whence did they come last?

Twenty-five years later, in the summer of 1902, Jack London answered James's questions. Joining the thousands of homeless men who thronged the West End at night, London found himself continually moved on every time

he attempted to sleep in one of the doorways along Piccadilly, until, at around four in the morning, the authorities opened the gates of Green Park:

It was raining again, but they were worn out with the night's walking, and they were down on the benches and asleep at once. Many of the men stretched out full length on the dripping wet grass, and, with the rain falling steadily upon them, were sleeping the sleep of exhaustion.

James was scathing about Piccadilly's southern extreme, apologizing on the behalf of all lovers of London 'for so bungled an attempt at a great public place as Hyde Park Corner… The place is the beating heart of the great West End, yet its main features are a shabby, stuccoed hospital, the low park-gates in their neat unimposing frame [and] the drawing room windows of Apsley House.' The 'shabby stuccoed hospital' was St George's Hospital, now converted

into the Lanesborough Hotel. As a student in the early 1980s, the novelist Nicholas Royle worked in the next-door building, Pizza on the Park, as a waiter, and discovered that from a window at the rear of the restaurant he could enter and explore the abandoned hospital. To date, St George's has featured in two of his novels. In *Counterparts* (1993) the tightrope walker Gargan breaks into the empty hospital using the same window, and performs a daring rope walk between it and Constitution Arch. In *The Matter of the Heart* (1997) London is portrayed as a massive circulation system, with a room in the Lanesborough Hotel, where 150 years earlier a surgeon has performed an experimental heart transplant, its psychic centre.

In the spring of 1909, the caricaturist Max Beerbohm had an encounter in Piccadilly which seemed to say something about the relationship between art and life. The young Beerbohm was hurrying to the Savile Club where he was looking forward to reading the latest Henry James story, 'The Velvet Glove', when he recognized the familiar portly figure of James himself coming towards him. In the conversation that followed, James invited Beerbohm to accompany him to an art exhibition, but Beerbohm pleaded a previous engagement.

Later, Beerbohm asked himself why he had instinctively lied.

It wasn't merely shyness and the fear that what I might have to say would sound cheap and tawdry to Henry James, that profoundly fastidious critic of men … It was mainly my impatience to be

reading 'The Velvet Glove'. And here I was now in the Savile reading it. It was, of course, a very good story, and yet, from time to time, I found my mind wandering away from it. It was not so characteristic, not so intensely Jamesian a story as James would have founded on the theme of what had just been happening between us, a theme of the disciple loyally, or unloyally, preferring the Master's work to the Master.

ST JAMES'S

The thin slice of land between the Mall and Piccadilly Circus is known above all for its timeless, exclusive gentlemen's clubs, most of them concealed behind anonymous, dignified façades in St James's Street and Pall Mall. Few, if any, deign to advertise their existence with a sign.

White's Club (37 St James's Street), is the oldest of them all, dating back over 250 years. In its early days it enjoyed a disreputable reputation: in *The Dunciad* (1728) Alexander Pope defined it as a place to 'teach oaths to youngsters and to nobles wit'. Swift, who at various times had lodgings in nearby Bury Street and Suffolk Street, took a violent dislike to White's and its members, shaking his fist at the building every time he passed it. White's was also infamous as a gambling den. According to Horace Walpole, a man once collapsed in the street outside and the members immediately started betting on his chances of survival.

Novelists, of course, have invented their own clubs as and

'*Going to White's*', from an 1823 illustration by SW Fores. Jonathan Swift considered the club '*the bane of the English nobility*'.

when it suited them. Dorothy L Sayers probably had several military establishments in mind when she wrote the early Lord Peter Wimsey mystery *The Unpleasantness at the Bellona Club* (the club would have been an easy walk from Lord Peter's elegant apartments at 110a Piccadilly). In the James Bond novels, 'M' is a member of Blades – an amalgam of White's and Boodle's (28 St James's Street). At the beginning of *You Only Live Twice* 'M' is to be found in Blades, 'sitting in the bow window looking out over St James's Street', smoking a pipe and worrying that 007 might be cracking up.

In the Graham Greene novel *It's a Battlefield* (1934) the Assistant Commissioner of Scotland Yard takes a leisurely walk along Pall Mall, unaware that he is being trailed by an assassin.

He could not help a momentary pride in London, the gentle gleam of autumn on the buildings, the gentle movement of Sunday in the streets, only one bus in sight, nobody hurrying.... The buildings seemed to him then to lose a little of their dignity;

the peace of Sunday in Pall Mall was like the peace which follows a massacre, a war of elimination; poverty here had been successfully contested, driven back on the one side towards Notting Hill, on the other towards Vauxhall.

Pall Mall boasts two more famous clubs, the Reform and the Athenaeum. Jules Verne's *Around the World in Eighty Days* (1872) begins with Phileas Fogg's famous wager in the drawing room of the Reform Club (104 Pall Mall), exactly 576 paces from Fogg's home in Savile Row. Patrick Hamilton's unpredictable father Bernard, who was known unaffectionately to his sons as the OD, or Old Devil, once cornered Arnold Bennett at the Reform Club and gave him a public ticking off for encouraging Patrick to pursue a career in literature. (In *Twenty Thousand Streets under the Sky*, Ella's stepfather's ability to slam doors open was derived from Bernard.) Surprisingly, perhaps, for the creator of one of the best-known fictional clubs, The Drones (see Mayfair), PG Wodehouse privately hated clubs and never went into them, though

The lobby of the Athenaeum in Pall Mall, likened by Rudyard Kipling to 'a cathedral between services'.

he belonged to at least half a dozen of them. 'I loathe clubs,' he told the writer Richard Usborne in 1956. 'The trouble is, it's so difficult to resign.'

Historically, the ultimate writers' club is probably the Athenaeum (107 Mall), founded in 1824 as a meeting place for London's intellectual élite. The Athenaeum was also the scene of a famous literary reconciliation. In 1858, a journalist named Edmund Yates published an article in which he criticized William Makepeace Thackeray. Thackeray, like Yates, was a member of the Garrick Club in Covent Garden and attempted to get the younger man blackballed. A third member, Charles Dickens, supported Yates, and Thackeray was left looking thoroughly foolish. For the next five years the two great novelists studiously avoided each other – until a chance meeting at the door of the Athenaeum. A witness, who was speaking to Thackeray, described how Dickens entered the club and passed Thackeray without speaking to him. But Thackeray ran after Dickens and caught up with him just as he was about to climb the main staircase. 'Dickens turned to him, and I saw Thackeray speak and presently hold out his hand to Dickens. They shook hands, a few words were exchanged, and immediately Thackeray returned to me, saying "I'm glad I have done this."'

Anthony Trollope was working on one of the monthly instalments of *The Last Chronicle of Barset* in the drawing room of the Athenaeum one day when two clergymen came in. Settling themselves on either side of the fire, they began a spirited discussion of Trollope's work, his inability to create new characters, and in particular the deficiencies of one of the characters in his latest serial, Mrs Proudie. Trollope was

unable to remain silent any longer. 'I got up, and standing between them, I acknowledged myself to be the culprit. "As to Mrs Proudie," I said, "I will go home and kill her before the week is over." And so I did.'

When Rudyard Kipling was invited to join in 1897, his first impression was of 'a cathedral between services', though he did grow to love its 'dear, dingy, old downstairs billiard-room'. However, the ultimate accolade came from Henry James. For him, the Athenaeum was nothing less than 'the last word of a high civilization'. A fellow member, Ezra Pound, recalled James's presence there: 'The massive head, the slow uplift of the hand… the long sentences piling themelves up in elaborate phrase after phrase, the lightning incision, the pauses…' No one paused like Henry James. A young actress, Ruth Draper, once asked him for advice. Should she concentrate on her stage career, or develop her talents as a writer? His reply, with its trademark stops and starts, was memorable: 'No, my dear child, you – you have woven – you have woven your own – you have

The famous wager in the Reform Club. David Niven (left) was perfectly cast as Phileas Fogg in the 1956 film of Jules Verne's Around the World in Eighty Days.

I an Fleming (1908–64), the creator of James Bond, in characteristic pose. He garnered much of his background information for the Bond books from his time working as a senior naval intelligence officer during the Second World War.

woven your own beautiful – beautiful little Persian carpet. Stand on it!'

On another occasion he offered her what was then a rare treat for a woman: a glimpse within the hallowed portals of the Athenaeum.

He asked me if I'd mind stopping at the Athenaeum to get a little money, and I shrank back in the back of the cab, having been told that I must never look at the outside of a gentleman's club. Presently he came out and said: 'My dear child, would you like to see the Athenaeum?' I was terrified and very shy and I said: 'Oh, Mr James, would I be allowed to go in?'

I was very much embarrassed. He said: 'Come with me,' so I believe I am one of the few women who has ever been in the inside of the Athenaeum Club. He took me all over the library and into the room where the beautiful books are, and showed me Thackeray's chair… It was a great thrill.

Of nearby St James's Palace, James was less complimentary – 'the queer, shabby old palace whose black, inelegant face stares up St James's Street' was his sniffy verdict in *English Hours*. Adjacent St James's Park reveals the Master at his most disdainful: 'There are few hours of the day when a thousand smutty children are not sprawling over it, and the unemployed lie thick on the grass and cover

the benches with a brotherhood of greasy corduroys.'

St James's has had a major role to play in the world of espionage – both real and fictional. During the Second World War, Graham Greene was working for MI6 in an office at 7 Ryder Street. One of his colleagues was Kim Philby, with whom Greene used to go drinking at lunchtime in the various pubs around St James's Street. It would be more than 30 years before Greene transmuted this material into fiction. In *The Human Factor* (1978), the veteran spy Maurice Castle has joined the Special Intelligence Service as a young wartime recruit and is still working there in the 1970s, lunching every day 'in a public house behind St James's Street, not far from the office'. In the same novel, Colonel Daintry, the head of security, lives in a small flat over a restaurant in St James's Street itself – as did Greene just after the war, when he and his mistress Catherine Walston had flats next door to each other, at numbers 5 and 6 respectively.

Some of Ian Fleming's wartime exploits around St James's tend to confirm Groucho Marx's dictum that 'military intelligence is a contradiction in terms'. On one occasion Fleming arranged for some captured German officers from the battleship *Bismarck* to be allowed a special day pass so that he could take them to the fashionable restaurant L'Ecu de France in Jermyn Street and encourage them to divulge naval secrets over the port. On the night, however, it was Fleming and his party who got drunk first and became dangerously expansive about operational matters of their own.

WESTMINSTER

Westminster has been a seat of political power since the reign of Edward the Confessor. As a lowly clerk in the Exchequer, Samuel Pepys began his diary at his 'garret' in Axe Yard, off Whitehall, where he lived with his French-born wife Elizabeth and their servant, Jane. Shortly afterwards, Pepys was given a far more lucrative position at the Navy Office and moved to Seething Lane near the Tower of London, but 23 April 1661 saw him back in Westminster, celebrating the coronation of Charles II in time-honoured fashion, by getting paralytically drunk:

To Axe Yard, in which, at the further end, there was three great bonfires and a great many great gallants, men and women; and they laid hold of us and would have us drink the King's health upon our knee, kneeling upon a faggot... I wondered to see how the ladies did tipple. At last I sent my wife and her bedfellow to bed, and Mr Hunt and I went in with Mr Thornbury (who did give the company all their wines, he being yeoman of the wine-cellar to the King) to his house; and there we drank the King's health and nothing else, till one of the gentlemen fell down stark drunk and lay there spewing ... No sooner in bed with Mr Sheply but my head began to turn and I to vomit, and if ever I was foxed it was now – which I cannot say yet, because I fell asleep and sleep till morning – only, when I waked I found myself wet with my spewing. Thus did the day end, with joy everywhere.

The original Houses of Parliament which were destroyed by fire in 1834.

The coronation of Charles II in 1661 was witnessed by Samuel Pepys, who had also seen the execution of his father, Charles I, 12 years earlier.

Built in 1097, Westminster Hall is the only surviving part of the original Palace of Westminster. After his first article was published in Monthly Magazine, *Dickens turned in here to pause for a moment, overcome by joy and pride.*

In 1666, shortly after the worst ravages of the plague had passed, Pepys was disturbed by a story from Mr Caesar, his manservant's lute-master, who told him how at the height of the plague 'bold people' were habitually visiting Westminster 'to go in sport to one another's funerals. And in spite to well people, would breathe in the faces (out of their windows) of well people going by.'

The following year, Pepys was among a large crowd in Westminster Hall, waiting to hear

Hall, crying "Repent! Repent!"' For centuries, the Hall acted as an indoor version of a Roman forum, housing various law courts as well as dozens of booksellers' stalls. In his preface to *The Pickwick Papers*, Dickens describes how on the day he saw his first article published in the *Monthly Magazine*, he 'walked down to Westminster Hall, and turned into it for half an hour, because my eyes were so dimmed with joy and pride, that they could not bear the street, and were not fit to be seen

there'. The hall is now the vestibule of the House of Commons.

Of the goings-on in the Houses of Parliament – 'the great pinnacled and fretted talking-house on the edge of the river' according to Henry James, 'the best club in London' according to Charles Dickens's Mr Twemlow – there have been relatively few literary chroniclers. Among the exceptions are Anthony Trollope's *Phineas Finn* and *The Prime Minister*, CP Snow's *Corridors of Power* and Michael Dobbs's *House of*

Charles II address Parliament, when he was startled by 'a man, a Quaker [who] came naked through the Hall, only very civilly tied about the privities to avoid scandal, and with a chafing-dish of fire and brimstone burning upon his head did pass through the

Cards. In William Morris's futuristic fantasy *News from Nowhere*, the Palace of West-minster is used as a dung market.

Since the early eighteenth century, 10 Downing Street has been the Prime Minister's official residence. Tobias Smollett practised (not very successfully) as a surgeon in Downing Street during the 1740s. Shortly after his arrival in London in November 1762, James Boswell found lodgings in a house opposite number 10 (since demolished), for the reasonable rent of 40 guineas a year (plus a shilling a go for dinner with the landlord and his family). Benjamin Disraeli had considerable success as a novelist (especially with his 1840s trilogy *Coningsby*, *Sybil* and *Tancred*) but he put his literary career on hold as his political career advanced him to high office; he was Prime Minister for ten months in 1868, and again from 1874–80. His last completed novel, *Endymion*, was published shortly after he left office and was based on the early part of his political career between the 1830s and 1850s. Mary Wilson, the wife of the Labour Prime Minister Harold Wilson, published *Selected Poems* in 1970. In 'The Parrot's Cry' she describes an official gathering in which the minor officials and hangers-on slaver like wolves. Writer MPs have included Geoffrey Chaucer, Sir Thomas More, Sir Walter Ralegh, Joseph Addison, John Buchan and Sir Winston Churchill, who published a single novel, *Savrola*, in 1900. Churchill is the only

resident of number 10 to have won the Nobel Prize for Literature, though in his case the award was mainly on the strength of his wartime speeches and for historical works such as his six-volume *The Second World War*. Among the more recent MPs-turned-novelists are Jeffrey Archer, Douglas Hurd, Rupert Allason (who writes espionage non-fiction under the name Nigel West) and Ann Widdecombe. The diaries of Richard Crossman, Barbara Castle and (most readable of the three) Tony Benn offer detailed, if contradictory, accounts of the Labour administrations of the 1960s and 1970s.

Downing Street was closed as a public thoroughfare in 1990, when Margaret Thatcher was in residence. Arguably the ultimate novel of the Thatcher years is Ian McEwan's *The Child in Time* (1987), set in a London of the near future in which beggars are licensed to operate under the terms of the 'leaner, fitter Charity Sector' but are strictly banned from Westminster, Whitehall and Parliament Square. The opening scene is an encounter with a girl beggar in Millbank, near Vauxhall Bridge. In the course of the novel McEwan achieves the technically difficult feat of including the Prime Minister among the characters without once disclosing his/her name or sex.

Benjamin Disraeli (1804–81), who forsook literature for a career in politics. His first novel, Vivian Gray, *was written to pay off debts.*

The Prime Minister's official residence, 10 Downing Street, pictured when it was still a public thoroughfare. Sir Winston Churchill is the only resident of Downing Street to have won the Nobel Prize for Literature.

When Westminster Bridge was opened in 1750, local bylaws stipulated that anyone found defacing the parapet would be sentenced to death without benefit of clergy. There were no laws against fornicating on it, however, and on 9 May 1763, James Boswell took advantage of the dim lighting and irregular police patrols:

At the bottom of the Haymarket I picked up a strong, jolly young damsel, and taking her under the arm I conducted her to Westminster Bridge, and then in armour complete [i.e. he wore a condom] did I engage her upon this noble edifice. The whim of doing it there with the Thames rolling below us amused me much.

On arriving home at his Downing Street lodgings, he discovered he was locked out.

Wordsworth's 'Lines Composed

upon Westminster Bridge' (1802) give a snapshot of central London in the days when it was still surrounded by countryside and untouched by the air pollution which would envelop the city in his own lifetime:

Earth has not anything to show more fair:
Dull would he be of soul who could pass by
A sight so touching in its majesty:
The City now doth, like a garment, wear
The beauty of the morning: silent, bare,
Ships, towers, domes, theatres, and temples lie
Open unto the fields, and to the sky,
All bright and glittering in the smokeless air.

Since it was consecrated in 1065, Westminster Abbey has been the scene of the coronation, and often the burial, of kings and queens. In his 'Ode on the Abbey Tombs', Francis Beaumont found this a source of irony:

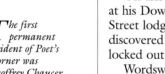

Mortality, behold and fear
What a change of flesh is here!
Think how many royal bones
Sleep within this heap of stones.

Beaumont was himself buried in Poets' Corner, near the south transept, in 1616, joining Geoffrey Chaucer (died 1400) and Edmund Spenser (died 1599), who had both lived in cottages in the grounds. Ben Jonson, who spent his last years in poverty in the Abbey precincts, was promised a grave by the Dean. The playwright replied: 'Six foot long by two foot wide is too much for me; two feet by two feet will do for all I want.' He was buried standing up. Over the next three and a half centuries, Poets' Corner was gradually filled with memorials – including those of Johnson, Dickens, Browning and Tennyson. In an article in the *Spectator* in 1711, Joseph Addison described going to the Abbey one day and watching a grave-digger at work.

I saw in every shovel-full of it that was thrown up, the fragment of a bone or skull intermixed with a kind of fresh mouldering earth that some time or other had a place in the composition of a human body ... When I look upon the tombs of the great, every motion of envy dies in me; when I read the epitaphs of the beautiful, every inordinate desire goes out; when I meet with the grief of parents upon a tombstone, my heart melts with compassion; when I see the tomb of the parents themselves, I consider the vanity of grieving for those whom we must quickly follow.

From 1370 until 1776, the Gatehouse Prison stood in Broad Sanctuary, which is now an open space between Westminster Abbey and the Middlesex Guildhall. The Abbey janitor traditionally acted as jailer, for which he received a loaf of bread and a flagon of ale every day and a new robe once a year. In October 1618 Sir Walter Ralegh

was held here on the night before his execution at the Tower of London. The poet Richard Lovelace was jailed at the Gatehouse in 1642 for supporting Charles I and wrote his famous poem 'To Althea': 'Stone walls do not a prison make, / Nor iron bars a cage.'

Samuel Pepys spent a short time there in 1679, after trumped-up charges of spying were laid against him.

Thomas Hardy's funeral arrangements in 1928 were unusually complicated: his heart was removed shortly after his death and temporarily stored in a biscuit tin before being buried near Dorchester. The rest of him

When I am in serious humour, I very often walk by myself in Westminster-abbey ... When I read the several dates of the tombs ... I consider that great day when we shall all of us be contemporaries and make our appearance together.' Joseph Addison, The Spectator, 1711.

was buried in Westminster Abbey, but for decades rumours circulated that the biscuit tin had been left uncovered on the Hardy kitchen table and that the cat had eaten it. Indignant denials by one of his former servants diminished the rumours, but failed to extinguish them completely.

Several distinguished writers who might reasonably have expected a place in Poets' Corner had their posthumous applications vetoed by deans who objected to their unchristian personal lives. Robert Burns (died 1796) was refused entry until 1885; as was DH Lawrence (died 1930; admitted 1985) and Oscar Wilde (died 1900; admitted 1995). Dylan Thomas, who died in 1953, was given his place in Poet's Corner in 1982, after the former US President Jimmy Carter expressed surprise that there was no mention of him in the Abbey.

William Blake too was refused a place, though a memorial to him was installed on the bicentenary of his death in 1957. In fact, Blake loved the Abbey – his mastery of colour may owe something to its stained-glass windows and colourful mosaics. As a 17-year-old apprentice engraver, he was sent to draw some of the royal tombs in the presbytery and in the chapel of Edward the Confessor. While he was working from a scaffold one day, some boys from nearby Westminster School started making fun of him. One boy climbed on to the scaffold to continue the jeering at close range – an unwise move, given Blake's legendary temper. His response was to knock the boy off the scaffold, sending him crashing to the ground. Shortly afterwards, in May 1774, Blake was present when the body of Edward I was exhumed so that antiquarian scholars could view the body. According to one of these witnesses, the King's face 'was of a dark-brown, or chocolate colour, approaching to black; and so were the hands and fingers. The chin and lips were intire, but without any beard.' During the hour-long exhumation, Blake completed two sketches which he later worked up into more finished drawings, 'The body of Edward ye 1st as it appeared on first opening the Coffin' and 'The body as it appeared when some of the vestments were remov'd'.

William Caxton, Nicholas Udall and Sir Walter Ralegh are all buried at St Margaret's, the official parish church of the House of Commons.

One of the finest scenes in literature to take place in the Abbey is in Anthony Trollope's first 'Barchester' novel *The Warden*. The conscientious Reverend Septimus Harding is the subject of malicious gossip suggesting that he is receiving an over-generous salary for his role as warden of a Barchester almhouse. Against the advice of his bishop and of his family, Harding travels to London to resign his position, knowing that doing so will reduce him to near penury. In the chapter 'A Long Day in London', he whiles away many hours in the Abbey, walking up and down the nave and aisles as he considers the step he is about to make, and ignoring the 'reverential stares' of the vergers.

In Our Mutual Friend, *Dickens memorably described St John's Church in Smith Square as 'a very hideous church with four towers at the corners, generally resembling some petrified monster, frightful and gigantic, on its back with its legs in the air'.*

The church was badly bombed in the Second World War, and is now a public hall.

Once likened to 'a promising child standing next to an indulgent parent' (*Time Out London Guide*), St Margaret's Church is a similar shape to Westminster Abbey, but far smaller. Samuel Pepys, John Milton and Sir Winston Churchill were all married here. One of the rectors (1876–95) was Frederick Farrar, author of the school story *Eric, or Little by Little*, which the young Eric Blair loathed so heartily that he later adopted the pseudonym George Orwell. Westminster School in Little Dean's Yard dates from medieval times. Among its headmasters was Nicholas Udall, who wrote the first known stage comedy in English, the crude but energetic *Ralph Roister Doister* (1522). Udall had earlier been removed from Eton for his paedophile activities. He was also an enthusiastic flogger; one victim, Thomas Tusser, later complaining of having been beaten by Udall 'for fault but small, or none at all'. Other Westminster old boys have included Ben Jonson, John Dryden, Robert Southey (expelled in 1792 for producing a satirical school magazine, *The Flagellant*), Patrick Hamilton and Angus Wilson. During his last year, in 1931, Wilson played Miss Prism in a school production of Wilde's *The Importance of Being Earnest*. The performance was attended by Lord Alfred Douglas, and

Vincent Square has changed little since Somerset Maugham lodged here in the 1890s, while studying to become a surgeon. By the 1910s, at the height of his fame as a West End playwright, he was living in luxurious Mayfair at Number 6, Chesterfield Street.

door) in his espionage satire *Our Man in Havana*.

Petty France, at the top of Broadway, is named after the French wool merchants who used to live there. In 1652 John Milton moved into a pleasant house with a garden backing on to St James's Park. Despite being totally blind, he worked as one of Oliver Cromwell's ministers and wrote most of *Paradise Lost* here, but in 1660 the monarchy was restored and Milton was forced to go into hiding. The house was later owned by Jeremy Bentham, who rented it out to William Hazlitt. The house was demolished in 1877. John Cleland died in a house in Petty France in 1789. The author of the erotic classic *Fanny Hill* had been receiving a pension from the Privy Council 'on his engaging to write nothing more of the same description'.

As a medical student at St Thomas's Hospital, Somerset Maugham lived in a flat at 11 Vincent Square, overlooking the centre of the square with its cricket grounds (used by boys from Westminster School). In the evenings, when his work at the hospital was over for the day, he worked on his first novel, *Liza of Lambeth*. In 1964, three other young writers – the novelists Derek Marlowe and Piers Paul Read, and the playwright Tom Stoppard – shared a second-floor flat at 10 Vincent Square Mansions, on the west side of the square.

emboldened by some after-performance drinks, Wilson asked the ageing 'Bosie' if he thought Wilde would have preferred Shakespeare's plays when the women's roles were played by boys. Douglas changed the subject to horseracing.

During the Second World War, the head of the Special Intelligence Service, Sir Stewart Menzies ('C'), had his office on the fourth floor of 54 Broadway. This inner sanctum was guarded by a well-spoken, middle-aged secretary named Kathleen Pettigrew. Ian Fleming, then a naval intelligence officer, later recreated 'C' as 'M' and Kathleen Pettigrew as Miss Moneypenny. Graham Greene, who also served in wartime intelligence, used C's office (complete with light which turns from red to green outside the

BLOOMSBURY

Of all the areas in London, Bloomsbury has the strongest claim to be the city's intellectual heart. Two of its most august institutions – the British Museum and the University of London – are to be found there. In addition, Bloomsbury gave its name to the most celebrated group of British writers and artists of the early years of the twentieth century. Although Bloomsbury's popularity among writers as a place to live and work waned after the Second World War, for over two centuries practically every author who was anybody seemed to put in some time there.

Bloomsbury's big, leafy squares help to explain its early popularity. In Jane Austen's *Emma*, the heroine's vapid sister Isabella offers an unsolicited testimonial to one of them. 'Our part of London is so very superior to most others!' she informs a not particularly interested family gathering. 'The neighbourhood of Brunswick Square is very different from almost all the rest. We are so very airy! I should be unwilling, I own, to live in any other part of the town; there is hardly any other that I could be satisfied to have my children in: but we are so remarkably airy!'

Queen Square, off Southampton Row, was airier still. When the novelist and playwright Fanny Burney was living there with her father, the musicologist Dr Charles Burney, in the 1770s, the north side of the square still had an unbroken vista of the hills of Hampstead and Highgate. On the eastern side of the square was an exclusive girls' school, whose pupils – among them James Boswell's daughter Veronica – had

their own gallery in the church of St George the Martyr. The girls invariably travelled to church by coach, despite the fact that it was only a few yards away, so they could practise getting in and out in the correct manner.

The Queen's Larder pub takes its unusual name from a poignant episode in history. When George III was being treated for mental illness at the home of Dr Willis, who lived in the square, Queen Charlotte arranged to have some

The classical façade of the British Museum. When it opened in 1759, entry was by appointment only.

The University of London Senate House housed the Ministry of Information during the Second World War and was Orwell's model for the Ministry of Truth in Nineteen Eighty-Four.

The nineteenth-century politician Charles James Fox sitting, as Louis MacNeice described him, 'on his arse in Bloomsbury Square'.

The portico of the eighteenth-century church of St George the Martyr in Queen Square, which James Boswell's daughter Veronica attended.

of his favourite food stored in the pub's cellar. (In the 1980s, the king's travails were the subject of Alan Bennett's play *The Madness of George III.*) At the end of the nineteenth century, Robert Louis Stevenson – another chronic invalid, who did much of his writing in his sick bed – also praised the atmosphere of Queen Square, considering it to have been set aside for 'the humanities of life and the alleviation of all hard destinies'. Queen Square is still associated with healing. The National Hospital for Neurology and Neurosurgery is in the square, and the Royal London Homoeopathic Hospital and Great Ormond Street Hospital for Sick Children are close by.

In the late seventeenth century, Bloomsbury Square was so determinedly fashionable that visiting royalty were taken to view it during state visits. Surveying the scene on an autumn day in 1962, the Ulster poet Louis MacNeice found the square faintly depressing and its statue of a nineteenth-century politician in Roman garb unimpressive:

> Charles James Fox
> unconcerned in a bath
>   towel sits
> on his arse in Bloomsbury
> Square
> While plane tree leaves flop
> gently down and lodge in
>   his sculptured hair.
>   October in Bloomsbury

William Makepeace Thackeray moved to Coram Street in 1837 and much of his sprawling novel *Vanity Fair* takes place in Bloomsbury. The Sedleys live in Russell Square, and their name may be a subconscious echo of the seventeenth-century dramatist Sir Charles Sedley, who also lived in Bloomsbury Square around 1690. The novel was particularly admired by another novelist, Charlotte Brontë, who dedicated *Jane Eyre* to Thackeray in 1849. Thackeray was touched but also embarrassed

22

by the gesture, as *Jane Eyre* contained an unsettling echo of his own life. Brontë had never met Thackeray and could not know that his wife Isabella had had a nervous breakdown shortly after the birth of their daughter, Harriet, and was living in a mental hospital. Harriet became the first wife of Leslie Stephen, the editor of the *Dictionary of National Biography*. One of his daughters by his second marriage was Virginia Woolf.

Coram Street plays a part in one of Dickens's novels: in *Little Dorrit* (1855), Mr Meagles's wayward adopted daughter Tattycoram is a former 'Foundling' – one of the children taken in by the Foundling Hospital in nearby Guilford Street, founded by the philanthropist Thomas Coram as a refuge for abandoned women and their children. Dickens is rightly criticized for his unconvincing female characters, but his portrait of Tattycoram – part affectionate towards her adopted family, part resentful that she can never be quite one of them – is an acute one. So too is his portrayal of her patient and loving adopted father, whose exhortation to her to calm down – 'Count five and twenty, Tattycoram' – echoes through the novel. Although all but the front entrance of the hospital has disappeared, part of the grounds, in Coram Fields, are still used as a children's playground. (Note: Adults are not admitted unless accompanied by a child.) In Graham Greene's *The Ministry of Fear* (1943) Arthur Rowe's house in Guilford Street receives a direct hit during an air raid, leaving him lying dazed in the wreckage and idly watching the incendiary bombs 'sailing slowly, beautifully down, clusters of spangles off a Christmas tree'.

Dickens liked Bloomsbury enough to live there twice: first at 48 Doughty Street, where he lived from March 1837 until the end of 1839, then (following an interlude at 1 Devonshire Terrace, Regent's Park) in Tavistock Square, between 1851 and 1860.

Dickens arrived at Doughty Street just as he was starting to become famous through the monthly serialization of *The Pickwick Papers*. While he was there he wrote the final chapters of *Pickwick*, the whole of *Oliver Twist* and most of *Nicholas Nickleby*. (In *Oliver Twist*, Fagin's den is in Field Lane, only a few

Children playing in Coram Fields in 1947. The grounds used to be part of the Foundling Hospital which appears in Little Dorrit.

Mary Hogarth, depicted shortly before her death at the age of 17.

minutes' walk from Doughty Street.) It was by far the largest house Dickens had lived in – until then, he and his family had had to squeeze in to Dickens's bachelor chambers at Furnival's Inn, Holborn. The 25-year-old author was clearly rather overwhelmed by his new domain, describing his luxurious new quarters to a friend as a 'frightfully first class family mansion, involving awful responsibilities'. Chief among these responsibilities was the sheer size of Dickens's household, which now comprised not only his wife Kate and son Charley, but Kate's 17-year-old sister, Mary Hogarth, Dickens's brother Frederick, and four servants. Always a dominant character, Dickens personally supervised the household accounts and held frequent parties, where he would sing comic songs and

imitate the famous actors and writers of his day (throughout his life he was an inveterate, and occasionally cruel, mimic). One visitor, his brother-in-law Henry Burnett, recorded a rare sight: Dickens writing in public.

One night in Doughty Street, Mrs Charles Dickens, my wife and myself were sitting round the fire, cosily enjoying a chat, when Dickens, for some purpose, came suddenly from his study into the room. 'What, you here!' he exclaimed; 'I'll bring down my work.' It was his monthly portion of Oliver Twist *for* Bentley's. *In a few minutes he returned, manuscript in hand.*

Dickens retired to a table in the corner of the room, telling his guests to carry on talking among themselves, while he himself

every now and then (the feather of his pen still moving rapidly from side to side) put in a cheerful interlude. It was interesting to watch, upon the sly, the mind and the muscles working (or, if you please, playing) in company, as new thoughts were being dropped upon the paper. And to note the working

Dickens's drawing room at 48 Doughty Street.

brow, the set mouth, with the tongue slightly pressed against the closed lips, as was his habit.

The domestic idyll was short-lived. On 7 May 1837, less than two months after they had moved in, Mary Hogarth, collapsed and died in her bedroom, from undiagnosed heart failure. Her sudden death plunged Dickens into a depth of grief that, in the words of his biographer Peter Ackroyd, 'amounted almost to hysteria'. He cut off a lock of Mary's hair and kept it in a special case; he removed one of her rings and wore it himself; he kept all her clothes and occasionally took them out to look at them, and told friends he wanted to be buried in her grave. As Ackroyd drily observes, 'To keep the clothes of a seventeen-year-old girl, and to desire to be buried with her, are, even in the context of early nineteenth-century enthusiasm, unusual sentiments.'

Over the years, Mary Hogarth would appear, in various guises, in Dickens's novels; the most complete portrait is probably Agnes, in *David Copperfield*. The Dickenses had two more children in Doughty Street, but their arrival only made Charles's depression worse: at one point he complained to a friend that the house was 'nothing but a hospital ward'. The family finally moved out at the end of 1839 and moved to 1 Devonshire Terrace, in Marylebone Road.

By the time Dickens returned to Bloomsbury in 1851 he was in his late thirties and about to embark upon the dark London novels of the 1850s, *Bleak House* and *Little*

Stanislawa de Karlowska's 'Russell Square from Montague Street', painted around 1934, shows off the leafy, 'airy' nature of Bloomsbury.

Dorrit. His view of the city was more jaundiced now. 'London is a vile place, I sincerely believe,' he wrote to Edward Bulwer-Lytton. 'Whenever I come back from the country now, to see that great heavy canopy lowering over the housetops, I wonder what on earth I do here, except on obligation.' The 'great heavy canopy' was choking, sulphurous fog, a by-product of the Industrial Revolution, which he evoked in one of the most vivid passages he ever wrote – the opening of *Bleak House*:

Fog everywhere. Fog up the

Charles Dickens seated at his writing desk in 1860.

boy on deck. Chance people on the bridges peeping over the parapets into the nether sky of fog, with fog all round them, as if they were in a balloon, and hanging in the misty clouds.

One house guest at Dickens's new home, Tavistock House in Tavistock Square, was Hans Christian Andersen, who noticed the fog from his bedroom window, overlooking the garden: 'Over the tree-tops I saw the London towers and spires appear and disappear as the weather cleared or threatened.'

Dickens started *Bleak House* shortly after moving in to Tavistock House. (The building was on the present site of the British Medical Association headquarters, BMA House.) But he found his work constantly interrupted: by strangers bearing letters of introduction; by street musicians, for whom Dickens had a long-standing aversion (he later campaigned for government legislation against street bands and organ grinders); by a neighbour's dogs, which barked continuously and which he had to be dissuaded from silencing with the aid of a shotgun; and, on one occasion, by a baker's roundsman whom he caught one morning urinating against his front gates. Dickens, who seems to have had a lifelong habit of getting involved in heated arguments in the street (he once performed a citizen's arrest on a man for swearing in public) threatened to have the baker arrested. When the man demanded to know what Dickens would have done in the same circumstances, the novelist was, for once, lost for words.

Dickens, however, used the garden of Tavistock House to

river, where it flows among green aits and meadows; fog down the river, where it rolls defiled among the tiers of shipping, and the waterside pollutions of a great (and dirty) city. Fog on the Essex marshes, fog on the Kentish heights. Fog creeping into the cabooses of collier-brigs; fog lying out on the yards, and hovering in the rigging of great ships; fog drooping on the gunwales of barges and small boats. Fog in the eyes and throats of ancient Greenwich pensioners, wheezing by the firesides of their wards; fog in the stem and bowl of the afternoon pipe of the wrathful skipper, down in his close cabin; fog cruelly pinching the toes and fingers of his shivering little 'prentice

indulge in one of his greatest pleasures: amateur dramatics. He built a tiny theatre at the back of the house, where he and his friend Wilkie Collins performed plays they had written. Other roles went to members of the Dickens family. Dickens's eldest son Charley, now in his teens, later recalled the disturbing passion with which his father played the lead role in Collins's play *The Frozen Deep*:

In the last act he had to rush off the stage, and I and three or four others had to try and stop him. He gave us fair notice, early in the rehearsals, that he meant fighting in earnest in that particular scene, and we very soon found out that the warning was not an idle one. He went at it after a while with such a will that we really did have to fight, like prize-fighters, and as for me, being the leader of the attacking party and bearing the first brunt of the fray, I was tossed in all directions and had been black and blue two or three times before the first night of the performance arrived.

The ferocity of his acting may have had something to do with the state of his marriage, which was beginning to disintegrate. Dickens and his wife Catherine had been together since their early twenties, but Catherine's quiet temperament, tendency to depression and (in Dickens' term) 'lassitude' had over the years made him an increasingly intolerant husband. A few months after acting in *The Frozen Deep* he had part of their bedroom walled up, sleeping from then on in 'his' portion of the room. Shortly afterwards, Dickens got up at two

in the morning and walked 30 miles to Gad's Hill Place, the house near Chatham which he was in the process of buying. In the event, only Charles lived there. When the couple formally separated, Catherine was, in effect, banished to a house in Camden Town.

Dickens's anger was aimed not only at Catherine, but at her family too. When he discovered that her mother had been spreading rumours that he had been having an affair, he ordered his children never to see, or speak to, their grandmother again. In her old age, his eldest daughter Kate recalled how she and her sisters used to avoid their mother so as not to incur Dickens's wrath. She told an interviewer 'My father was a wicked man, a very wicked man.'

A painting by Augustus Egg of Dickens as Captain Coldstream in an amateur dramatics production of Used Up *by Dion Boucicault in the early 1850s. His love of acting was such that he attempted to join a company in Covent Garden, but, on the day of the audition, a bad cold and inflammation of the face saved him from 'another kind of life'.*

When the writer and editor Leslie Stephen died in 1904 he left behind four children – Vanessa, Virginia, Thoby and Adrian – all of them in their twenties. With both their parents now dead, the Stephen children decided to begin a new life on their own, by selling the family home in Kensington and buying a larger house, 46 Gordon Square, in unfashionable Bloomsbury. Unlike most of their contemporaries, who were still answerable to their parents, the Stephenses were free to entertain whoever they liked in their new home. Naturally, their inclination was to mix with young intellectuals like themselves – among them the economist John Maynard Keynes, the essayist and biographer Lytton Strachey, the artist Roger Fry and the novelists David Garnett and Leonard Woolf. From this nucleus, the Bloomsbury Group was born.

The group was always a fluid assortment, partly because of the frequent changes of address by the Stephen family. For a time the group had two centres. When Vanessa Stephen married the art critic Clive Bell in 1907, her two surviving siblings, Virginia and Adrian, moved to 29 Fitzroy Square (previously occupied by Bernard Shaw), while Vanessa and Clive remained in Gordon Square. (The fourth brother, Thoby, had died the previous year, from typhoid fever contracted on a family holiday in the eastern Mediterranean.)

As Virginia described in a letter, she was talking to Vanessa one spring evening at 46 Gordon Square when Lytton Strachey entered the room. He pointed at a stain on Vanessa's white dress. 'Semen?' he said.

> *Can one really say it? I thought & we burst out laughing. With that one word all barriers of reticence and reserve went down. A flood of the sacred fluid seemed to overwhelm us. Sex permeated our conversation. The word bugger was never far from our lips. We discussed copulation with the same excitement and openness that we had discussed the nature of good. It is strange to think how reticent, how reserved we had been, and for how long.*

Vanessa's son Quentin Bell would later identify this as a signal moment, not only for the Bloomsbury Group, but for a whole generation. After a century

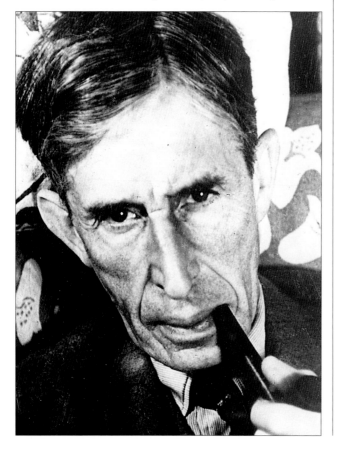

Publisher and novelist Leonard Woolf (1880–1969) was one of the original members of the Bloomsbury Group.

or more of self-imposed repression, the middle-class intelligentsia had discovered sex – or at least the desire to talk about it.

When Virginia and Adrian began to get on each other's nerves at Fitzroy Square, they decided to move to a bigger house and share it with some friends. At 38 Brunswick Square, Maynard Keynes had the ground floor, Adrian the first, Virginia the second and Leonard Woolf the third. Domestic expenses were shared, but the idea was for the four 'Inmates', as they called themselves, to lead separate lives. That was the theory, anyway; but soon Virginia and Leonard had developed their own programme of writing 500 words in the morning, then having lunch together or sitting talking in Bloomsbury Square. Virginia's decision to marry Woolf in 1912 would be described by her nephew Quentin Bell as 'the wisest decision of her life'.

Shortly after their marriage, Virginia Woolf had a nervous breakdown – the first of the bouts of mental illness which would dog her for the rest of her life. These bouts were characterized by acute anxiety, suicidal depression alternating with a state of near mania, and, worst of all, hallucinations – the 'horrible voices' which had first manifested themselves during her first breakdown at the age of 13 (see Kensington) and which eventually drove her to suicide at 59. The inner monologue of Septimus Warren Smith, the shell-shocked soldier in Woolf's 1925 novel *Mrs Dalloway*, came directly from her own experience. In the novel, Septimus hears the birds singing in Ancient Greek as he walks in Regent's Park – just as had Woolf while experiencing a breakdown. Septimus eventually jumps to his death from an upstairs window, as had Woolf on her first attempt to take her own life.

When the Woolfs sold their Richmond home, Hogarth House, in 1924 and moved to 52 Tavistock Square, their publishing business, the Hogarth Press moved with them. In a BBC interview after her death, a friend, Ralph Partridge, recalled her at work in the mid-1920s:

Sometimes in the summer, when I was working in the printing room, she'd wander in and set up type or distribute it with her quick, sensitive fingers, looking like a dishevelled angel – her bare feet shuffling about in bedroom slippers, in a nightdress with a great tear down the side, and a dressing gown vaguely thrown over it, but her mind far, far away from her mechanical task.

Quentin Bell likened Woolf to 'some fantastic bird, abruptly throwing up her head and crowing with delighted amusement at some idea, some word, some paradox,

Virginia Woolf was a story-teller from her childhood and wrote prolifically throughout her life. Along with James Joyce, she is regarded as one of the great innovators of the modern novel.

that took her fancy. Her conversation was full of surprises, of unpredictable questions, of fantasy and laughter – the happy laughter of a child who finds the world more strange, more absurd and more beautiful than anyone could have imagined possible; laughter seemed in those years to be her natural element.'

By encouraging her writing and involving her in his publishing business, Leonard Woolf managed to maintain a fragile truce with his wife's mental illness. But in 1939, the truce began to break down. When plans were announced to knock down and redevelop their home at 52 Tavistock Square, the Woolfs moved again, to 37 Mecklenburgh Square, near Gray's

Angus Wilson (1913–91), 'that testy elderly female voice in the Reading Room'.

Inn Road. Within a year both it and 52 Tavistock Square had been bombed, and the couple spent their last few months together at their country home, Monk's House, near Lewes. By this time, Virginia was ill again, and the 'horrible voices' were back. Convinced that this time she could not recover, she drowned herself in the river Ouse, on the morning of 28 March 1941.

Born in St Louis, Missouri, Thomas Stearns Eliot arrived in Britain in the summer of 1914. Then 26, Eliot had already written some of his most brilliant poetry, including 'Portrait of a Lady' and 'The Love Song of J Alfred Prufrock', but had made no attempt to publish it; instead, he intended to become a philosopher. With a few months to spare before embarking on a postgraduate degree at Oxford, where he intended to write a thesis on the philosopher FH Bradley, Eliot moved in to lodgings at 28 Bedford Place. Like many other expatriate Americans (among them Henry James), Eliot felt ill at ease on his first visit to London. The First World War had just been declared, and the whole city was on edge. However, Eliot was back in London for the Christmas vacation, renting a room in Gordon Square and studying at the British Museum Reading Room.

Within a year, Eliot's plans had changed completely. He met and swiftly married the beautiful but highly strung Vivienne (later Vivien) Haigh-Wood, and abandoned Oxford, taking a job as a teacher at Highgate Junior School in order to earn some money. The marriage was a disaster and Eliot was left bewildered and helpless in the face of his wife's increasing mental illness, which was characterized by paranoia, obsessive cleanliness and, occasionally, violence. He finally left her in the early thirties.

By then, he was working daily at the Faber and Faber offices in Russell Square, where Vivien would turn up unannounced in the waiting room, hoping to persuade her husband to come home. While his secretary gently told her that Mr Eliot was well, thank you, but it was not possible for her to see him, Eliot himself would slip quietly out of the building.

Eliot did, however, make time to see fellow writers who were in need of support. The poet Roy Campbell once described one of the periodic borrowing raids he used to mount with Dylan Thomas, in which they would systematically tap all the newly wealthy poets who had been given lucrative wartime jobs in government offices. First they tried the Ministry of Information, in the University of London Senate House, but soon found themselves standing empty-handed in Malet Street. It then occurred to Campbell to take their quest to the highest level.

> *'What about His Grace?' I asked. 'He lives around here.'*
> *'You mean the Archbishop?' gasped Dylan. 'I wouldn't dare.'*
> *'Come on, you'll see. He's not only a saint in his poems, he's a bloody saint in his life too.'*
> *We went to see Eliot, and the great man helped us so lavishly that it lasted till by some curious coincidence we both got our first radio jobs,*

almost simultaneously, and were able to pay Eliot back. Dylan never forgot his kindness. Neither did I.

Eliot's guiding hand would give Faber a reputation as Britain's premier publishers of poetry. It was largely through his influence that the careers of WH Auden, Louis MacNeice, Ted Hughes, Thom Gunn and others were established and nurtured. Meeting Eliot for the first time, the American publisher Robert Giroux

In the thirties and forties the Lamb in Lamb's Conduit Street was a favourite watering hole of the Bloomsbury Group. The pub had no toilets: patrons were obliged to use the public conveniences at the end of the street.

One of the Angry Young Men of the 1950s, Colin Wilson (1931–) received early encouragement from Angus Wilson (no relation). His largely auto-biographical novel Adrift in Soho *(1961) describes his entry into London's bohemian literary scene.*

asked him whether he agreed that most editors are failed writers. 'Perhaps,' Eliot replied. 'But so are most writers.'

Shortly before the outbreak of the Second World War, a camp, rather theatrical assistant cataloguer at the British Museum's Department of Printed Books moved into a small flat (number 3/11) on the top floor of Endsleigh Court, a mountainous block of flats on the north-east corner of Tavistock Square. At 25, Angus Wilson had yet to show the slightest interest in becoming a writer (that would come at the end of the war, when he was recovering from a nervous breakdown). But, though he didn't realize it at the time, he was already gathering material for two of his future novels. As war approached, Wilson was among those charged with the task of packing up the British Museum's treasures and transporting them by train for safe keeping at various secret locations around the country. Many years later he would rework this experience of the queasy, uncertain weeks of pre-war and phoney war in his novel *The Old Men at the Zoo*, in which the packaging of museum

exhibits is changed to the evacuation of animals as London prepares for the Third World War. Wilson, for reasons nobody ever quite understood, was fascinated by the notion of the Third World War, to which he makes a casual, almost surreal, reference in his novel *Anglo-Saxon Attitudes*.

Although Wilson never saw any action in the war, he had an eventful time as a code-breaker at Bletchley Park in Buckinghamshire. (On his way to meet friends in Kensington one night during the blackout, he was approached by an elderly man. 'Madam, I see you are lost,' he told Wilson. 'May I escort you?' Taking his arm, he proceeded to do just that.) After the war, as Deputy Superintendent of the British Museum Reading Room, the bouffant-haired Wilson would sit resplendent on a raised dais in the centre of the room, directly under the apex of the famous dome – 'a colourful bird in a vast circular cage', as his friend and biographer Margaret Drabble describes him, 'bow-tied, blue-rinsed, chattering loudly to readers and staff and friends on the telephone… a spider at the centre of his own web'. (He prided himself on never once saying 'Shh!') Another friend, Graham Reynolds, also remembered him vividly as 'that testy elderly female voice in the Reading Room' – not a description that would have pleased Wilson, who was only 42 when he left to become a full-time writer.

It was only a matter of time before the British Museum, with its gallery of eccentrics, would find its way into one of his novels. *Anglo-Saxon Attitudes* was partly inspired by the Piltdown Man affair, in which the remains of the so-called missing link between primitive man and homo sapiens, excavated in 1912, had been exposed as a fake. Wilson's novel is about a scholar, Gerald Middleton, who uncovers a similar forgery, and is peopled with characters whom Wilson remembered from the British Museum, right down to Middleton's cleaning lady, Mrs Salad, whom he based on the Reading Room ladies lavatory attendant, Mrs Manwaring. A minor character, Elvira Portway, was based on George Orwell's second wife Sonia, then on the staff of Cyril Connolly's literary magazine *Horizon*. Sonia had been instrumental in getting Wilson's first short stories published, and she was not amused to find herself caricatured as the hair-twirling, intellectually lightweight Elvira. Friendly relations would not be restored for nearly 20 years.

Among the Museum eccentrics not included in the novel was Colin Wilson, who wrote his Jack the Ripper novel *Ritual in the Dark* in the Reading Room and

camped on Hampstead Heath to save on rent. Nor did Wilson include his friend, Willie King, who worked in the Museum's ceramics department by day and hosted literary salons in the evenings. Every now and again he would exclaim 'I'm sick of all this fucking rubbish!' and sweep a deskload of priceless artefacts on to the floor.

John Keats was the first of many writers to pay tribute to the British Museum. A friend, the painter Benjamin Robert Haydon, described how he loved to take Keats to the Museum and hear him 'expatiate... on the glories of the antique'. Keats returned the favour by dedicating his two sonnets on the Elgin Marbles to Haydon. Keats's 'Ode on a Grecian Urn' was also inspired by a visit to the Museum.

Later writers had a more mixed response to this Bloomsbury institution. Virginia Woolf loved it: 'Stone lies solid over the British Museum, as bone lies cool over

Louis MacNeice (1907–63) wrote memorable verse about the British Museum and the nearby Museum Tavern.

Opened in 1900, the vast Russell Hotel features prominently in Alan Hollinghurst's The Swimming Pool Library.

wander in an eternity of vain research along the endless shelves. Or again, the readers who sat here at these radiating lines of desks, what were they but hapless flies caught in a huge web, its nucleus the great circle of the Catalogue?' Arguably the most enjoyable Reading Room scene in fiction is the one in Max Beerbohm's story 'Enoch Soames', about a talentless but grossly conceited poet who makes a pact with the devil to see if his work is remembered in a hundred years' time. Granted five hours in the Reading Room on 3 June 1997, Soames finds a single, passing reference to himself – as a character in a story by Max Beerbohm.

Writing just before the outbreak of the Second World War, the poet Louis MacNeice took a jaundiced view of the 'hive-like dome' with its ranks of 'stooping haunted readers':

> *Some on commission, some for*
> *the love of learning,*
> *Some because they have*
> *nothing better to do*
> *Or because they hope these*
> *walls of books will deaden*
> *The drumming of the demon*
> *in their ears.*

Surveying the Museum again in 1962, MacNeice again found himself overwhelmed by it:

> *...the Museum*
> *Spreads its dead hands wide,*
> *a pigeon scores an outer*
> *On a scholarly collar, the*
> *menu in the pub says Butter*
> *Beans Greens Peas,*
> *Black men and schoolchildren*
> *rummage for culture, the*
> *tutelary spirits are hard*
> *to please.*

the visions and heat of the brain' she wrote in *Jacob's Room.* For George Gissing, however, the Museum, and especially the Reading Room, could be a desolate place, a prison for solitary toilers. In *New Grub Street* (1891), Marian Yule sits in the Reading Room on a foggy November day, reflecting on the futility of her task of writing literary reviews – writing about writing – when all around her there is already more literature than anyone will ever have time to read. Looking up at the great dome, Marian notices one of the librarians walking along the upper gallery. 'In pursuance of her grotesque humour, her mocking misery, she likened him to a black, lost soul, doomed to

The pub was almost certainly the Museum Tavern, opposite the main entrance, where Karl Marx accidentally broke one of the mirrors, and where Angus Wilson once had a massive nosebleed followed by an equally spectacular fainting fit.

The Museum apart, Bloomsbury's other architectural landmarks have been put to good use by novelists. In George Orwell's *Nineteen Eighty-Four*, Winston Smith has a job falsifying history at the Ministry of Truth. The building, 'an enormous pyramidal structure of glittering white concrete [which] towered vast and white above the grimy landscape', was inspired by the University of London Senate House, then the tallest building in London. In John Wyndham's 1951 novel *The Day of the Triffids*, a cluster of survivors adopts the Senate House as its headquarters, at one point firing a volley of shots at a group of blind people who try to gain entry. The novel's narrator, William Masen, later puts in a spot of triffid gun practice in Russell Square, remarking on the deceptive normality of 'the absurdly grandiose hotels on the other side of the Square'. The most grandiose of them all is the massive, terracotta-coloured Russell Hotel, which dominates Alan Hollinghurst's novel *The Swimming Pool Library*, published in 1988. Set in the summer of 1983 – 'the last summer of its kind there was ever to be', before the onslaught of AIDS – the novel's gay narrator enjoys afternoon trysts on the roof of the hotel (ironically renamed the Queensberry, after Wilde's persecutor), high above the tinkling fountains of Russell Square, and at the swimming pool of the nearby 'Corinthian Club' – easily recognizable as the YMCA in Great Russell Street.

Two Bloomsbury churches are worth seeking out for their literary connections. St George's, in Bloomsbury Way, is a well-known central London landmark, with its unique, pyramid-shaped steeple, topped by a statue of George I. Horace Walpole described the design as 'a masterpiece of absurdity', and in his 1985 novel *Hawksmoor* Peter Ackroyd's highly strung detective Nicholas Hawksmoor stands beneath the tower one night, and considers ascending 'its cracked and broken stone, and then from its summit screaming down at the silent city as a child might scream at a chained animal'.

The dramatist James

St George's Church in Bloomsbury took 15 years to build, but was condemned in the 1876 London Guide as 'the most pretentious and ugliest edifice in the metropolis'.

So many bodies were buried at St Giles in the Fields during the Great Plague that the church suffered structural damage.

Shirley is buried, with his wife, at the church of St Giles in the Fields, in St Giles High Street. His tombstone notes that he 'died after shock and exposure in the Great Fire of London', of which he was one of the few casualties. Another plaque celebrates the life of a contemporary, the poet Andrew Marvell, in words which would be embarrassing if they were not so patently sincere:

Near unto this place lyeth the body of Andrew Marvell Esq, a man so endowed by nature, so improved by education, study and travell [sic], so consummated by practice and experience; that joining the most peculiar graces of wit and learning with a singular penetration, and strength of judgment, and exercising all these in the whole course of his

*W*B Yeats burnt the midnight oil in Woburn Walk.

life, with an unalterable steadiness in the ways of virtue, he became the ornament and example of his age; beloved by good men, fear'd by bad, admir'd by all.

In Gerald Kersh's 1938 novel *Night and the City*, the small-time criminal Harry Fabian crosses St Giles High Street and enters 'one of those innumerable back-doubles which spring, like tortuous capillaries, out of the larger, congested arteries of ancient cities'. There, he enters the shabby International Political Club, whose proprietress, Anna Siberia, Kersh describes with Dickensian relish:

Imagine the death-mask of Julius Caesar, plastered with rouge, and stuck with a pair of eyes as small, as flat, and as bright as newly cut cross-sections of .38 calibre bullets; marked with eyebrows that ran together in a straight black bar; and surmounted by a million diabolical black hairs that sprang in a nightmarish cascade up out of her skull, like a dark fountain of accumulated wickedness squeezed out by the pressure of her corsets.

Perhaps the most enduring image of Bloomsbury as the intellectual focal point of London is one by the novelist Dorothy Richardson. In 1906 she was living on the top floor of a lodging house at 2 Woburn Buildings in Woburn Walk. At night, she would occasionally glance across at another lodging house, at number 18, where WB Yeats could be seen working by candlelight.

FITZROVIA

It wasn't until the outbreak of the Second World War that people thought to put a name to the approximate square formed by Oxford Street, Great Portland Street, Euston Road and Gower Street. The name Fitzrovia was taken from Fitzroy Square, one of the area's few green spaces, or possibly from the Fitzroy Tavern in Charlotte Street, which in the 1940s was the area's most fashionable drinking place. The writer who did most to define the area's character, Patrick Hamilton, never even used the term Fitzrovia in his books, but in *The Plains of* Roads, the criminal patches and Belgian penury of Charlotte and Whitfield Streets, the vast palace of pain known as the Middlesex Hospital, the motor salesman's paradise in Great Portland Street, the august solemnity of Portland Place itself.

The first volume of the trilogy, *The Midnight Bell*, is the story of Bob, a waiter at a pub on the Euston Road – this was in the

The Fitzroy Tavern was a Victorian pub which later became extremely popular with London's bohemians and regulars included Dylan Thomas and Augustus John.

Fitzroy Tavern
In the 1920's The Fitzroy Tavern was a very famous literary-Artistic Pub. As a result The Fitzroy gave it's name to this area of London we now call "Fitzrovia".

Cement, the third part of his London trilogy *Twenty Thousand Streets under the Sky*, he points out the area's defining features with a mordant but not wholly unaffectionate eye:

> *The respectable, residential precincts of Regent's Park, the barracks and lodging-houses of Albany Street, the grim senility of Munster Square, the commercial fury of the Euston and Tottenham Court*

days when pubs had waiters. Bob's infatuation with a young prostitute, Jenny Maple, begins when she comes into the pub complaining of a stomach ache, which he remedies with a dose of gin and peppermint. Jenny was based on a prostitute named Lily Connolly, whom Patrick Hamilton met around 1927, when he was living at 50a New Cavendish Street. It's not clear whether he met Lily 'professionally', but several of their meetings found

Maple Street may have inspired the name of one of Patrick Hamilton's characters in Twenty Thousand Streets under the Sky.

*H*G Wells's Invisible Man, Griffin, is living in a 'big, ill-managed lodging house in a slum near Great Portland Street' when he turns invisible for the first time. James Boswell (1740–1795) lived out his last lonely years at Number 122 Great Portland Street.

the Midnight Bell, that Hamilton truly excels himself. The final part of the trilogy, *The Plains of Cement*, focuses on Ella, the barmaid at the Midnight Bell, her unspoken love for the preoccupied Bob and her courtship by the pub bore Mr Eccles, who is described by the critic Michael Holroyd as 'one of the most dreadful admirers in English literature'. As Doris Lessing, a resident of Langham Street, wrote in 1968, six years after Hamilton's alcohol-induced death at the age of 58, 'His novels are true now. You can go into any pub and see it going on.'

You can also see where much of it happened, since Fitzrovia was left relatively unscathed by both forties bombs and sixties planners. The Midnight Bell was modelled on several pubs, particularly the Prince of Wales Feathers in Warren Street. Though much changed, the basic layout – main bar on the right near the doors, seating area at the back, where Bob waits on the tables – has been left intact. Fitzroy Square is also much the same as it was in the thirties. Two of Hamilton's minor characters live here: 'Illegal Operation', one of the customers at the Midnight Bell, and Johnnie, the friend who vainly attempts to keep George Bone on the right side of sanity in Hamilton's wartime thriller *Hangover Square*. Fitzroy Square had earlier been the scene of one of the more surreal incidents in English literary life. Late one night, Bernard Shaw, who was then living at number 29, was on his way home after attending a ballet when he got into conversation with a policeman. According to Shaw, he and the constable then pirouetted round the square.

Great Portland Street, 'the motor salesman's paradise', also

their way into *The Midnight Bell* – particularly in the scene where Bob goes for tea with Lily and other street girls in a slum house in Bolsover Street. Writing to his brother Bruce (who was later to provide the germ of Patrick's play *Gaslight*), he described, with just a hint of pride, how 'I had tea with them all on a foggy day in a filthy little room at the top of a house in Bolsover Street – just opposite Great Portland Street station... they all three slept in the same bed, and syphilis was in the air. Not that there was any air, or anything but the heavy odour of carbolic soap, gone bad.'

It is in his portrait of pub life, through the staff and customers of

makes an appearance in Graham Greene's 1936 novel *A Gun for Sale*. On the run, the hired killer Raven takes a taxi to Euston Station, along Euston Road 'where all the bicycles had been taken in for the night and the second-hand car dealers from that end of Great Portland Street were having a quick one, before they bore their old school ties and their tired tarnished bonhomie back to their lodgings'.

Cleveland Street, too, has earned a couple of footnotes in literary history. Number 22 is where Charles Dickens lived, between the ages of three and five, when his parents first moved to London from the south coast. He subsequently had no recollection of the place – a pity, as the building is largely unchanged. A few years later, when the family fell on hard times, Dickens's mother opened a 'Young Ladies' Academy' in Gower Street North: a perplexing decision, since, as far as could be ascertained, no young ladies ever went there, and there were no attempts to encourage them to do so. At the other end of the century, in the summer of 1889, the Cleveland Street Scandal was centred on a

homosexual brothel in which telegraph boys entertained various members of the aristocracy, one of whom, Lord Somerset, was forced to flee the country. The episode whetted the public appetite for the Oscar Wilde revelations a few years later, and eventually found its way into Paul West's 1991 novel, *The Women of Whitechapel*. Harold Biffen, one of the penniless writers in George Gissing's novel *New Grub Street* (1891) lives in nearby Clipstone Street – 'a thoroughfare discoverable in the dim district which lies between Portland Place and Tottenham Court Road' – and buys his humble supper of pease pudding and faggots in adjoining Cleveland Street. Gissing himself had lived in poverty at 22 Colville Place, near the southern end of Tottenham Court Road and gave an account of his wretched existence there in his last novel, *The Private Papers of Henry Ryecroft*.

Tottenham Court Road itself was the scene of one of the more ludicrous episodes in the life of the Irish writer Brendan Behan. A teenage member of the IRA, Behan was sent to

Charles Dickens's first London home, 22 Cleveland Street.

George Gissing (1857–1903), who vividly described Fitzrovia before the area had even acquired its name.

39

Goodge Street Station, where Brendan Behan was nearly arrested for the wrong crime.

London in 1939 to act as a courier during a bombing campaign. His instructions were to meet a contact outside Goodge Street tube station who would be carrying a copy of *Picture Post*, and Behan was to ask, 'Can I have a look at your magazine?' When he arrived, the only person carrying a copy of *Picture Post* was a middle-aged woman. Following orders, Behan approached her and murmured 'Can I have a look at your magazine?' Incandescent with rage, the woman roared, 'You will see the inside of Cannon Row Police Station, young man!' then started to shout 'Pick up! Pick up!' at the top of her voice. At this point the real IRA contact arrived and whisked the red-faced Behan away in a car. Behan was arrested a short while later and spent the next three years in Borstal. He returned to London in triumph in the late 1950s, when his plays *The*

GOODGE STREET STATION

Hostage and *The Quare Fellow* were staged by Joan Littlewood's Theatre Workshop company, in Stratford, East London.

Michael Marshall Smith's 1994 short story 'Missed Connection' takes place at the next stop up the line from Goodge Street. It is the blackly funny tale of Lawson, an inoffensive Christmas shopper, who gets off the train and finds himself imprisoned inside a dark, topographically impossible version of Warren Street Station.

Behan launches into song at the Fitzroy Tavern in 1956. The other customers have obviously heard this one before.

Kindly and eccentric (her dyed purple hair was a novelty at the time), Lady Ottoline Morrell felt thwarted by her lack of artistic talent. 'It is so humiliating that one is so uncreative,' she wrote to a friend. 'Perhaps in another existence I may be.' During her earthly existence she compenstated for the defect by establishing a literary salon at her home at 10 Gower Street, where the finest writers and artists of the day were entertained for tea every Thursday. Among the regular guests were Henry James, WB Yeats, TS Eliot and Virginia Woolf.

Two other guests, DH Lawrence and Aldous Huxley were unable to resist parodying their hostess in print – Huxley through Mrs Wimbush in *Crome Yellow* and Mrs Aldwinkle in *Those Barren Leaves*; Lawrence, more unkindly, as Hermione Roddice in *Women in Love*. Lawrence's caricature caused the gentle Lady Ottoline lasting pain. Towards the end of her life, a late addition to her circle redressed the balance with a more sympathetic portrait. In Graham Greene's 1934 novel *It's a Battlefield*, she appears as Caroline Bury, whose 'passion to help' leads her to intervene on the behalf of a man who has been unjustly condemned to death. Lady Ottoline died in 1938, but Greene must have been reminded of her frequently in the early years of the Second World War, when he lived at 19 Gower Mews, directly opposite her old house. An air raid warden during the Blitz, Greene's ARP post was just up the road, outside the School of Tropical Medicine, and in *The Ministry of Fear* (1943) he offers a brief, authentic glimpse of a typical morning after a raid: 'In Gower Street they were sweeping up glass, and a building smoked into the new day like a candle which some late reveller has forgotten to snuff.'

Dylan Thomas became an habitué of Fitzrovia's pubs in the mid-1930s, shortly after his arrival in London. Two of his favourites were the Fitzroy Tavern, at 16 Charlotte Street, and the Wheatsheaf, at 25 Rathbone Place. A fixture of both pubs was the artist Nina Hamnett, who in her youth had been the model and lover of Modigliani. 'Modi said I had the best breasts in Europe,' she would drawl in her booze-roughened Carmarthen accent, obligingly hauling up her sweater to reveal the evidence to anyone who happened to be listening. 'Feel them, they're good as new.' Constantly broke, she worked the bar for free drinks or cash donations, which she carried around in a tin box. Contributors would be treated to anecdotes

After her first meeting with Lady Ottoline Morrell (above) in 1900, Virginia Woolf scribbled a record in a letter to a friend. 'We have just got to know a wonderful Lady Ottoline Morrell, who has the head of a Medusa; but she is very simple & innocent in spite of it, & worships the arts.'

The London home of the literary hostess Lady Ottoline Morrell, seen from Gower Mews, Graham Greene's address during the Second World War.

from her racy autobiography, *Laughing Torso*, and tales of Picasso and Hemingway, whom she had known in Paris.

Dylan Thomas's own favourite pub game was 'cats and dogs', a rather infantile pastime which he had developed at home in Swansea that involved crawling round the bar on his hands and knees and biting women's ankles. Once he snapped one of his front teeth biting a lamp post. It was at the Wheatsheaf, on 12 April 1936, that he first met Caitlin Macnamara, who was sitting on a stool at the bar. He walked over, put his head in her lap and told her she was beautiful and he was going to marry her. At the time, Caitlin was having an affair with the painter Augustus John, but she agreed to spend the night with Thomas at a hotel called the Eiffel Tower in Percy Street. Augustus John's daughter, Vivien, regularly stayed there and charged the bill to her father's account, and to Thomas's great satisfaction John picked up the bill on this occasion too. Dylan and Caitlin were married the following year at Penzance Registry Office. Their stormy marriage continued until Thomas's death, from alcohol poisoning, in New York, in 1953.

Another fixture of thirties and forties Fitzrovia was Quentin Crisp, though he tended to favour Fitzrovia's cafés rather than its pubs. In *The Naked Civil Servant*, Crisp recalled that on the frequent days when he had no work to do, he 'would gladly have drunk pale-grey coffees from midday to midnight if I could have found people to listen when I spoke'. It was in these Charlotte Street cafés that he perfected his 'café technique' of speaking – dry, sparkling 'Crisperanto' – which made the TV chat show appearances and one-man shows of his seventies and eighties such a delight.

In a 1993 story, 'Newman Passage, or J. Maclaren-Ross and the Case of the Vanishing Writers', the film director and novelist Christopher Petit identifies Newman Passage as 'the secret heart' of Fitzrovia – 'not a portal, like the archway into Soho in Manette Street, but a partly roofed, narrow alleyway with a hidden dog-leg, out of sight of either end'. In his unfinished autobiography, *Memoirs of the Forties*, Julian Maclaren-Ross recalled that Newman Passage was known locally as Jekyll and Hyde Alley, the hidden part conveniently 'piled high with cardboard boxes into which one sometimes guided girls in order to become better acquainted'.

Maclaren-Ross was one of those writers who is more talked about than read – he published only a handful of books, all of them more or less forgotten. But, with his trademark dark glasses, camel-hair coat and silver-topped walking stick, he was, with the possible exception of Dylan Thomas, Fitzrovia's most distinctive bohemian, appearing, with little or no embellishment, as the writer X Trapnel in Anthony Powell's novel *A Dance to the Music of Time*. In the early 1940s Dylan Thomas worked with him at Strand Films in Golden Square, where they were employed as script writers. On their first

meeting, in the office lift, Thomas recoiled at Maclaren-Ross's foppish attire of white corduroy jacket, cream silk shirt and peach tie, but softened slightly when his new colleague offered to take him for a drink at the Café Royal. As the drink flowed, Thomas's belligerence returned. 'Fucking dandy,' he scoffed. 'Why don't you try to look more sordid. Sordidness, boy, that's the thing!' They became close friends.

The short-story writer Dan Davin once described a typical Maclaren-Ross day, circa 1945: in the Wheatsheaf from midday until 3 o'clock closing; then a late lunch at the Scala in Charlotte Street – roast beef with lashings of horseradish and as much fat as possible to soak up the booze. Next, a stroll down to Charing Cross Road to browse around the bookshops and buy his cork-tipped cigarettes (Royalty, jumbo-size). Then, back to the pub until closing time, followed by a late supper at the Scala and a midnight tube home from Goodge Street. The rest of the night would, allegedly, be spent writing.

If Maclaren-Ross never quite fulfilled his literary promise, he had only himself to blame. As he admitted in *Memoirs of the Forties*, a seasoned Fitzrovian, the Ceylonese editor of *Poetry London* James Meary Tambimuttu ('Tambi') pointed out the pitfalls to him early on.

'Only beware of Fitzrovia,' Tambi said, 'It's a dangerous place, you must be careful.'
'Fights with knives?'
'No, a worse danger. You might get Sohoitis, you know.'
'No, I don't. What is it?'
'If you get Sohoitis,' Tambi said very seriously, 'you will stay there always day and night and get no work done ever. You have been warned.'

The Newman Arms pub and Newman Passage (left), known in the forties as 'Jekyll and Hyde Alley'.

The Green Man in Bolsover Street features in Patrick Hamilton's Twenty Thousand Streets under the Sky.

SOHO

'Of all quarters in the queer adventurous amalgam called London,' wrote John Galsworthy in *The Forsyte Saga*, 'Soho is perhaps least suited to the Forsyte spirit ... Untidy, full of Greeks, Ishmaelites, cats, Italians, tomatoes, restaurants, organs, coloured stuffs, queer names, people looking out of upper windows, it dwells remote from the British Body Politic.'

Soho is, by tradition, a private enclave for the initiated – even in its earliest days, it was set aside as a private hunting ground for Henry VIII ('So-ho!' was a hunting cry). Unlike most areas of London, its borders are clearly defined: Oxford Street to the north, Shaftesbury Avenue to the south, Regent Street to the west, Charing Cross Road to the east. In his 1993 novel *Robinson* Christopher Petit identifies the precise point of entry into Soho's eastern flank as the archway that links Manette Street to Greek Street – 'a border-post, the crossing- point where obligations could be left behind'. Originally called Rose Street, Manette Street was renamed after one of the characters in Dickens's *A Tale of Two Cities*, set during the French Revolution: 'The quiet lodgings of Dr Manette were in a quiet street-corner not far from Soho Square ... A quainter corner than the corner where the doctor

Gateway to Soho: the Manette Street archway.

lived was not to be found in London.'

For a while, Soho was almost respectable. The large houses surrounding Golden Square provided settings for several eighteenth- and nineteenth-century novels. Matthew Bramble lives here in Tobias Smollett's *The Expedition of Humphry Clinker* (1771). Dickens, who had loved the novel as a child, set Ralph Nickleby's house in Golden Square.

William Blake was born, in humbler circumstances, just north of Golden Square in 1757. His father ran a hosiery and haberdashery business on the corner of Broad Street (now Broadwick Street) and Marshall Street. William himself was a pugnacious, self-contained boy – according to his friend Frederick Tatham 'he despised restraints and rules so much that his father dare not send him to school'. Instead, he spent long hours exploring London – which was still a loose assortment of villages – and sketching and versifying as he went along. Blake never had any regrets about his lack of formal education. As a young man he would recall fondly how he 'roam'd from field to field / And tasted all the summer's pride'.

As a child he was already experiencing the intense visions – amounting to hallucinations – which would recur throughout his life – most famously of angels on Peckham Rye. The visions were not always pleasant. At the age of four, he was left screaming in terror after 'seeing' God looking in his bedroom window at Broad Street. Blake's practical, hard-working parents were unimpressed by his gift – on one occasion his mother beat him when he told her he had just seen the Prophet

Ezekiel sitting under a tree – but they had the good sense to realize he was never going to carry on the family business of selling stockings. Instead, he was sent to a drawing school in the Strand to train as a draughtsman and engraver. He returned to Broad Street in 1784, to set up a print shop, next door to the family hosiery shop, at number 27 (now number 72). There, he would sell prepared prints to customers by day, and work on his own creations at night, either in the shop, or at the lodgings at 28 Poland Street where he and his wife lived.

With works such as *Songs of Innocence and of Experience* and *The Book of Thel*, Blake achieved what few if any other writers have done before or since: he invented a completely new art form. In his 'illuminated books', words and images were combined to produce a work which was not so much written as made – text and pictures were laboriously engraved on copper plates. As publisher and retailer of his own work, Blake was free – artistically, if not financially – to do whatever he liked. For the most part, his efforts were either ignored or dismissed as the works of a lunatic. Even his friends, who grew used to his earthy dialogue, and casual references to 'conversations' with Milton, Socrates and the Angel Gabriel, routinely, and even affectionately, described him as 'mad'. When others criticized him Blake would hit back with vicious and occasionally obscene verses. Even when praising a kindred spirit, Blake was instinctively provocative – 'The only Man that e'er I knew / Who did not make me almost spew' – was his curiously endearing verdict on the Swiss artist Henry Fuseli. For all the beauty and sensitivity of his

work, Blake's natural environment was the raucous Soho tavern, rather than the Covent Garden coffee house, with its vapid literary gossip. However, he could when pressed offer a relatively measured self-justification. 'The ignorant Insults of Individuals will not hinder me from doing my duty to my Art,' he wrote in the advertisement for an exhibition of his paintings, at the family shop at 28 Broad Street. 'Those who have been told that my Works are but an unscientific and irregular Eccentricity, a Madman's Scrawls, I demand of them to do me the

Golden Square, with its 'mournful statue, the guardian genius of a little wilderness of shrubs'. Dickens's description in Nicholas Nickleby *still holds good today.*

justice to examine before they decide.' That justice would not come until after his death, when he was rediscovered by Swinburne and Yeats and declared a genius. Even Wordsworth was inclined to damn him with faint praise: 'There was no doubt that this poor man was mad, but there is something in the madness of this man which interests me more than the sanity of Lord Byron and Walter Scott.'

In 1811 it was Shelley's turn to seek lodgings in Poland Street, after he and his friend James Hogg had been expelled from Oxford for writing a provocative pamphlet, 'The Necessity of Atheism'. The house they briefly shared, at number 15, is now an Italian restaurant, but Shelley is commemorated in a huge mural, 'The Soho Mural: Ode to the

West Wind' at the end of the road, on the corner with Noel Street.

In 1802 the 17-year-old Thomas De Quincey ran away from Manchester Grammar School, where he was a boarder, and, after wandering aimlessly in Wales, ended up, virtually penniless, in Soho. There, as De Quincey recalls in *Confessions of an English Opium Eater*, he managed to find a lodging in a large empty house at 38 Greek Street (the house is long gone) – empty, that is, apart from a ten-year-old girl who had been living and sleeping in the house completely alone. De Quincey never discovered how she had come to be there.

On the same night that he wrote this account in *Confessions*, De Quincey returned to Greek Street.

About ten o'clock this very night, August 15, 1821, being

*B*lake was considered mad during his lifetime (like so many men of genius) and nicknamed the Cockney Nutcase, gaining recognition only after his death.

*T*he Soho Memorial shows a scene from Shelley's 'Ode to the West Wind', written mainly in a wood near Florence in 1819.

my birthday – I turned aside from my evening walk, down Oxford-street, purposely to take a glance at it: it is now occupied by a respectable family; and, by the lights in the front drawing-room, I observed a domestic party, assembled perhaps at tea, and apparently cheerful and gay. Marvellous contrast in my eyes to the darkness – cold – silence – and desolation of that same house eighteen years ago, when its nightly occupants were one famishing scholar, and a neglected child.

At some point during the 16 weeks he spent in the house, De Quincey became friends with a teenage prostitute named Ann. Both on the verge of starvation, they spent hours wandering up and down Oxford Street or taking shelter in shop fronts; one night Ann saved his life when he collapsed with hunger as they sat together on the steps of a house in Soho Square. Their last meeting was in Golden Square, where they arranged to meet a few days later at their usual rendezvous at the bottom of Great Titchfield Street. Ann never turned up and, despite making repeated efforts to trace her, De Quincey never saw her again. Nineteen years later, he wrote:

To this hour, I have never heard a syllable about her. This, amongst such troubles as most men meet with in this life, has been my heaviest affliction. – If she lived, doubtless we must have been sometimes in search of each other, at the very same moment, through the mighty labyrinths of London; perhaps, even within a few feet of each other – a barrier no wider in a London street, often amounting in the end to a separation for eternity!

In the early nineteenth century, De Quincey's only serious rival as a literary critic was William Hazlitt (between them, they pioneered the serious study of Shakespeare). Hazlitt died at 6 Frith Street, where his last words were 'Well, I've had a happy life.' This wasn't entirely true: both his marriages ended in separation, and at the age of 42 he became embroiled in a hopeless one-way love affair with a 16-year-old servant girl, a mid-life crisis which he recounts in *Liber Amoris*. His Frith Street home is now a small, exclusive hotel, from which Bill Bryson begins his odyssey around Britain in *Notes from a Small Island* (1995).

A 1731 view of Soho Square, with Hampstead and Highgate on the horizon.

In later life De Quincey lived in the Lake District with his wife and family, visiting London occasionally and contributing articles to various magazines.

Soho Square, where Thomas De Quincey nearly died from starvation, is now hemmed in by office blocks.

*A Paris ornament of 1803.
Let's make it go again,
let London know
That life and heart and
hope are in Soho.*

St Anne's also has a plaque commemorating Dorothy L Sayers, theologian and creator of Lord Peter Wimsey. Her ashes are buried under the tower.

Soho's reputation for physical and moral squalor can be glimpsed in Robert Louis Stevenson's 1885 classic *Dr Jekyll and Mr Hyde*. Around nine o'clock on a foggy morning, the lawyer, Utterson, takes a cab to Mr Hyde's home somewhere in 'the dismal quarter of Soho ... with its muddy ways, and slatternly passengers'. As the cab draws up in front of the address, the fog lifts slightly to reveal 'a dingy street, a gin palace, a low French eating-house, a shop for the retail of penny numbers and two-penny salads, many ragged children huddled in the doorways, and many women of many different nationalities passing out, key in hand, to have a morning glass'.

Hazlitt's commemorative stone can still be seen at the foot of the tower which is all that remains of St Anne's Church in Wardour Street (the rest of the building was destroyed during an air raid in 1940). The 1976 appeal to restore the tower to its present state was launched by John Betjeman. The poem he wrote for the occasion confirms the view that he was not at his best when writing to order:

*High in the air two barrels
interlock
To form the faces of this
famous clock.
Reduced to drawing
room size, this clock
would be*

In Joseph Conrad's novel *The Secret Agent* (1907), Mr Verloc's pornographic bookshop is the meeting place for a nest of anarchists plotting to blow up Greenwich Observatory. Conrad's description of edgy young men losing their nerve at the last moment and buying bottles of ink which they don't particularly need, can still be seen, with small variations, in similar establishments nearly a century on.

Gerald Kersh's classic low-life novel *Night and the City* (1938) pulled even fewer punches. Its central character, Harry Fabian, is a blackmailer and pimp, living off the immoral earnings of the prostitute Zoë, then multiplying the profits by blackmailing her clients. As Fabian leaves their flat

night had brought about some nightmarish mating-season of machines – some madman's vision of the coupling of panting iron beasts in a burning jungle of stone.

Fabian survives in the jungle because he is 'versed in the tortuous geography of the night-world and familiar

Hazlitt's hotel, formerly the final residence of the writer. While awaiting his burial, his landlady hid his body behind furniture to show his room to prospective tenants.

The tower of St Anne's in Wardour Street, rescued from dereliction by Sir John Betjeman.

in Rupert Street to trail another victim back to his home, he encounters a scene that could have been written yesterday:

In Rupert Street, jammed bonnet to bumper, a line of quivering cars waited for the lights to change. Under the shaky scarlet light of the neon signs, Chrysler nuzzled Austin and Morris sniffed at the hindquarters of Ford, as if that humid spring

with every rat-hole in West One and West Central ... He saw London as a kind of Inferno – a series of concentric areas with Piccadilly Circus as the ultimate centre.' Fabian's attempts to recruit the night-club hostess Helen as a prositute fail – not for

The seedier side of Soho detailed so vividly by Gerald Kersh and Patrick Hamilton is still there for all to see.

reasons of morality, but because as a night-club hostess she is already one step up in the Soho pecking order. Kersh's description of the Soho 'clip joint' where hostesses use Machiavellian skill to relieve punters of their money, is also familiar. 'Bear this in mind,' night-club boss Phil Nosseross tells Helen, 'any man who'll pay five shillings or seven-and-six entrance fee to go into a place, and then lay out two pounds for a bottle of Scotch and a syphon of soda is a fool. Therefore, skin him alive – but peel it off gently.' Only the prices have changed; the clip joints – and the all-night restaurants where their hung-over customers go to face the cold light of day – have not.

The pavements, though, have altered. Patrick Hamilton's *Twenty Thousand Streets under the Sky* gives a vivid impression of the

Soho of the 1930s, before legislation forced prostitution underground. The pub waiter Bob is fascinated by Wardour Street, 'because it was the principal resort of the women of the town ... they lurked solitary in shop doorways, or aimlessly crossed the road, or came down the street in couples absorbed by that frantic garrulity and backbiting which rend their kind'. At about the same time, Quentin Crisp was making his own precarious and dangerous living as a male prostitute. As he recalled in *The Naked Civil Servant*: 'Courtship consisted of walking along the street with a man who had my elbow in a merciless grip until we came to a dark doorway. Then he said, "This'll do."' The meagre proceeds of such liaisons would be spent in the Black Cat, a homosexual café in Old Compton Street, where, 'day after uneventful day, night after loveless night, we sat buying each other cups of tea, combing each other's hair and trying on each other's lipsticks.'

The 1957 Wolfenden Report finally drove prostitution off the streets and into seedy first-floor flatlets with hand-stencilled cards with the euphemism 'Model'. Out of sight did not, necessarily, mean out of mind. In *Robinson* Christopher Petit offers a snapshot of Soho vice, nineties style, as the narrator collides with 'a man ducking out after his swift transaction upstairs, already moving at street speed as he came through the door'.

Through the 1950s the two worlds of vice and bohemia continued to intermingle – particularly in the pubs. Regulars at the French Pub in Dean Street included writers Dylan Thomas, Brendan Behan, Julian Maclaren-

Ross, Colin Wilson and Jeffrey Bernard, as well as the painters Francis Bacon and Lucian Freud. By the early sixties, the ratio of vice to bohemia was beginning to rise alarmingly, as Soho's bohemians either died or moved to the suburbs. Soho in the sixties, when the Kray twins held sway, is convincingly recreated in Jake Arnott's 1999 novel *The Long Firm*. In Derek Raymond's last novel *Not Till the Red Fog Rises* (1994), a hitman with £17,000 in his pockets is forced to spend a night in Soho Square – the notes are all in fifties and he can't get change for the bus home.

One of the few bohemians who stayed on was the columnist Jeffrey Bernard, who had by now taken up almost permanent residence at the Coach and Horses on the corner of Greek Street and Romilly Street. Bernard's weekly column in the *Spectator*, was once described as a suicide note in weekly instalments. 'Low Life' chronicled the writer's crowded but narrow world of betting, booze and lunch. 'People have often asked me if drinking has ever interfered with my work,' Bernard

once observed, 'to which I always reply, no it has never interfered with my work, though my work has occasionally interfered with my drinking.' In the last decade of his life, Bernard belatedly found himself a celebrity, due largely to the success of Keith Waterhouse's play *Jeffrey Bernard is Unwell* (the title refers to the apologetic note the *Spectator* used to print when Bernard was too drunk or too hung-over to write his weekly

Leoni's Quo Vadis restaurant, which now occupies the building where Karl Marx once lived in two rooms in 'the greatest disorder'.

Dating from 1847, the Coach and Horses is a Soho institution, despite the passing of its most famous regular, Jeffrey Bernard.

*K*arl Marx *(1818–83), whose most famous work,* Das Kapital, *was completed by his friend Friedrich Engels.*

his final days in the tower block next to Berwick Street market. One of the last things he wrote was a typically pithy lonely hearts advertisement, which was published in the satirical magazine *Private Eye* (whose staff members regularly lunched at the Coach and Horses): 'Recent amputee seeks sympathy fuck.'

While he was writing *Das Kapital* in the 1850s Karl Marx lived with his large family in two of the upstairs rooms at 26 Dean Street (now Leoni's Quo Vadis restaurant). A visitor described his home: 'There is not one clean and good piece of furniture to be found; all is broken, tattered and torn, everywhere clings thick dust, everywhere is the greatest disorder; his manuscripts, books and newspapers lie beside the children's toys, bits and pieces from the wife's needlework basket, teacups with broken rims, dirty spoons, knives, forks, lamps, an ink-well, tumblers, Dutch clay-pipes, tobacco ash.' The general squalor gave Marx and his wife 'not the slightest embarrassment', though it does help explain his long hours at the British Museum Reading Room.

column). Well-meaning strangers would make the pilgrimage to the Coach and Horses to meet the irascible columnist; Bernard would accept the free drinks they offered, then order them to piss off. Inevitably, the vodka and endless cigarettes exacted their due. Circulation problems led to the amputation of both his legs and Bernard spent

In 1720 the historian John Strype wrote of Old Compton Street, 'This Street is broad, and the Houses well built, but of no great Account for its inhabitants, which are chiefly French.' The traditional Mediterranean shop and restaurant owners now vie for space with the gay community who have made the street their own.

Number 9 Gerrard Street (currently a Chinese newsagent and gift shop) was once the Turk's Head tavern, frequented by Johnson, Boswell (who lodged at number 22), Goldsmith, Burke and other eighteenth-century luminaries. Burke himself lived at number 37 and Dryden at number 43 (both houses are now Chinese restaurants). As a child, Charles Dickens used to visit his uncle, Thomas Barrow, who had lodgings in a bookshop in Gerrard Street. Dickens enjoyed long chats with the owner of a nearby barber's shop, who entertained him with colourful reminiscences of the Napoleonic Wars. In *Great Expectations* (1861), the lawyer Jaggers lives on the south side of Gerrard Street, in 'rather a stately house of its kind, but dolefully in want of painting, and with dirty windows'.

In the 1950s, Gerrard Street became the main thoroughfare of London's Chinatown. In Timothy Mo's 1982 novel *Sour Sweet* it is known simply as 'Chinese Street'. In the novel, Chen and his family have been living in Britain for four years – 'long enough to have lost their place in the society from which they had emigrated but not long enough to feel comfortable in the new'. Chen is a waiter at the Ho Ho restaurant in Gerrard Street, where the steep steps linking different floors, and uncompromising staff, bear a more than passing resemblance to the famous Wong Kei restaurant in Wardour Street. One night Chen loses heavily in one of the local gambling dens and is forced to borrow money from the Triads, whose casual, carefully controlled violence is neatly set down by Mo – particularly in the scene where a car is used to break a victim's legs

in Dansey Place. For Western readers, the novel is full of insights into a semi-hidden world. Mo reveals the inauthenticity of what most Westerners know as 'Chinese food' when the preoccupied Chen begins to confuse the orders, absent-mindedly bringing 'lurid orange sweet and sour pork with pineapple chunks to outraged Chinese customers and white, bloody chicken and yellow duck's feet to appalled Westerners'.

Fittingly, given the amount of writing that did manage to get done in Soho, Charing Cross

Narrow Lisle Street forms the southern boundary of Chinatown.

Charing Cross Road in 1958. The great bookselling road was made famous by Helene Hanff's 84, Charing Cross Road, (1970), the tale of her 20-year correspondence from 1949 to 1969 with London bookseller Frank Doel. Sadly the Marks & Co. bookshop where he worked is no longer there.

Here he hosted a series of dinner parties that were marked by his increasingly bizarre behaviour. On one occasion he told Osbert and Sacheverell Sitwell to ask the porter for 'the Captain', despite the fact that Eliot had never been in the armed forces. During the meal the guests noticed that Eliot was wearing pale green face powder, presumably to look more like a tragic poet. At another gathering here, to which he invited various members of the Bloomsbury Group, Eliot became paralytically drunk, threw up, then passed out, leaving his guests to see themselves out. The next morning he spent ten minutes apologizing on the phone to Virginia Woolf.

Road is lined with bookshops. Foyles, at number 119, is famous for its impenetrable shelving system and mountains of dusty, forgotten stock. During the first half of the twentieth century, the poet and diabolist Aleister Crowley (known, to his great satisfaction, as 'the most evil man in the world') could occasionally be seen browsing in the occult section. The 'mole hunt' in John Le Carré's espionage novel *Tinker Tailor Soldier Spy* (1974) takes place close by, in 'the Circus' – the dingy offices of MI6, in the northeast corner of Cambridge Circus.

In 1923, TS Eliot rented rooms at Burleigh Mansions at 20 Charing Cross Road, near Cecil Court.

The last word on Soho belongs to Quentin Crisp. After decades of being beaten up, arrested and generally harassed, Crisp experienced a moment of epiphany in the Coach and Horses, in the late 1960s. 'A man was asked to leave because he persistently made fun of me. When this happened I knew for sure that Soho had become a reservation from hooligans. We could at last walk majestically in our natural setting, observed but no longer shot at by the safaris that still loved to penetrate this exotic land.'

OXFORD STREET AND MARYLEBONE

As a teenage runaway at the very beginning of the nineteenth century, Thomas De Quincey walked endlessly up and down Oxford Street with his friend Ann, the young prostitute who had befriended him (see Soho). In middle age he would describe how 'Often, when I walk at this time in Oxford-street by dreamy lamplight, and hear those airs played on a barrel organ which years ago solaced me and my dear companion (as I must always call her) I shed tears, and amuse with myself at the mysterious dispensation which so suddenly and so critically separated us for ever.'

At times, De Quincey would rail against Oxford Street and its doleful influence on his life. In *Confessions of an English Opium Eater* he berated 'Oxford-street, stony-hearted step-mother! thou that listenest to the sighs of orphans, and drinkest the tears of children', but in reality he had mixed feelings about the street which shaped his life more than any other. It was in Oxford Street that he bought his first bottle of laudanum (basically heroin mixed with alcohol), recommended by a college friend as a cure for toothache. This single purchase – from a chemist's shop next door to the Pantheon Theatre (now the Marks & Spencer Pantheon store) – would lead to a lifetime of addiction. But, rather than seeing it as the first step on the road to ruin, De Quincey looked back on the purchase with reverent nostalgia.

It was a Sunday afternoon, wet and cheerless: and a duller spectacle this earth of ours has not to show than a rainy Sunday in London. My road homewards lay through Oxford-street; and near 'the stately Pantheon,' (as Mr Wordsworth has obligingly put

A busy Oxford Street, 1909. Fifteen years later, Denham Dobie, the out-of-town, eccentric heroine of Rose Macaulay's Crewe Train *(1926), is driven frantic by the swarming crowds on Oxford Street – 'as thick as flies over a dead goat' – and the 'thousands of omnibuses, taxis, vans and cars…mowing down with angry trumpetings such human life as crossed their path.' Denham concludes, 'the population needed thinning; but it seemed a curious way of doing it.'*

*it) I saw a druggist's shop.
The druggist – unconscious
minister of celestial pleasures!
– as if in sympathy with the
rainy Sunday, looked dull
and stupid, just as any
mortal druggist might be
expected to look on a Sunday;
and, when I asked for the
tincture of opium, he gave it
to me as any other man might
do: and furthermore, out of
my shilling, returned me what
seemed to be a real copper
halfpence, taken out of a real
wooden drawer. Nevertheless,
in spite of such indications of
humanity, he has since existed
in my mind as the beatific
vision of an immortal
druggist, sent down to earth
on a special mission to myself.*

Back in his lodgings with his
precious purchase, De Quincey
had his first taste of 'the abyss of
divine enjoyment'.

*Here was a panacea ... for all
human woes: here was the
secret of happiness, about*

*which philosophers had
disputed for so many ages, at
once discovered: happiness
might now be bought for a
penny, and carried in the
waistcoat pocket: portable
ecstasies might be corked up in
a pint bottle: and peace of
mind could be sent down in
gallons by the mail coach.*

The terrifying 'opium
nightmares', inability to work and,
consequently, chronic poverty and
debt would come later.

The Oxford Street that De
Quincey knew was on the
northern edge of London,
with a view along 'every avenue in
succession which pierces through
the heart of Marylebone to the
fields and the woods'. One such
avenue was Berners Street, where
another opium addict, Coleridge,
lived with his friends the Morgan
family in 1812–13. His visitors at
number 17 included Charles
Lamb and Wordsworth, with
whom he had recently (and, as it
turned out, irrevocably) fallen out;
the two poets, did,
however, walk to
Hampstead together.
Dickens knew Berners
Street well. As a child,
he once saw a mad
woman there, dressed
entirely in white and
with her hair in white
plaits; the incident
may have influenced
his friend Wilkie
Collins's suspense
novel *The Woman in
White*. Dickens's
friend Ellen Ternan
lived at 31 Berners
Street, with her sister
Maria, in the late
1850s, at about the
time Dickens

*Louis MacNeice
(right) with BBC
producer Frank
Hauser at the Stag's
Head in Hallam
Street, c.1950.*

separated from his wife.

The novelist John Buchan was living at 14 Portland Place in 1914 when he wrote his much-imitated spy thriller *The Thirty-Nine Steps*. His hero, Richard Hannay, also lives in Portland Place, in a first-floor flat 'in a new block behind Langham Place'. It is there that he stumbles across what was then a highly original scenario: a man lying on the smoking room carpet with a knife through his heart. Guessing correctly that the police may assume he had something to do with the murder, Hannay makes his escape dressed as a milkman.

Since 1932, the best-known landmark in Portland Place has been the BBC studios at Broadcasting House. Past employees have included Louis MacNeice, who was a radio producer and broadcaster from the Second World War until his early death in 1963, from pneumonia exacerbated by conducting an outside broadcast from a Yorkshire pot hole. During the war MacNeice's friend Dylan Thomas was given a poetry-reading slot on the Third Programme. On one occasion, Thomas's producer, Roy Campbell, found the poet sitting at the microphone in a drunken stupor, with only minutes to go before he was supposed to be on the air. When Campbell desperately shook him awake, Thomas almost jumped out of his skin with fright, but then delivered an almost perfect rendition of the first poem, bungling only the title, which came out as 'Ode on Shaint Sheshilia Day'. Thomas then seemed to get into his stride, then started waving his arms about to attract Campbell's attention. He had spotted another verbal booby trap, 'Religio Laici', in the text, and didn't know how to pronounce it. He made three attempts, then gave up and carried on. The next day, Campbell was duly carpeted by the Controller of the Third Programme.

Another BBC producer at the time was George Orwell, whose brief included broadcasting to India and south-east Asia with a view to stiffening their wartime resolve. To this end, TS Eliot was invited to the studio to read 'The Waste Land' and EM Forster to discuss the development of the novel. Orwell swiftly grew to dislike the bureaucracy and stuffiness of the BBC, which he described as 'halfway between a

Dylan Thomas (right) looks dangerously close to dropping off as he prepares a wartime radio broadcast.

The BBC canteen in 1943. Broadcasters who have complained about the food range from George Orwell to Terry Wogan.

girls' school and a lunatic asylum'. Orwell took his revenge in a number of ways – some of them rather childish, such as adopting a fake cockney accent and noisily slurping his canteen tea from the saucer – others more measured. In *Nineteen Eighty-Four*, written five years after he left the BBC, the bureaucracy and appalling canteen food at the Ministry of Truth were both modelled on the BBC. The scene in which Winston sits in the room above Mr Charrington's shop and listens to the 'prole woman' singing also had its origin at Broadcasting House. Orwell, who worshipped the working class, was enthralled by the sight and sound of the BBC charwomen at work: 'They sit in the reception hall waiting for their brooms to be issued to them and making as much noise as a parrot house, and then they have wonderful choruses, all singing together as they sweep the passages.'

Anthony Trollope spent the last month of his life in Welbeck Street. After suffering a stroke in Suffolk Street, on 3 November 1882 (it is said, after getting into an argument with a group of noisy street musicians), he was brought to a nursing home at 34 Welbeck Street, where he died on 6 December.

At one point in Iris Murdoch's *Under the Net* (1954) the narrator, Jake Donaghue, is sitting on a fire escape overlooking Welbeck Street, eavesdropping at the door of a third-floor flat. When a small group of onlookers gathers on the corner of Queen Anne Street, Donaghue descends the fire escape at a leisurely pace, then runs towards the crowd uttering a piercing hiss. The crowd scatters in terror.

Nearby Wimpole Street enjoys dual fame as the scene of a great friendship and, later, a great romance. The friendship was that of Alfred Tennyson and Arthur

Hallam. The two young men met at Cambridge, and in 1831 Arthur became engaged to Tennyson's sister Emily. Two years later, Hallam died suddenly at the age of 22, leaving Tennyson almost suicidal with grief. Over the next 17 years he wrote a series of verses inspired by the friendship, and his own loss, which were eventually published together as 'In Memoriam'. The lines 'The dark house by which once more I stand, / Here in the dark unlovely street' refer to Hallam's family home at 67 Wimpole Street.

In 1838, 32-year-old Elizabeth Barrett moved with her father, brothers and sisters to 50 Wimpole Street. Her life to date had been marred by a series of tragedies. At 15 she was seriously injured in a riding accident, since when her family had treated her as a semi-invalid. When Elizabeth was 20 her mother died, followed by her brother, drowned off the Devon coast. Elizabeth herself was a gifted scholar and poet: at eight she was reading Homer in the original, and at 13 she wrote an epic of her own, 'The Battle of Marathon', which her father, Edward Moulton Barrett, published at his own expense.

In Wimpole Street her 'delicacy', combined with her father's protective aut-horitarianism, kept her almost permanently confined to her room where, with her spaniel Flush for company, she read voraciously and wrote poetry. By then another poet, Robert Browning, had started corresponding with her, and soon after their first meeting they became engaged. The engagement had to be kept secret – Elizabeth's father had forbidden any of his children to marry. On 12 September 1846, the couple were married at St Marylebone Parish Church, after which Elizabeth returned home, alone, to Wimpole Street. After a week in which she had to pretend nothing had happened, she and Browning, accompanied by the faithful Flush, left for Italy, where they lived until her death in 1861. Nathaniel Hawthorne, who met the couple at their home in Florence, remembered Elizabeth Browning as 'a small, pale person, scarcely embodied at all … It is wonderful to see how small she is, how pale her cheek, how bright and dark her eyes. There is not such another figure in the world, and her black ringlets cluster down into her neck and make her face look whiter.'

Rudolph Besier's 1930 play *The Barretts of Wimpole Street* hinted at an incestuous motive in Edward Moulton Barrett's behaviour. In the film version Barrett was played by Charles Laughton. 'They can't censor the gleam in my eye,' was Laughton's response when he heard that this aspect of the play would have to

Emily Tennyson (above) was engaged to Arthur Hallam, the close friend of Alfred Lord Tennyson (below). The friendship between Tennyson and Hallam and the loss Tennyson felt at Hallam's untimely death were the inspiration for 'In Memoriam'.

Number 50 Wimpole Street, the family home of Elizabeth Barrett before she eloped with Robert Browning.

the Bayswater benches … pick themselves up, and drag their misery away from the pitiless daylight'. As for Fabian, he is on his way to blackmail (for £150) a harmless, broken man in a distant suburb.

Edgware Road, which runs north-west from Marble Arch, is now best known for its Lebanese restaurants and for its ceaseless traffic heading for the M1. In the early 1770s, Oliver Goldsmith had lodgings in a nearby farm cottage, where he wrote his most successful play, *She Stoops to Conquer*. Charles Dickens was walking down Edgware Road one day in the spring of 1849 with his friend Mark Lemon, when a youth picked Lemon's pocket. Dickens and Lemon gave chase, handed the man over to the police and subsequently gave evidence at his trial. The youth indignantly told the court that his pursuers were criminals themselves and made their living fencing stolen goods.

be toned down for cinema audiences. In 1933 Virginia Woolf wrote a now obscure novel, *Flush*, written from the dog's point of view, 'to cool myself' as she put it, after a bout of intense mental effort on *The Years*.

The westernmost point of Oxford Street is marked by Marble Arch, originally erected in front of Buckingham Palace and moved to its present position in 1851. The arch now forms the centre of a formidable road junction. In Gerald Kersh's *Night and the City* (1938), the amoral Harry Fabian sits in a taxi there at dawn, listening to a remote bird singing 'the notes of an ecstatic song' as 'the broken outcasts of

Elizabeth Barrett Browning (1806–61) wrote her first epic while still a teenager.

Greene's ghost story 'A Little Place off the Edgware Road' (1939) is set in a silent-film cinema near Marble Arch.

Best known for his epic paintings and his gossipy journals, Benjamin Robert Haydon was living at 116 Lisson Grove when he hosted one of the most embarrassing literary dinner parties on record. The guests included Keats and Wordsworth, who had met only once before, Charles Lamb, and a number of others. Prominently on display was Haydon's unfinished painting 'Christ's Entry into Jerusalem', in which Keats and Wordsworth can be seen in the crowd.

The evening started promisingly enough, with a spirited group discussion of Homer, Virgil, Shakespeare and Milton, followed by an impromptu recital of Milton's poetry by Wordsworth. The trouble started when another guest, John Kingston, the Deputy Comptroller of the Stamp Office, arrived late. Wordsworth, who had been earning some extra income as a local Distributor of Stamps in the Lake District, was a junior colleague of Kingston, though the two men had never met. By then Charles Lamb, who had no head for alcohol, was already inebriated and he took an instant dislike to the new arrival. Thirty years later, Haydon recalled the toe-curling scene which followed:

> Lamb got up and, taking a candle, said, 'Sir, will you allow me to look at your phrenological development?' He then turned his back on the poor man, and at every question of the comptroller he chanted –
> Diddle diddle
> dumpling, my son John

Went to bed with his breeches on.

The man in office, finding Wordsworth did not know who he was, said in a spasmodic and half-chuckling anticipation of assured victory, 'I have the honour of some correspondence with you, Mr Wordsworth.' 'With me, sir?' said Wordsworth. 'Not that I remember.' 'Don't you, sir? I am comptroller of stamps.' There was a dead silence; – the comptroller evidently thinking that was enough. While we were waiting for Wordsworth's reply, Lamb sung out
> Hey diddle diddle,
> The cat and the fiddle.

'My dear Charles!' said Wordsworth, –
> 'Diddle diddle
> dumpling, my son John,'
chanted Lamb, and then rising, exclaimed, 'Do let me have another look at that gentleman's organs.' Keats and I hurried Lamb into the painting-room, shut the door and gave way to inextinguishable laughter. Monkhouse [an MP] followed and tried to get Lamb away. We went back but the comptroller was irreconcilable. We soothed and smiled and asked him to supper. He stayed, though his dignity was sorely affected. However, being a good-natured man, we parted all in good humour, and no ill-effects followed. All the while, until Monkhouse succeeded, we could hear Lamb struggling in the

'*I* love your verses with all my heart, dear Miss Barrett' wrote Robert Browning (1812–89) to Elizabeth Barrett after reading her volume of Poems 1844.

painting-room and calling at intervals, 'Who is that fellow? Allow me to see his organs once more.'

In July 1822, Coleridge was living with the Gillman family in Highgate when his 26-year-old son Hartley came to stay for a few days. Hartley was Coleridge's eldest son – the 'babe' to whom many years earlier he had addressed one of his finest poems, 'Frost at Midnight'. During the visit, father and son went into London on some errand. Hartley suddenly announced that he had a bill to pay and arranged to meet his father at six o'clock outside a shop in York Street. He then disappeared into the crowd, and at the appointed time he failed to appear. Coleridge never saw him again.

Charles Lamb (1775–1834), like his sister, was prone to bouts of mania. In 1796 he wrote to his old schoolfriend Coleridge: 'The six weeks that finished last year and began this, your humble servant spent very agreeably in a mad house at Hoxton – I am somewhat rational now and don't bite anymore.'

Four of the greatest Victorian novelists – Dickens, Collins, Gissing and Eliot – all lived at various times in Marylebone. In 1839, Dickens moved his growing family to 1 Devonshire Terrace, on the corner of Marylebone Road and Marylebone High Street. It was here that he wrote *The Old Curiosity Shop*, *Barnaby Rudge*, *Martin Chuzzlewit*, *A Christmas Carol*, *Dombey and Son* and *David Copperfield*. An additional member of the family who was acquired at Devonshire Terrace was a pet raven named Grip, who used to nip the children's ankles; he appears, name unchanged, in *Barnaby Rudge*. Dickens moved out in 1851, and the whole of Devonshire Terrace was pulled down in the 1950s. Ferguson House, which stands on the site, has a bust of Dickens and bas-reliefs of some of his characters. Dickens's next – and last – permanent London home was in Tavistock Square, but between February and June 1864 he lodged at 57 Gloucester Place, writing the early instalments of *Our Mutual Friend*.

Dickens's friend Wilkie Collins began and ended his career in Marylebone. They met in 1850, when Collins became a member of Dickens's touring amateur theatre company. He and Dickens acted in Edward Bulwer-Lytton's comedy *Not So Bad As We Seem* and subsequently wrote plays together. Dickens seems to have been intrigued by, and perhaps a little envious of, Collins's (for its time) outrageous lifestyle. Despite his unusual appearance – he was short, near-sighted and had an enormous head which was concave on one side and convex on the other – Collins was a prolific and highly successful womanizer, enjoying numerous one-off sexual encounters while maintaining two mistresses, and several illegitimate children, in separate households.

Collins's first published work – a biography of his father, the landscape painter William Collins – was written at 38 Blandford Square in 1848, where he was living with his mother and brother. In 1850 the family moved to the august surroundings of 17 Hanover Terrace, on the south-eastern edge of Regent's Park, where Collins began writing for

Dickens's journal *Household Words*. His classic short story 'The Traveller's Story of a Terribly Strange Bed' was written here in 1852, as was his spellbinding 'novel of sensation' *The Woman in White*.

In 1867, Collins moved to 65 Gloucester Place – a few doors along from Dickens's temporary lodging a few years earlier – and wrote his second-best book *The Moonstone*. His hero, Sergeant Cuff, was not, as has often been claimed, the first literary detective – Edgar Allan Poe's Dupin ('The Murders in the Rue Morgue') and Dickens's Inspector Bucket (*Bleak House*) both got there before him – but TS Eliot was correct when he described *The Moonstone* as 'the first, the longest and the best of modern English detective novels'.

By now, Collins's most productive years were over. Although he went on to publish 15 more novels, the quality of his work began to decline when he ill-advisedly switched from the sensation novel, which was his natural metier, to the 'social problem' novel, which was not. Algernon Swinburne – another Marylebone neighbour, at 22 Dorset Street – summed up his decline in a couplet:

What brought good Wilkie's genius nigh perdition? Some demon whispered – 'Wilkie! have a mission.'

Collins's health was also failing. He suffered acute pain from a variety of ailments – chiefly gout, compounded by unspecified neuralgic problems – from which he sought relief in laudanum. By the end of his life he was taking the drug in enormous quantities; it is said that one of his servants

died after helping himself to half his employer's usual dose. Collins himself died in 1889, at 82 Wimpole Street, at the surprisingly advanced age of 65.

In 1860, George Eliot and her partner George Henry Lewes took a three-year lease on a house at 16 Blandford Square. Eliot was a reluctant Marylebone dweller. 'I languish sadly for the fields and the broad sky; but duties must be done,' she wrote to a friend. The 'duties' involved acting as a surrogate mother to Lewes's sons and living a conventional domestic existence, which Eliot hoped would limit the opprobrium that inevitably followed her setting up home with a married man.

Charles Dickens described his home at 1 Devonshire Terrace as 'a house of undeniable situation and splendour', but the building was demolished in the 1950s.

Wilkie Collins was as prolific as a womanizer as he was as a novelist.

The ostracism was comprehensive – Eliot's own brother, Isaac, did not speak or write to her again until after Lewes's death some 20 years later – but it was also based on a profound misunderstanding. Lewes's marriage had foundered not through his own infidelity but that of his wife. Agnes Lewes had had four children by Thornton Leigh Hunt (son of the editor Leigh Hunt), whom Lewes had unselfishly brought up as his own children. One of the boys was even named Thornton after his real father.

The precise terms of the ostracism were doubly curious by today's standards. According to Victorian convention, it was unacceptable for a 'fallen woman' like Eliot to consort with members of her own sex, but quite permissible for her to receive gentlemen callers. Hence, when she and Lewes threw a house-warming party at their next home, the Priory at 21 North Bank, on the edge of Regent's Park, it was attended by Anthony Trollope, but boycotted by his wife.

Over the years, George Gissing lived at more than a dozen addresses in London, but between 1884 and 1890 he was at 7k Cornwall Residences, a block of flats behind Madame Tussaud's in Marylebone Road. Probably because of this long residence in the area, Gissing's most enduring novel, *New Grub Street*, has scenes in Marylebone and Regent's Park. Like Collins and Eliot, George Gissing conducted life very much on his own terms, though in his case it seems to have been dictated by something approaching masochism. Even the normally non-judgemental *Dictionary of National Biography* noted drily that Gissing 'showed a curious inability to do the sane, secure thing in the ordinary affairs of life'. As a student at Owen's College, Manchester, he won awards for his poetry, and for classical and Shakespearian scholarship, but was expelled from the university and jailed for a month after being caught stealing. Gissing had planned to use the money to help a young prostitute, Helen Harrison, whom he subsequently married. He endured several years of marital discord and poverty before Helen drank herself to death, and in *New Grub Street* he wrote feelingly about the unhappy marriage of the intellectual Alfred Yule and his unintellectual, 'unpresentable' wife. Yet, while the novel was still at the printers, he married a second working-class girl, Edith Underwood, an action which one of his future biographers would describe as 'another of those acts of self-mortification that Gissing committed from time to time with the subconscious motive of putting himself at a disadvantage'. A further act of 'self-mortification' was his refusal to accept lucrative journalistic work, even though by doing so he condemned himself to a life of near-penury. Gissing did write a couple of articles for the *Pall Mall Gazette*, through the intervention of a friend, the philosopher Frederic Harrison, but then refused to write any more. Harrison's son Austin recalled that 'at any time after 1882, Gissing could have obtained a place as critic or writer on some journal, which could have enabled him to write [fiction] at leisure. But he would never hear of such a thing … Gissing positively chose to live in strife.'

In *New Grub Street*, Edwin Reardon lives in a flat near Regent's Park, where he struggles to provide for his family by writing populist novels. Too worried about money to construct a new novel, but knowing that if he does not produce something soon his family will go hungry, Reardon spends sleepless nights in which he contemplates either finding a new occupation, or committing suicide.

The various sounds which marked the stages from midnight to dawn had grown miserably familiar to him; worst torture to his mind was the chiming and striking of clocks. Two of these were in general audible, that of Marylebone Parish Church, and that of the adjoining workhouse; the latter always sounded several minutes after its ecclesiastical neighbour, and with a difference of note which seemed to Reardon very appropriate – a thin, querulous voice, reminding

one of the community it represented. After lying awake for a while he would hear the quarters sounding; if they ceased before the fourth he was glad, for he feared to know what time it was. If the hour was complete, he waited anxiously for its number. Two, three, even four, were grateful; there was still a long time before he need rise and face the dreaded task, the horrible four blank slips of paper that had to be filled ere he might sleep again.

Eventually, some of Gissing's own wilfulness paid off. Although the marriage to Edith predictably ended in separation, Gissing's prolific writing eventually enabled him to live in reasonable comfort. One of his last books was *By the Ionian Sea* (1900), an account of his travels in Italy with HG Wells. Coming from a similar back-

George Eliot came to London after the death of her father and quickly found herself at the centre of a literary circle whose members included Herbert Spencer and George Henry Lewes.

St Marylebone Parish Church appears in the novels of George Gissing and Patrick Hamilton.

ground in provincial 'trade' (Gissing's father was a Wakefield pharmacist), Wells got the measure of his friend early on: 'He felt that to [court] any woman he could regard as a social equal would be too elaborate ... so he flung himself at a social inferior, whom he expected to be eager and grateful.'

Reardon is not the only fictional character to be tormented by St Marylebone Parish Church. In Patrick Hamilton's *Twenty Thousand Streets under the Sky* (1935) Bob the barman has arranged to meet Jenny Maple outside the Green Man pub, opposite the church, at a quarter past three. Bob's thought process will be familiar to anyone who has ever been on a first date.

By five and twenty past he was growing disturbed. It seemed that only five minutes stood between him and an almost unthinkable dilemma. For at half past he would have to give up hope. His mind and soul concentrated on the hands of the clock, trying to stay their movement. In walking up and down he was careful to look at the dial only when farthest to the right of it. In that way you gained, by the angle, about half a minute. But there came a time when no angle could mitigate the facts of the case. It was half-past three. He would now wait as a formality until four.

The address of Sherlock Holmes, 221b Baker Street, is probably the most celebrated in literature. When Sir Arthur Conan Doyle published the first Holmes mystery, 'A Study in Scarlet', in 1887, he was practising as an oculist in South-sea. In 1891 he moved his practice to 2 Upper Wimpole Street. As he recalled later, 'Every morning I walked from the lodgings at Montague Place, reached my consulting room at ten and sat there until three or four with never a ring to disturb my serenity.' To while away the time, he wrote more of the Holmes stories. What Doyle later described as 'the first fruits of a considerable harvest' enabled him to abandon medicine and devote himself to writing. He was eventually to receive the then considerable sum of £2,500 per story for the British rights alone. The last Holmes adventure, 'Shoscombe Old Place'. appeared in March 1927, three years before Doyle's death.

Holmes's knack of immediately identifying the character and recent activities of his clients was derived from the surgeon Joseph Bell, under whom Doyle had done his medical training in Edinburgh. One of the best stories, 'The Adventure of the Speckled Band', has a typical example of Holmes' powers of on-the-spot deduction. Visited at Baker Street by a distraught client, Holmes gives her 'one of his quick, all-comprehensive glances'.

'You have come in by train this morning, I see.'
'You know me, then?'
'No, but I observe the second half of a return ticket in the palm of your left glove. You must have started early, and yet you have had a good drive in a dog-cart, along heavy roads, before you reached the station.'
The lady gave a violent start, and stared in bewilderment at my companion.
'There is no mystery, my dear madam,' said he, smiling. 'The left arm of your jacket is spattered with mud in no less than seven places. The marks are perfectly fresh. There is no vehicle save a dog-cart which throws up mud in that way, and then only when you sit on

the left hand side of the driver.'

In *Baker Street Byways*, published to mark the centenary of Doyle's birth, James Edward Holroyd celebrated the cosy sitting room in Baker Street, with its solid, uncomfortable-looking armchairs, bearskin rug, chemical apparatus in the corner, pipes, dressing gown and the jack-knife which Holmes uses to secure correspondence to the mantelpiece. As Holroyd remarks, 'all these became, and for large numbers of people have remained, as immediately recognizable as the furniture in the homes of close friends'.

Identifying the actual location of 221b Baker Street is surprisingly difficult. When Doyle chose the 'address', the street

Sir Arthur Conan Doyle eventually tired of his most famous character, Sherlock Holmes and killed him off in 'The Final Problem' by having him fall into the Reichenbach Falls. He resurrected him reluctantly after much public clamour. 'The old dog always returns to his vomit,' Doyle is reputed to have explained.

The archetypal Holmes and Watson, as illustrated in the original Strand *magazine stories by Sidney Paget.*

numbers in Baker Street only went up to 85: Doyle, like many other novelists, habitually gives addresses consisting of fictitious numbers in real streets. To complicate matters further, in a notebook which Doyle used to jot down some early thoughts on Holmes and Watson he gave the address as 221b *Upper* Baker Street (which then ran from Paddington Street to Marylebone Road), and repeated the address in his stage version of 'The Adventure of the Speckled Band'. Number 221b didn't exist until the 1930s, when the buildings were renumbered and *Upper* Baker Street officially ceased to exist. The Abbey National Building Society was given the hallowed number 221, and still receives up to 50 letters a month from people asking for Holmes's assistance. As part of the Festival of Britain in 1951, the Abbey National housed an exhibition of Holmesiana, complete with a reconstruction of the 221b sitting room. Afterwards, the exhibition

was moved to the Sherlock Holmes pub in Northumberland Street (see Strand), where it remains.

One of Holmes's greatest fans was TS Eliot, who liked to amuse his friends by quoting lengthy passages from memory. (In *Keep the Aspidistra Flying* George Orwell attributes the same habit to his fictional poet Gordon Comstock, which may or may not have been a deliberate dig at Eliot.) In 1916, Eliot and his wife Vivien moved in to a cramped, noisy flat just off Baker Street, at 18 Crawford Mansions, Crawford Street. Shortly after their arrival, Eliot received a court summons for showing too much light around his blackout curtains (London was being subjected to regular Zeppelin raids). Crawford Street was then a poor, run-down area, and Eliot's nerves – already fragile as a result of Vivien's psychiatric illness – were made worse by the incessant noise from a pub across the street. The Eliots managed to stick it out for four years before moving to Flat 9, Clarence Gate Gardens, a mansion block next to Regent's Park. Over the next 12 years they would live in various other flats in the same block, finishing at 68 Clarence Gate Gardens, which was the last home they shared. A neighbour, the novelist Elizabeth Bowen, visited the Eliots there in 1932 and found it a 'sinister and depressing' place – 'two highly nervous people shut up together in grinding proximity'. By then, Vivien had taken to biting people and her nurses were under instructions to keep her away from the windows. In September Eliot departed on a lengthy tour of North America, and on his return he decided to live alone. Vivien remained at 68 Clarence Gate Gardens, from where she would make frequent visits to her husband's offices in Russell Square hoping to see him (see Bloomsbury). On the second anniversary of his departure, Vivien placed an advertisement in *The Times* which read: 'Will T S Eliot please return to his home 68 Clarence Gate Gardens which he abandoned Sept. 17th 1932.' In 1938 she was confined in a mental hospital in Finsbury Park, where she died nine years later.

The publisher who narrates Julian Barnes's witty ghost story 'A Self-Possessed Woman' (1975) begins by announcing, 'I have always disliked those large blocks of flats at the northern end of Baker Street. They epitomize for me the deadness of high material comfort.' It is in one of them that he meets Mrs Beesley, a medium who is receiving messages from beyond the grave from a variety of writers, including Coleridge, Byron, Gissing, and James. Realizing he is on to something, the publisher starts preparing an anthology of their posthumous literary efforts as they appear – an arrangement which works well until the authors start squabbling with each other and with literary critics who have misrepresented them.

Barnes's first novel, *Metroland* (1980), is told by a schoolboy who travels from his home in outer suburbia ('Metroland') to Baker Street Station on the Metropolitan Line, taking in 'the grimy, lost stations between Baker Street and Finchley Road; the steppe-like playing fields at Northwick Park; the depot at Neasden, full of idle, aged rolling-stock; the frozen faces of passengers glimpsed in the windows of fast Marylebone trains'. The term Metroland had already been made familiar by John Betjeman, who in his verse autobiography *Summoned by Bells* recalled childhood expeditions on the Underground with his father:

> The expeditions by North
> London trains
> To dim forgotten
>   stations, wooden shacks
> On oil-lit flimsy
>   platforms among fields
> As yet unbuilt-on,
>   deep in Middlesex ...

Similar trips were taken with his school friend Ronnie Wright. During pauses between stations, the pair would wait for silence to descend on the compartment and then launch into animated gibberish, so other passengers would think they were foreign.

One of Sherlock Holmes's greatest fans was TS Eliot, who lived just off Baker Street for four years, at 18 Crawford Mansions.

COVENT GARDEN

When the ten-year-old Charles Dickens arrived in London with his family from Chatham in 1822, it was Covent Garden that he wanted to visit first. Dickens's enthusiasm had been fuelled by the books he had read at home in Chatham, among them George Colman's verses on Covent Garden:

John Gay's The Beggar's Opera was first performed in Covent Garden in 1728, in a production by the theatrical manager John Rich. Its enormous success was said to make Gay rich and Rich gay.

Centrick, in London noise,
and London follies,
Proud Covent Garden
blooms, in smoky glory;
For chairmen, coffee-rooms,
piazzas, dollies,
Cabbages, and comedians,
famed in story.

Dickens also remembered the earthier description of the market in one of his favourite novels, Tobias Smollett's *The Expedition of Humphry Clinker:*

I saw a dirty barrow-bunter
in the street, cleaning her
dusty fruit with her own

spittle and who knows but
some fine lady of St James'
parish might admit into her
delicate mouth those very
cherries, which had been
rolled and moistened between
the filthy, and perhaps
ulcerated chops.

Clearly, Dickens wasn't disappointed by what he found. In his first book, *Sketches by Boz,* published when he was 24, he describes the street life of Seven Dials – gin shops and their brawling customers, out-of-work labourers leaning against lamp posts and 'streets of dirty straggling houses, with now and then an unexpected court composed of buildings as ill-proportiond and deformed as the half-naked children that wallow in the kennels'. As he approached the end of his career 30 years later, Dickens was still drawing inspiration from Covent Garden. In the last novel he completed, *Our Mutual Friend,* Mr Venus, the collector of anatomical specimens, was based on a taxidermist named Willis whose shop Dickens had visited in St Andrew's Street, near Seven Dials.

Until the mid-nineteenth century, Covent Garden was famous for its street ballad writers and publishers. One of the most successful of these was John Gay, whose *Beggar's Opera* (1728) was based on a series of street songs. His description of Seven Dials, written in *Trivia* in 1716, is still recognizable today:

Here to seven streets, seven
dials count the day,
And from each other catch the
circling ray;
Here oft the peasant with
enquiring face

*Bewildered trudges on from
place to place;
He dwells on every sign
with stupid gaze,
Enters the narrow alley's
doubtful maze,
Tries every winding court
and street in vain,
And doubles o'er his weary
steps again.*

Times haven't changed much, except that the bewildered peasants have been replaced by bewildered tourists. In his 1985 novel *Hawksmoor*, Peter Ackroyd's eponymous detective lives alone in a flat near Seven Dials.

If Seven Dials was the disreputable nexus of Covent Garden, the area around the Piazza was its fashionable centre, where the great scenes of its literary heyday were played out. One of the more endearing of these took place on 9 May 1662, when Samuel Pepys watched London's first ever Punch and Judy show, under the portico of St Paul's Church. (The same portico provides the rainswept opening scene of Bernard Shaw's *Pygmalion*, with pedestrians sheltering from the rain.) In 1665 Pepys came across the first visible signs of the plague which was soon to sweep London:

This day, much against my Will, I did see in Drury Lane see two or three houses marked with a red cross upon the doors, and "Lord have mercy upon us" writ there – which was a sad sight to me, being the first of that kind that to my remembrance I ever saw. It put me into an ill conception of myself and my smell, so that I was forced to buy some roll tobacco

to smell to and to chaw – which took away the apprehension.'

Designed in the 1620s as a development for 'Gentlemen and men of ability', the Piazza was subsequently dominated by its fruit and vegetable market and by the newly fashionable coffee houses which sprang up nearby. By the mid-eighteenth century, Inigo Jones's carefully designed houses were rapidly going downmarket, inhabited not by gentlemen but by the patrons of seedy taverns, Turkish baths, gambling dens and brothels. Press gangs and footpads (muggers) roamed the streets, and the local inns were notorious for brawls and duels. In 1772, Richard Brinsley Sheridan fought a duel at the Castle Tavern in Henrietta Street. Sheridan had

The fruit, vegetable and flower market was held at Covent Garden from 1656 until 1974, when it moved to Vauxhall. When he had no money, Charles Dickens would come to the market to gaze at the pineapples.

*B*ernard Shaw's Pygmalion *begins under the portico of St Paul's Church (top), with 'cab whistles blowing frantically in all directions'.*

*C*ovent Garden *flower women (circa 1870). When Henry Higgins meets Eliza Doolittle she is selling flowers in Covent Garden.*

Attempting to keep some semblance of order in and around Covent Garden were the famous Bow Street magistrates, one of whom was the novelist Henry Fielding. It was Fielding who, in 1750, established the rudimentary police force known as the Bow Street Runners. Though famously incorruptible, Fielding was no prude: the bawdiness of his novel *Tom Jones* (1749) earned the wrath of Dr Johnson. Fielding's assistant was his stepbrother John, who succeeded him as magistrate in 1754. Known to local villains as 'the blind beak', John did not allow his disability to interfere with judicial efficiency: he was said to be able to recognize 3,000 footpads by their voices.

The original courthouse from which the brothers used to dispense justice, at 4 Bow Street, was pulled down in the 1880s. The present-day Bow Street Magistrates' Court, which replaced it, is roughly opposite. In April 1895, Oscar Wilde was brought here to be committed for trial after being arrested at the Cadogan Hotel in Chelsea (see Chelsea).

Number 1 Bow Street was the address of one of London's most famous coffee houses, Will's, opened about 1660 by one William Urwin. Looking into Will's one day in 1668 on the way to meet his wife, Pepys found Will's a place of 'very witty and pleasant discourse'. Much of the discourse was provided by Will's star turn, the poet and dramatist John Dryden, who had his own seat by the fire in winter, and

befriended a young woman, Eliza Linley, who was being pursued by an unwanted admirer, Major Mathews, and when Sheridan escorted her to France and subsequently married her Mathews publicly denounced his rival as 'a treacherous scoundrel'. Both men survived the duel, though they wounded each other so badly that pistols subsequently replaced swords as the weapons of choice for such contests. Sheridan seems to have mellowed with age. In 1809, the Theatre Royal, Drury Lane, where his play *The School for Scandal* had been a huge success, caught fire and burnt to the ground. Sheridan had shares in the theatre and knew that its destruction meant economic ruin, so a friend was surprised to come across him calmly sipping a glass of port while watching the flames lick around his theatre. 'Surely,' the playwright protested, 'a man may be allowed to take a glass of wine by his own fireside?'

another on the balcony during the summer months. On the night of 18 December 1679 Dryden was on his way home from Will's when he was set upon by a masked gang outside the Lamb and Flag tavern in Rose Alley (now Rose Street). His assailants had almost certainly been hired by the Earl of Rochester, in the mistaken belief that he was the author of the 'Essay on Satire' in which Rochester had been ridiculed. The true culprit was the Earl of Mulgrave, who later put up a monument to Dryden in Westminster Abbey.

Another regular at Will's was the elderly satirist Samuel Butler, whose appearance was described by a casual visitor shortly before his death in 1680 as 'an old paralytic claret drinker, a morose surly man except elevated with claret, when he becomes very brisk and incomparable company'. (Three centuries later he was reincarnated as the vodka-drinking Jeffrey Bernard.) The dramatist William Wycherley recommended Will's to a rising young poet, Alexander Pope, 'out of pure

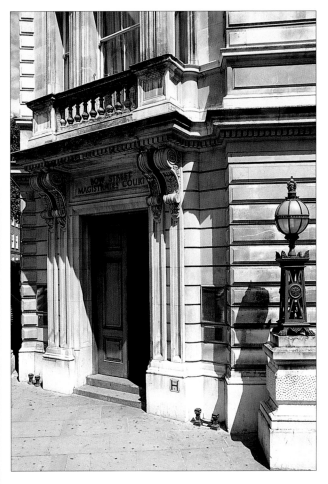

compassion for his exotic figure, narrow circumstances and humble appearance' (see Twickenham). Wycherley's fellow dramatists Addison, Steele and Congreve were also familiar faces at Will's in the early 1700s, but when Addison defected to a rival coffee house, Button's in Russell Street, Will's went into a decline.

A few doors away from Button's, at 8 Russell Street, was a bookshop run by a man named Tom Davies. Writing up his journal for 16 May 1763, a young Edinburgh lawyer named James Boswell described a memorable encounter in the shop:

Visitors to Bow Street Magistrates' Court have included Oscar Wilde (1895) and Jeffrey Archer (2000).

The rebuilt Theatre Royal, Drury Lane was opened in 1812 with an address written by Lord Byron. When it burnt down in 1809, the flames could be seen from the House of Commons. Jane Austen visited the theatre soon after, while staying with her brother in nearby Henrietta Street.

The Lamb and Flag in Rose Street. One evening in 1679, Dryden was set upon here by a masked gang hired by the Earl of Rochester, who believed Dryden had written a pamphlet entitled 'Essay on Satire' ridiculing him.

'Characters at Button's Coffee House' – Martin Folkes, a numismatist who published various books on coinage (left) and Joseph Addison (right).

I drank tea at Davies' in Russell Street, and about seven came in the great Mr Samuel Johnson, whom I have so long wished to see. Mr Davies introduced me to him. As I know his mortal antipathy at the Scotch, I cried to Davies, 'Don't tell where I come from.' However, he said, 'From Scotland.' 'Mr Johnson,' said I, 'indeed I come from Scotland, but I cannot help it.' 'Sir,' replied he, 'that, I find, is what a very great many of your countrymen cannot help.' Mr Johnson is a man of most dreadful appearance. He is a very big man, is troubled with sore eyes, the palsy, and the king's evil [scrofula]. He is very slovenly in his dress and speaks with a most uncouth voice. Yet his great knowledge and strength of expression command vast respect and render him very excellent company. He has great humour and is a worthy man. But his dogmatical roughness of manners is disagreeable. I shall mark what I remember of his conversation.

Johnson's anti-Scottish remarks were not based on simple chauvinism. The 1745 Jacobite Rebellion was a recent memory, and when Boswell arrived in London in 1762 the heads of two of its leaders (preserved by boiling in salt) were still displayed over Temple Bar. What is more surprising is Boswell's humility. Only a few months before, he had been at the Covent Garden Theatre (later the Royal Opera House) when people in the gallery spotted two Highland officers in the pit. Roaring 'No Scots! No Scots! Out with them!' the mob began to pelt the men with apples. On this occasion, Boswell's Scottish blood boiled with anger, and he leapt up to the gallery, shouting, 'Damn you, you rascals!'

The incident was far from unique. In the same year, the Covent Garden Theatre was the scene of a full-scale riot, when the management refused to honour the custom of selling half-price tickets after the third act. When the price of admission was increased in 1809 to help pay for rebuilding, 'Old Price Riots' raged for 61 nights until the prices were lowered again.

In the winter of 1810, Coleridge spent several miserable weeks at the Hudson Hotel at 43 King Street. He had just learnt that his closest and most valued friend, Wordsworth, had made a series of remarks about him to a mutual friend, saying he had 'no hope of him' and describing him as 'an absolute nuisance' who was 'rotting out his entrails by intemperance'. Coleridge was devastated by the rejection. As Wordsworth's criticisms echoed around his brain, he confided in his notebook: 'Sunday Night. No Hope of me! absolute Nuisance! God's mercy, it is a Dream!' Coleridge remained at the hotel, barely venturing out, until a friend, John Morgan, came looking for him and found him distraught and alone in his upstairs bedroom. He packed Coleridge into his carriage and drove him to his home, 7 Portland Place (now Addison Bridge Place) in Kensington. Coleridge later expressed his gratitude and relief. 'If it be allowed to call anyone on earth Saviour,' he wrote, 'Morgan & his Family have been my Saviours, Body and Soul.'

In 1821 Thomas De Quincey was living at 36 Tavistock Street while writing his autobiographical *Confessions of an English Opium Eater*. A keen opera-goer, as well as an opium user, he would frequently indulge in the latter in order to enhance his appreciation of the former. In *The Years* (1937), Virginia Woolf describes the awkward juxtaposition between Opera House patrons and the porters and stallholders in Covent Garden market.

In Iris Murdoch's 1954 novel *Under the Net* the wastrel writer Jake Donaghue and his cronies fetch up in the market early one summer morning, nursing ferocious hangovers after a night's drinking in the City. After restoring themselves with coffee from a market stall, the group wander into 'an avenue of crated blossoms', where they help themselves to armfuls of roses, peonies, violets, anenomes and pansies, still wet with dew, 'until our sleeves were drenched and we were half suffocated with pollen'. The passage is one of the last outstanding descriptions of the market to be written before it closed in 1974.

The first meeting of Boswell and Johnson took place at Davies's Bookshop, 8 Russell Street, now a coffee shop.

*T*homas De Quincey wrote his autobiography Confessions of an English Opium Eater at 36 Tavistock Street.

Other novelists associated the area with more indoor pleasures. In his autobiography HE Bates recalled meeting Graham Greene for lunch in 1933, at 'that splendidly Edwardian pub in the heart of London's theatre-land, all brass and red plush and mirrors and beer engines and snug corners, the Salisbury in St Martin's Lane. Graham, as impecunious as I was, had discovered with delight that for one-and-ninepence you could get some soup, a large plate of boiled or roast beef, roast lamb or pork, some sort of pudding or cheese with perfectly magnificent celery. It was all excellent.'

Forty years later, writers were still being impressed by the fare at The Salisbury. When the novelist Julian Symons was playing host to the husband-and-wife American crime novelists Ross Macdonald and Margaret Millar in the early 1970s, he decided to take them to his favourite pub for lunch. It was Millar's first visit to Britain.

Settled on the red plush, I diverted Margaret from the idea that she could order a cup of tea. She settled for cider, but what was she to eat? Looking around with great interest at the people around us and the food being handed over the bar counter, she asked suddenly, 'Is it shepherd's pie I see over there? That's what I'd like.' The shepherd's pie was pronounced the best food she'd had since leaving the States, and on a trip they took afterwards they asked for it whenever they stopped at a pub for lunch.

A quiet moment at the Salisbury in St Martin's Lane. The fare at the pub has impressed HE Bates, Graham Greene, Ross Macdonald and Margaret Millar.

THEATRELAND

Although London's first purpose-built theatre was opened in 1576 (see Shoreditch), theatre-going was widely viewed as only marginally more respectable than bear-baiting or frequenting brothels, and actors and playwrights tended to be viewed with contempt. Attitudes began to change during the Restoration, when theatre began to edge towards respectability. Charles II enjoyed plays and in 1662 he gave his name to the King's Company, based at the Theatre Royal in Drury Lane.

An orange seller is believed to have started the fire which destroyed the building in 1672, by searching for fruit by candlelight in a store under the wooden staircase. The theatre was rebuilt, then demolished and rebuilt again before being burnt down a second time, during the tenure of Richard Brinsley Sheridan (see Covent Garden). Reopened in 1812, the Theatre Royal became permanently associated with the actor Edmund Kean (1789–1833), whose performances as Shylock and Richard III helped stimulate critical interest in Shakespeare.

Less celebrated but in some respects more ambitious, the Fortune Theatre in Russell Street made its name in 1926 with productions of Sean O'Casey's *Juno and the Paycock* and *The Plough and the Stars*. In 1961 it mounted *Beyond the Fringe*, written and performed by Peter Cook, Dudley Moore, Jonathan Miller and Alan Bennett, which paved the way for irreverent satire.

The Albery opened in St Martin's Lane in 1903. In the 1950s it staged a series of ground-breaking dramas,

The auditorium at The Ambassadors Theatre, which was the first home of Agatha Christie's long-running success The Mousetrap.

among them TS Eliot's *The Cocktail Party* and Willis Hall's wartime melodrama *The Long and the Short and the Tall*.

Opened during the First World War, the Ambassadors in West Street is best known as the first home of Agatha Christie's whodunnit *The Mousetrap* the longest-running play ever staged in London (or indeed anywhere else). After a run of nearly 50 years, *The Mousetrap*'s record is unlikely to be surpassed. The play opened on 25 November 1952 and remained there until 1974, when it moved a few yards up the road to the St Martin's Theatre, where it remains.

The Garrick, named after Dr Johnson's friend, the actor David Garrick (1717–79), is situated in Charing Cross Road. The theatre has tended to specialize in comedy. In the 1990s, however, JB Priestley's 1945 play *An Inspector Calls* settled down for a long run, triggering glowing reviews, particularly for the brilliant, if impractical, stage set.

One of the few theatres to be found within Soho is the tiny Comedy Theatre in Panton

David Garrick, after whom the Garrick theatre is named, playing Richard III. One of the greatest English actors and a close friend, and former pupil, of Dr Johnson, he was manager of the Theatre Royal, Drury Lane for 30 years from 1747, before handing the reins to Richard Brinsley Sheridan.

Street, opened in 1881. In its early years it specialized in comic opera. In the 1950s, the theatre restyled itself as the New Comedy Club so as to circumvent regulations which outlawed the portrayal of homosexuality in British theatres. Arthur Miller's *A View from the Bridge*, Robert Anderson's *Tea and Sympathy* and Tennessee Williams's *Cat on a Hot Tin Roof* were all staged at the theatre between 1956 and 1958.

Built in 1720, the Haymarket Theatre (now the Theatre Royal, Haymarket) was briefly managed by Henry Fielding but closed down when the authorities objected to the satires he was staging. In the late nineteenth century, the Haymarket enjoyed two monster hits, first with an adaptation of George du Maurier's *Trilby*, then with Oscar Wilde's *A Woman of No Importance* and *An Ideal Husband*.

Her Majesty's Theatre, on the opposite side of Haymarket, was built by the architect-cum-playwright Sir Thomas Vanbrugh in 1705. Despite being jointly managed by Vanbrugh and his fellow playwright William Congreve, the theatre was not a success and closed after two years. A contemporary, Colley Cibber, blamed Vanbrugh's design: 'Every proper quality and convenience of a good theatre has been sacrificed or neglected to show the spectator a vast piece of architecture,' he complained. The building was burnt down in 1789 and was rebuilt in the 1890s by the architect Charles Phipps, of whom Bernard Shaw wrote: 'He has had the good sense – a very rare quality in England where artistic matters are in question – to see that a theatre which is panelled, and mirrored, and mantelpieced like the first-class saloon of a Peninsula and Oriental liner or a Pullman drawing room car, is no place for *Julius Caesar*, or indeed for anything except tailor-made drama and farcical comedy.' It was, however, the perfect venue for Andrew Lloyd Webber's *The Phantom of the Opera*.

The Adelphi Theatre, in the Strand, started out life as 'The Sans Pareil', built by a trader John Scott in 1806 for his daughter, an aspiring actress. It enjoyed huge profits in the 1830s from dramatized versions of Dickens's novels *The Pickwick Papers*, *Oliver Twist* and *Nicholas Nickleby*.

When a new road, Aldwych, was built in 1905 to link the Strand with Kingsway, it came with a brand new playhouse: the Aldwych Theatre. Until the 1930s, the Aldwych was known almost exclusively for its farces, most of them written by Ben Travers, and including *Rookery Nook* (1926) and *A Cup of Kindness* (1929). In 1949 the Aldwych staged the first London production of Tennessee Williams's *A Streetcar Named Desire*, in which Vivien Leigh gave her finest stage performance. The theatre was the home of the Royal Shakespeare Company from 1960 until its relocation to the Barbican in 1982.

HOLBORN

Named after the Holebourne, a tributary of the river Fleet, Holborn is sandwiched between Theobald's Road and the eastern section of the Strand. The area dominates Dickens's greatest novel, *Bleak House*, starting from its arresting opening, with London in 'implacable November weather', and 'as much mud in the streets as if the waters had but recently retired from the face of the earth, and it would not be wonderful to meet a Megalosaurus, forty feet long or so, waddling like an elephantine lizard up Holborn Hill'. In the novel, the sinister lawyer Mr Tulkinghorn has chambers at Lincoln's Inn Fields, 'in a large house, formerly a house of state ... let off in sets of chambers now; and in those shrunken fragments of its greatness, lawyers lie like maggots in nuts'. Dickens is actually describing the home of his closest friend, 'the Lincolnian

mammoth' John Forster, at 58 Lincoln's Inn Fields. In his brilliant biography, *Dickens* (1990), Peter Ackroyd points out that it was to Forster that Dickens had entrusted the private auto-biography detailing his early life at the Marshalsea Prison and at Warren's Blacking, which may be the reason he portrays Forster's home as the repository of potentially explosive secrets.

It was also at Forster's home that Dickens read his Christmas story 'The Chimes' to a group of friends and reduced several of them to tears. The discovery that he possessed mesmerizing powers as a storyteller encouraged Dickens to embark on the public readings which dominated his final years, and which would induce a state of near-hysteria in both the audience and the reader.

Dickens reads his Christmas story 'The Chimes' to a group of friends at John Forster's house in December 1844.

Lincoln's Inn itself was one of the four Inns of Court (see Temple), built piecemeal between the late fifteenth and early seventeenth

Lincoln's Inn Fields, the home of Dickens's closest friend, John Forster, and one of his most sinister characters, the lawyer Tulkinghorn in Bleak House.

The Old Curiosity Shop, supposed to be the model for Dickens's establishment, has stood in Portsmouth Street for over 400 years.

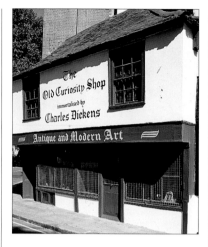

Bleeding Heart Yard. 'A place much changed in feature and in fortune, yet with some relish of ancient greatness about it … It was inhabited by poor people who set up their rest among its faded glories, as Arabs in the desert pitch their tents among the fallen stones of the Pyramids.'
Dickens: Little Dorrit, 1855.

centuries. Among the workers was a young bricklayer, later a playwright, Ben Jonson. Among the lawyers who have lived and practised in Lincoln's Inn over the centuries were Thomas More, John Donne, Benjamin Disraeli, H Rider Haggard and John Galsworthy. The foundation stone of the chapel was laid by Donne, who became the first chaplain when the building was consecrated in 1623.

The 'Old Curiosity Shop' at 13 Portsmouth Street, on the south-

west corner of Lincoln's Inn Fields, has long claimed to be the inspiration for Dickens's 1841 novel. Whether or not it formed the model for Little Nell's establishment, it is probable that Dickens at least knew the place. Built in 1567, it is believed to be the oldest shop in London.

Other Dickens locations in Holborn are better documented. At the age of 15, Dickens became a clerk at a firm of lawyers, Ellis and Blackmore, in Holborn Court, off Chancery Lane. The desk he used is now on display at the Dickens House Museum in Doughty Street. On his very first day Dickens got into a fight in the street. As he was crossing Chancery Lane, wearing a brand new suit and a military-style cap, a burly young man said 'Hello, soldier!' and knocked his cap off. Dickens punched him and received a black eye in return. A few months later, Ellis and Blackmore moved to new premises in Raymond Buildings. Here the young Dickens would amuse himself by leaning out of the window and spitting cherry stones onto the heads of passers-by, calmly pleading his innocence if anyone complained.

A few years later, when he was beginning to make a name for himself as a reporter on the *Morning Chronicle*, Dickens moved into chambers at one of the Inns of Chancery, Furnival's Inn, initially with his brother Frederick then, following his marriage, with his wife Catherine Hogarth. It was here that he began *The Pickwick Papers*, and the surrounding streets, courts and alleys would continue to feature in his work long after he had moved away. Hatton Garden is the scene of Mr Fang's police court in *Oliver Twist*, Bleeding

Heart Yard is the hunting ground of Pancks, the snorting, hair-tugging rent collector in *Little Dorrit*, and Furnival Street (formerly Castle Street) is where David Copperfield's old school friend Tommy Traddles has lodgings. Furnival's Inn itself was demolished in 1897 to make way for the vast, terracotta-coloured Prudential Assurance building which dominates Holborn between Brooke Street and Leather Lane. There is a small bust of Dickens, under glass, at the far end of the main courtyard.

and Sir Philip Sidney. Charles Lamb called them 'the best gardens of any in the Inns of Court, my beloved Temple not forgotten'.

In 1795 Lamb was 20 years old and living with his family at 7 Little Queen Street (now the site of a disused church, Holy Trinity, in Kingsway) when his sister Mary stabbed their mother to death during a bout of mental illness. For a short while Mary was confined to an asylum in Hackney, but she was soon released into the

Dickens is commemorated in the courtyard of the Prudential building in Holborn.

Gray's Inn lies between High Holborn and Theobald's Road. Like the other Inns of Court, it traditionally sponsored new drama. Shakespeare's *The Comedy of Errors* had its first performance in the hall in 1594, before his patron the Earl of Southampton, who was a member of the Inn. The dramatist James Shirley, who later perished in the Fire of London, was also a member. He wrote the lyrics for a masque, *The Triumph of Peace*, which was performed at Gray's Inn in 1634.

The philosopher Francis Bacon entered the Inn as a student in 1576. His chambers were in Verulam Buildings, on the north-east corner of the Gray's Inn Square. Bacon is believed to have planted the catalpa tree which still stands in Gray's Inn Gardens, behind 4 Raymond Buildings. The gardens were once popular for gentlemanly strolling and conversation; visitors included Samuel Pepys, Sir Walter Ralegh

The gardens of Gray's Inn, once popular with Samuel Pepys, Sir Walter Ralegh and Sir Philip Sidney, are open to the public at lunchtime.

St Andrew's Church, Holborn Circus, where Charles Lamb had an embarrassing fit of giggles at William Hazlitt's wedding ceremony.

care of Charles, who took care of her for the rest of his life. (She outlived him by 13 years, dying in 1847.) They wrote two children's books together: *Tales from Shakespear* (1807) and *Mrs Leicester's School* (1809). In 1808, Charles was best man and Mary bridesmaid at the wedding of William Hazlitt at St Andrew's Church in Holborn Circus. As the ceremony began, Charles let out a peal of nervous laughter but managed to regain his composure.

In Gerald Kersh's 1930s lowlife thriller *Night and the City*, Mr Figler is a businessman whose Byzantine dealings keep him just on the right side of legality and solvency. Figler is 'usually to be found somewhere in the residential area between Southampton Row and Gray's Inn Road – that sombre, comfortless jungle of smoky apartment-houses, inhabited by a shifting population of men without property who arrive in a hurry and frequently leave by night; where tradesmen give no credit, and rent is payable strictly in advance'.

Now an anonymous office building, 39 Brooke Street was the site of one of literature's great tragedies: the suicide, on 25 August 1770, of the 17-year-old poet Thomas Chatterton.

Chatterton had already garnered a certain reputation in his native Bristol after writing a series of pseudo-archaic poems purporting to be the work of, among others, an imaginary fifteenth-century monk named Thomas Rowley. Chatterton had sent some of the poems to Horace Walpole, who was briefly taken in by them until some friends pointed out that they were full of factual and stylistic anachronisms.

In April 1770 Chatterton's apprenticeship to a Bristol attorney, John Lambert, was abruptly cancelled when he left on his employer's desk a document announcing his suicidal intentions entitled 'The Last Will and Testament of Me, Thomas Chatterton of Bristol'. Having deposited the document, Chatterton immediately took a coach to London. By the time he arrived, he was in a more optimistic frame of mind. He immediately visited several editors, who had already published some of his poems and articles, and secured new commissions. He

then holed himself up in a lodging house in Shoreditch, and subsequently in Brooke Street, and wrote furiously for the next three months. By July the various poems and songs he published in the *Town and Country Magazine* and *Freeholders' Magazine* had earned him £12 – much of which he spent on presents for his family in Bristol. He wrote excitedly to his sister: 'Almost all the next "Town and Country Magazine" is mine!' It wasn't: most of his new pieces were held over, and when his employers delayed paying him for the articles which they had used, Chatterton was left penniless and alone in London. Unaccountably, he refused to accept his landlady's offer of food. The same night Chatterton locked himself into his garret – much as he had done at home as a child, when he used to lock himself into the lumber room for hours on end to write and draw. He was found dead the next morning, with an empty phial of arsenic still in his hand and with tiny paper fragments strewn over the floor – the wreckage of his remaining, unpublished manuscripts. He was buried in the workhouse cemetery in Shoe Lane under the name 'William Chatterton'. Horace Walpole did not learn of his death until Oliver Goldsmith mentioned it to him a year later, during a banquet at the Royal Academy.

The 'Rowley' hoax continued to cause confusion. Twelve years after Chatterton's death, the Society of Antiquaries published a lavish quarto edition of the poems, with elaborate notes 'proving' their authenticity. But later he was idolized by a new generation of poets, including Blake, Shelley, Coleridge and Keats, who wrote to a friend: 'I always somehow associate Chatterton with autumn. He is the purest writer in the English language.'

The Victorian novelist George Meredith posed as the poet Thomas Chatterton for the painting The Death Of Chatterton (1856) by Henry Wallis.

Former residents of Chester Square include Mary Shelley, author of Frankenstein *and wife of Percy Bysshe Shelley.*

BELGRAVIA

To Benjamin Disraeli, Belgravia was 'as monotonous as Marylebone, and so contrived as to be at the same time insipid and tawdry'. With its massive houses and neat private squares, Belgravia has tended to attract writers who have already made it big – sometimes in fields other than literature. Matthew Arnold lived at 2 Chester Square from 1858 to 1868, when he was working as an inspector of schools and writing some of his finest poetry, such as 'Dover Beach' and 'Rugby Chapel'. He didn't particularly want to leave Belgravia, reporting that he was 'fairly driven out of Chester Square, partly by the number of our children, partly by the necessity of a better school for the boys' (they moved to Harrow). The diplomat and writer Harold Nicolson and his wife, the novelist, poet and garden designer Vita Sackville-West, lived at 182 Ebury Street in the late 1920s. Their 'open' marriage was daring for the time (they married in 1913), especially as it included same-sex affairs on both sides. Sackville-West's relationship with Virginia Woolf inspired the latter's 1928 novel *Orlando*.

Although Percy Bysshe Shelley died in 1822, his legend was perpetuated well into the Victorian era by two of those closest to him. Many years after his death, his second wife, Mary Shelley, lived at 24 Chester Square, which she shared with her stepsister Claire Clairmont, a one-time lover of Byron. Chiefly remembered now as the author of *Frankenstein* (1818), Mary devoted much of her last few years editing her husband's poems, essays and letters. In the late 1830s Shelley's friend Edward Trelawny was living at 17 Eaton Square. Trelawny, who was a member of Shelley's Italian circle at the time of his death, later published a volume of reminiscences of his famous friends, *Records of Shelley, Byron and the Author*.

In 1936 a young stockbroker named Ian Fleming moved into the upstairs flat at 22 Ebury Street, a former school built in pseudo-classical style and looking like a mini-Parthenon. Fleming's flat, 22B, had previously been occupied by the fascist leader Sir Oswald Mosley.

Fleming, who had previously been living with his mother in Cheyne Walk, had been on the look-out for bachelor accommodation where he could indulge in his favourite pastimes – collecting first editions and surrealist art, and seducing upper-class women. With the help of an interior designer, the flat became the last word in avant garde masculinity, with grey walls, hidden lighting and no windows. The seductions followed a set pattern: dinner, consisting of Fleming's limited culinary repertoire (either salmon kedgeree or sausages), an invitation to examine his large collection of French erotica, and finally a swift adjournment to the bedroom.

Fleming was back in Belgravia in the early 1950s, following his marriage to the society hostess Ann Charteris. At 16 Victoria Square, Fleming was irritated by his wife's intellectual salons, especially when he came home one evening to find Ann, the Labour Party leader Hugh Gaitskell, the warden of All Souls College, Oxford and the novelist Angus Wilson holding hands on the sofa and reciting WB Yeats. He responded by reciting a Cossack nursery rhyme before stomping off to bed. The Bond novels were mainly written at Goldeneye, his beloved holiday home in Jamaica.

A favourite Belgravia neighbour,

and one of Fleming's guests at Goldeneye, was Noel Coward. From the mid-1930s on, he lived in a sprawling, rustic-looking house at 17 Gerald Road, where he wrote the play *Cavalcade* (1931), the wartime screenplays *This Happy Breed* (1942) and *Brief Encounter* (1944), and three volumes of autobiography, *Past Imperfect*, *Present Indicative* and *Future Indefinite*.

The literary establishment has always been divided about the quality of Fleming's books. On his death in 1964 one critic compared him favourably with Robert Louis Stevenson. On the other hand, in his history of crime fiction

*I*an Fleming moved into a flat in this pseudo-classical building in Ebury Street in 1936.

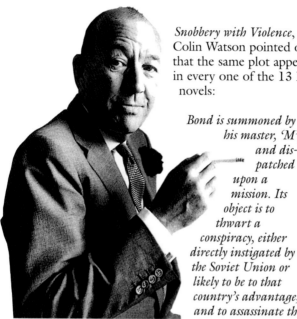

Snobbery with Violence, Colin Watson pointed out that the same plot appears in every one of the 13 Bond novels:

Bond is summoned by his master, 'M', and dispatched upon a mission. Its object is to thwart a conspiracy, either directly instigated by the Soviet Union or likely to be to that country's advantage, and to assassinate the sinister guiding genius. Bond penetrates the villain's stronghold, is captured and tortured. He escapes, with or without the help of the nymphomaniacal young woman who by this time has drawn thrustingly abreast of him. He engineers the destruction of plot, villain and all, fulfilling his personal norm of three murders per book, and bows out to an interlude of peaceful fornication until 'M' gets another idea.

*I*an Fleming was one of the few people who could insult Noel Coward and get away with it. 'Have you ever noticed,' Fleming once asked him, 'that when you perspire the sweat runs off your face and drops off your first chin on to your second?'

O*ne of the few works of literature that really conveys Belgravia's atmosphere of respectable melancholy is Graham Greene's 1935 story 'The Basement Room'. Seven-year-old Philip's parents have gone on holiday, leaving him in the care of the servants, Mr and Mrs Baines. As he prowls round the huge Belgravia house, Philip becomes 'caught up in other people's darkness' – the kindly Mr Baines is having an affair, and Philip unwittingly

*C*oward's home in Gerald Road, a few minutes' walk from Fleming's. Coward also had a Jamaican home near Fleming's beloved Goldeneye.

betrays him. When the story was filmed (as *The Fallen Idol*) in 1949, the setting was changed to an embassy. After just 14 years, the notion of a privately owned mansion in Belgravia was increasingly out of date.

Nigel Balchin's 1945 novel *Mine Own Executioner* is similarly indicative of the fate of many of Belgravia's private residences. In the novel, a private psychiatric clinic is based at '47 Laston Square'. Unfortunately, the clinic has barely any money, so the enterprise is kept ticking over with 'plenty of good intentions and the services of anybody who was prepared to work for nothing'. One of those is Felix Milne, a psychoanalyst who, against his better judgement, agrees to treat a shell-shocked former fighter pilot who has tried to kill his wife. Milne's realization that he is out of his depth and losing control of his patient forms the crux of this minor classic.

VICTORIA

Dominated by its huge railway terminus and characterized by endless rows of cheap hotels and restaurants, Victoria is the travellers' quarter of London. Oscar Wilde's *The Importance of Being Earnest* ends with the crucial revelation that Jack (also known as Ernest) was mislaid as a baby, in a handbag, at Victoria Station ('Brighton Line').

In 1893, Joseph Conrad came to Victoria for a short holiday after nearly 20 years spent almost continuously at sea. He found lodgings just off Vauxhall Bridge Road, at 17 Gillingham Street, where he completed his first novel, *Almayer's Folly*. When the novel was accepted by the publishers Fisher Unwin, Conrad was able to retire from the sea and devote himself to writing; his second novel, *An Outcast of the Islands*, appeared in 1896. In *The Secret Agent*, published in 1907, Conrad was almost certainly thinking of his home in Gillingham Street where he notes that Mr Verloc's mother-in-law is providing for her widowhood by 'letting out furnished apartments for gentlemen near Vauxhall Bridge Road'.

At the age of eight, Richard Church caught a glimpse of Queen Victoria's funeral, while he and his family were on their way from Battersea to Highgate to visit relatives. 'We were caught near Victoria station, and took our stand on a step, in the private doorway of a shop at the corner of Buckingham Palace Road,' he wrote in his autobiography *Over the Bridge*. 'We saw the coffin on a gun-carriage, followed by the princes of the blood, and the strange new King, on dark horses.

I remember most clearly the Kaiser, because he rode a white horse, a nonconformity which caused the crowd to murmur with astonishment and dismay.'

In 1913, the newly married Virginia Woolf was attending a cookery class in Victoria Street. In John Wyndham's *The Day of the Triffids* (1951), set in a post-apocalyptic London, William Masen discovers that the Army and Navy Stores in Victoria Street have been stripped of provisions, with a man rolling a large cheese along the middle of Victoria Street. Masen searches for his girlfriend Josella in the dozens of small hotels around the station, before getting information on her

The blue plaque outside Conrad's home in Gillingham Street, near Victoria Station.

Joseph Conrad (1857–1924) was Polish by birth but wrote all his novels in English. Despite his command of the language, he occasionally confused English with French. In Nostromo *he writes 'they were arrested' (from the French verb, s'arrêter) when he means 'they stopped'.*

whereabouts from an old woman sitting on a doorstep near the corner of Buckingham Palace Road.

Angus Wilson's ambitious 1967 novel *No Laughing Matter* tells the story, over 50 years, of a shabby-genteel family, the Matthews, living at '52 Gillbrook Street' in Victoria. As Margaret Drabble reports in her biography of Wilson, a real-life family, the Mastermans, whom Wilson had known since his schooldays in Westminster, immediately recognized the house as their own

Victoria station, where Jack in Oscar Wilde's The Importance of Being Earnest *was mislaid as a baby.*

family home at 46 Gillingham Street – 'a house "long in the same family" with its dark kitchen, its coal hole, its area into which passers-by vomited, its background noises of quarrelling prostitutes and drunks"? The background noises have not entirely disappeared from this part of Victoria, but sadly the house has: it has since been obliterated by an office block.

In a diary entry for July 1967, the playwright Joe Orton described getting on a number 19 bus to go to Victoria Station with his partner, Kenneth Halliwell.

> *The bus was full. A rather fat girl (blind to everyone but her own breasts) wearing a mini-skirt got on and had to stand*

next to me. She kept rubbing up against my leg. I got a hard on. It showed through the jeans I was wearing. I asked Kenneth as we got off the bus if he'd noticed the girl. 'Yes,' he said, 'the man next to me was getting v. excited.' 'You mean me?' I gasped. 'No,' Kenneth said, 'the other side.' 'I was getting excited too,' I said, blushing and feeling foolish. 'She was rubbing her thighs up and down in a v. bold way. What d'you suppose would've happened if I'd followed her off the bus?' 'She'd've charged you three quid, I expect,' Kenneth said in a cold manner. 'I've never seen a more obvious pro on a 19 bus before.'

PIMLICO

'**B**lind with mascara and dumb with lipstick, I paraded the dim streets of Pimlico.' So wrote Quentin Crisp in 1968, recalling the period in the early thirties when he was living in a room in Denbigh Street, and demonstrating to all and sundry – despite the risk to

rows of solid, dazzling-white terraced houses were built in and around Belgrave Road, and in Anthony Trollope's *The Small House at Allington*, Lady Alexandrina is nearly fooled by her new husband into thinking Pimlico as respectable as Belgravia. 'Her geographical knowledge of Pimlico had not been perfect, and she had very nearly fallen into a fatal error. But a friend had kindly intervened. "For Heaven's sake, my dear, don't let him take you anywhere beyond Eccleston Square!"' In the twentieth century, many of the Georgian terraces fell into disrepair and were divided up into bedsits and cheap hotels, though others (particularly in Moreton Place and St George's Drive) have been beautifully maintained. In 1955 Richard Church, whose loyalties lay firmly south of the river in his native Battersea, wrote of 'the sinister labyrinth of Pimlico, where row after row, through street after street, of mid-Victorian houses with pillared porticos still stand flaking away gradually into a squalor that is not even brutal. A kind of lethal greyness, like the scurf of leprosy on doomed human skin, covers the whole district.'

Pimlico's southern boundary is formed by the Thames, and from Vauxhall Bridge

life and limb – that he was not ashamed of being gay. 'Sometimes I wore a fringe so deep that it completely obscured the way ahead. This hardly mattered. There were always others to look where I was going.'

For a committed social outcast like Crisp, Pimlico was a natural stamping ground: Pimlico has always rather prided itself on its raffishness, compared with neighbouring Belgravia and Westminster. (The writer TEB Clarke cleverly tapped into the Pimlico psyche in his screenplay for the film *Passport to Pimlico*, where the entire area declares itself independent from the United Kingdom.) It is somehow typical of Pimlico that there is no clear definition of its boundaries, and at least four different explanations as to how it required its very un-English name.

Samuel Pepys was one of the first writers to describe Pimlico's charms in print. One day in August 1667 he went there with his wife and his mistress, Mrs Knipp the actress, 'and there, in a box, in a tree, we sat, and sang, and talked, and eat; my wife out of humour as she always is when this woman is by'. In the 1830s, long

Covering seven acres, Dolphin Square was the largest residential development in Europe when it was completed in 1937. Former residents include CP Snow and Radclyffe Hall.

The Embankment benches, where Orwell attempted to sleep whilst researching Down and Out in Paris and London. *In Iris Murdoch's* Under the Net *Jake Donaghue discusses the impossibility of spending a comfortable night on the benches because they are divided in the middle.*

there's a good view of the Millbank foreshore, where David and Mr Peggotty follow the prostitute Martha in *David Copperfield*. About half a mile to the west, Dolphin Square is a vast art deco residential block, complete with its own shops and restaurant. Its earliest residents included the novelist CP Snow, best known today for coining the term 'corridors of power', and Radclyffe Hall, who died at Dolphin Square in 1943, 15 years after the banning of her lesbian novel *The Well of Loneliness* (the book was championed at the time by, among others, Virginia Woolf , though privately she considered it a 'meritorious dull book').

The novelist Angus Wilson

moved in to a one-bedroomed flat in Dolphin Square in 1948. Flat 07 Frobisher House faced on to the large central gardens, where on fine days Wilson would sit and write, imagining that a thousand eyes were looking down on him. He invariably disconnected the phone when he was working in the flat, partly because he didn't want to be disturbed, partly because callers frequently mistook his high-pitched voice for that of a woman. (In the flesh, he had a passing resemblance to the actress Margaret Rutherford.) As for the flat itself, one friend, the book illustrator Philippe Jullian, was dismissive, describing it as 'cynically petit-bourgeois: a bare room, badly decorated, with nothing aesthetic about it'. Nevertheless, Wilson remained at Dolphin Square for over ten years, latterly in a slightly larger flat in Greenville House, which he shared with his partner, Tony Garrett.

In 1959, when homosexuality was still a criminal offence, Garrett was given an ultimatum by his employers, the Probation Service. He could keep his job, provided he agree to live not less than 40 miles away from the 'known homosexual' Angus Wilson, or he could resign. Forced to choose between his career and Angus Wilson, he chose Wilson. The partnership ended only with Wilson's death, in 1991.

VICTORIA EMBANKMENT

This narrow strip of land between the Strand and the river Thames is one of the newest areas of London. It dates from the 1860s, when Victorian engineers reclaimed 37 acres of land from the river.

The rows of benches facing the river have traditionally been colonized at night by society's outcasts. In the Somerset Maugham novel *Liza of Lambeth* (1897), Liza and her married lover Jim regularly cross the river to escape the prying eyes of their neighbours, and spend a November evening shivering on a bench while a homeless tramp sleeps 'like a dead man' nearby. George Orwell tried his hand at sleeping on the Embankment in about 1930, when he was gathering material for *Down and Out in Paris and London*. He was kept awake by the trams going along the Embankment and by the neon signs on the other side of the river. On another occasion Orwell was crossing Westminster Bridge with one of the local pavement artists when the man stopped at one of the alcoves on the bridge and gave Orwell an impromtu astronomy lesson.

In Iris Murdoch's exuberant first novel *Under the Net* (1954), the narrator Jake Donaghue offers the following advice:

If you have ever tried to sleep on the Victoria Embankment you will know that the chief difficulty is that the seats are divided in the middle. An iron arm-rest in the centre makes it impossible to stretch oneself out. I am not sure whether this is an accidental phenomenon or whether it forms part of an LCC campaign against vagrancy. In any case it is very inconvenient. Various systems are possible. One may try to use the arm-rest as a pillow, or one may lie with one's knees raised over it and one's feet on the other side. Or again one may resign oneself to curling up on one half of the seat.

Although the LCC (London County Council) is long gone, the divided benches are still very much in evidence.

One writer who would not have been seen dead among the down and outs was the notoriously snobbish Ian Fleming. At about the same time that George Orwell was sleeping rough on the Embankment, Fleming was working for the Reuters press agency in Carmelite Street, in a first-floor office overlooking Blackfriars Bridge.

The Embankment's most prominent landmark plays a small but memorable role in children's literature. In Hugh Lofting's 'Dr Dolittle' series, the cockney sparrows Cheapside and his wife Becky habitually meet on the tip of Cleopatra's Needle.

*V*ictoria Embankment Gardens are one of the best kept secrets of central London.

*D*ating from around 1500 BC, Cleopatra's Needle has earned itself a footnote in the annals of children's literature.

STRAND AND TRAFALGAR SQUARE

Until the construction of the Victoria Embankment in the 1860s, the Strand was, literally, that – the muddy northern margin of the Thames foreshore. Yet it was one of the most important thoroughfares in London, linking the political centre, Westminster, with the commercial one, the City. The junction of Strand, Whitehall and Cockspur Street, at Charing Cross, was particularly busy. In his diary for 13 October 1660, Samuel Pepys describes coming to Charing Cross to see Major General Thomas Harrison hung, drawn and quartered, 'looking as cheerfully as any man could do in that condition'. The scene had a special significance for Pepys. Eleven years earlier he had also witnessed the beheading of Charles I in Whitehall, in which Harrison had been personally involved. Another diarist, John Evelyn, missed the execution of Harrison and his eight fellow regicides, but he did see the aftermath. In the Strand he 'met their quarters, mangled and cut and reeking as they were brought from the gallows in baskets'.

In the early eighteenth century, the Strand was renowned for its eating houses. The Grecian Coffee House in Devereux Court, off Essex Street, has been called 'the Athenaeum of its day' because of its popularity among men of letters. Regulars included Addison and Steele, who soaked up the gossip and retailed it in their newspaper, the *Spectator*. (The site is now occupied by a pub, the Devereux.) For newcomers to the city, such as James Boswell, who arrived from Edinburgh in November 1762, these coffee houses were highly convenient. For only a few pence, it was possible to sit by a warm fire, with free newspapers to hand and a good chance of some stimulating conversation (even if it was somebody else's). Like other men of limited means, Boswell would usually go to one of the Strand chop houses for meals. One of his favourites was the New Church, near St Clement Danes, where a good dinner cost a shilling. (Henry James's nervous visit to a chop house in Piccadilly shows that the ambience had changed little a century later.)

The Strand taverns were more expensive, and out-of-towners like Boswell needed to be on their guard: waiters and prostitutes would combine forces to fleece the unwary. Boswell did

The Charing Cross Hotel was built in 1864, on the site of Hungerford Market, which is mentioned in David Copperfield.

his best to avoid temptation. A few days after his arrival he resolved in his journal that he would 'have nothing to do with whores, as my health is of great consequence to me'. Nevertheless, on the same day he 'picked up a girl in the Strand and went into a court with intention to enjoy her in armour [wearing a condom]. But she had none. I toyed with her. She wondered at my size, and said if I ever took a girl's maidenhead, I would make her squeak. I gave her a shilling, and had command enough of myself to go without touching her. I afterwards trembled at the danger I had escaped. I resolved to wait cheerfully till I got some safe girl or was liked by some woman of fashion.'

No such woman presented herself, and by the following summer Boswell was casting caution to the winds. His journal entry for 4 June 1763 does not reflect well on him: 'In the Strand I picked up a little profligate wretch and gave her sixpence. She allowed me entrance. But the miscreant refused me performance. I was much stronger than her, and *volens nolens* pushed her up against the wall. She however gave a sudden spring from me; and, screaming out, a parcel of more whores and soldiers came to her relief.' Boswell only managed to escape by claiming to be an army officer.

It seems unlikely that Boswell mentioned these escapades to his friend Samuel Johnson, whose

every word and deed he was already recording for posterity. Johnson, who was more than 30 years Boswell's senior, seems to have treated women of the streets with a degree of sensitivity which Boswell lacked. When the pair were strolling along the Strand one evening and 'a woman of the town came enticingly near us', Johnson was kind but firm. 'No, no, my girl,' he told her. 'It won't

do.' Afterwards he and Boswell discussed the wretched lives of the street girls, and the misery produced by casual sex, before parting, as usual, at Temple Bar, at the Fleet Street end of the Strand.

Johnson was a religious man, with his favourite pew in the gallery of St Clement Danes. Boswell went there with him on Good Friday 1773 and was impressed by his friend's 'solemnly devout' behaviour. 'I never shall forget the tremulous earnestness

*F*rom Boswell's accounts of his life as a young man in London, it seems hard to believe that as a boy he was bashful in company, priggish, puritanical and prone to fits of depression.

*E*ssex Street, south of the Strand, where the publishers Chapman and Hall, Methuen and Macmillan once had their offices.

Charles Dickens is perhaps the only novelist to have truly got the measure of London in all its glory and squalor. If there was one street that can be said to have shaped his life and work more than any other, it was the Strand.

Its influence on his life began before he was born. His father, John Dickens, worked as a Navy clerk at Somerset House, and he and Dickens's mother Elizabeth were married in the church of St Mary le Strand in 1809. John Dickens was irredeemably improvident, but until Charles was 11 he somehow managed to keep one step ahead of his creditors. When they finally caught up with him, John Dickens was arrested for debt and sent to the Marshalsea Prison in the Borough. While he was incarcerated, Charles worked in a factory making boot polish at Hungerford Stairs, roughly where Embankment tube station now stands, in 'a crazy, tumbledown old house, abutting of course on the river, and literally overrun with rats'. Dickens's job was to cover the pots of blacking with paper, tie it on with string, clip the paper to shape with scissors, and paste on a label. He did this for ten hours a day, six days a week, and at the end of each working day he would walk to Blackfriars Bridge, cross the river and make his way through the streets to the Marshalsea to visit his father.

The experience of being deprived of his education, forced to work alongside 'low' company (deeply humiliating in the class-conscious 1820s) and, above all, the sense of being abandoned by his parents were to haunt Dickens for the rest of his life. Yet, with the probable exception of his wife, he seems to have spoken of these

Samuel Johnson would probably have had mixed feelings about the statue which depicts him and his friends outside St Clement Danes.

with which he pronounced the awful petition in the Litany: "In the hour of death, and at the day of judgement, Good Lord deliver us.'" Shortly before his death in 1784, Johnson wrote to his friend, Hester Thrale: 'After a confinement of 129 days, more than the third part of a year, and no inconsiderable part of human life, I returned this day to God in St Clement's Church for my recovery.' A not very flattering statue of Johnson was erected outside the church in 1910, with reliefs of Boswell and Mrs Thrale on the base.

years to just one person, his friend John Forster. No one else, even Dickens's own children, knew anything about this phase of their father's life until Forster's biography appeared two years after the novelist's death.

He did, however, leave clues. At a Christmas party shortly before his death Dickens took part in a word game in which the participants had to contibute long strings of words which then had to be memorized by the other players. When it was Dickens's turn, he gave the name 'Warren's Blacking, 30 Strand'. His son Harry, who was present, later described the 'odd twinkle and strange inflection in his voice' as he said the words.

Dickens left literary clues too. His alter ego, *David Copperfield*, undergoes much the same experience as his creator, though in the novel Dickens moved the location of the blacking factory a mile or so upriver to Blackfriars and changed it to a wine warehouse, Murdstone and Grinby. The real location does appear, however, at the end of the novel – but as a scene of impending escape rather than one of misery and imprisonment. On the eve of their emigration to Australia, Mr Micawber and his family briefly lodge at Hungerford Stairs, in 'a little, dirty, tumbledown public house', with protruding wooden rooms overhanging the river.

Fate, or perhaps an unconscious desire to return and tame the scene of his childhood misery, would bring the adult Dickens again and again to the Strand and its side streets. As a young parliamentary reporter, he had lodgings in Buckingham Street, as does his alter ego: the young David lodges with Mrs Crupp the landlady in a set of chambers at the end of Buckingham Street, overlooking the Thames. To complete the parallels, David Copperfield, like his creator before him, goes for invigorating early morning dips at the 'Roman' bath in Strand Lane, off Surrey Street. (The bath's Roman origins have since been disputed, but it can still be visited, by prior arrangement with its owners, the National Trust.) What Dickens almost certainly didn't realize was that Buckingham Street already had an impressive literary pedigree. From 1679 to 1688 Samuel Pepys lived at number 12, and in 1688 he moved briefly to number 14 – next door to Mrs Crupp's establishment – before retiring

Buckingham Street looks much the same as it did when Coleridge had lodgings here over two centuries ago.

to Clapham. And, by odd coincidence, Samuel Taylor Coleridge worked, like Dickens, as a political journalist when he moved into lodgings at 21 Buckingham Street in 1799.

Even while he was packing his childhood experiences into *David Copperfield*, Dickens was making plans which would entail visiting the environs

The 'Roman' bath at Strand Lane where Dickens and his alter ego David Copperfield used to bathe in the morning.

on the corner of Drury Lane and Russell Street, it is now an open-air basketball court.

Dickens was working at Wellington Street North when his son Charley saw him for the last time, writing what proved to be one of the last completed chapters of *The Mystery of Edwin Drood*. Intent on his work, Dickens did not notice his son as he entered the room, and rather than disturb him, Charley withdrew and left him alone. Less than a week later, Dickens was dead.

Unlike many of his contemporaries, Dickens was not for a moment fooled by the author of *Scenes of Clerical Life*. As soon as he read the novel he realized that 'George Eliot' must be a woman.

In 1850 Marian Evans moved in to John Chapman's boarding house at 142 Strand, hoping to establish a foothold in literary London. Chapman's was no ordinary establishment. The ground floor consisted of his bookshop and publishing business, while the upper storeys were occupied by Chapman, his wife Susanna, their two children Beatrice and Ernest, and the children's governess, Elizabeth Tilley, who was Chapman's long-standing mistress. Soon after moving in, Marian became the fourth member of an uneasy *ménage à quatre*, with the sexually prodigious Chapman constantly playing his three partners off against each other.

Chapman, however, proved to be highly useful to Eliot when he published her first book, a translation of Friedrich Strauss's *Das Leben Jesu* (*The Life of Jesus*). When he took over a literary journal, the *Westminster Review*, Marian became his assistant editor,

of the Strand several days a week for the rest of his life. In 1850, while he was writing the novel's monthly instalments, he took out a lease on an office at 16 Wellington Street North and started a new weekly journal *Household Words*, in which he would serialize not only his own works but those of up-and-coming novelists such as Elizabeth Gaskell and Wilkie Collins. Dickens had his own private quarters at 16 Wellington Street North, and his walks to and from the office yielded further locations for novels. In his vivid biography, *Dickens*, Peter Ackroyd pinpoints the real location of the burial ground where Esther Summerson's mother dies in *Bleak House*. About a minute's walk from the *Household Words* offices,

shaping editorial policy, commissioning articles and checking text. One of the sub-editors, William Hale White, remembered her vividly: 'I can see her now, with her hair over her shoulders, the easy chair half sideways to the fire, her feet over the arms, and a proof in her hands, in that dark room at the back of No 142.' Although her affair with Chapman didn't last, their professional relationship did, and she contributed scores of reviews herself, among them the caustic and self-explanatory 'Silly Novels by Lady Novelists', before making her own novelistic debut with *Scenes of Clerical Life*.

The painter William Rossetti (brother of the poets Dante Gabriel Rossetti and Christina Rossetti) once worked for the Inland Revenue in Somerset House. In conversation with Henry James one day, Rossetti claimed to have seen the philosopher Herbert Spencer proposing to George Eliot on the terrace of Somerset House, which overlooks the Thames. James had no reason to disbelieve the story (though he chastised Rossetti for telling it badly), but the truth was that far from proposing to Eliot, Spencer had jilted her on the grounds that she was ugly. Contemporary photographs reveal that he wasn't exactly an oil painting himself.

When Rudyard Kipling moved to London in 1889 after working as a journalist in India, he found lodgings at 43 Villiers Street, next door but one to what is now Gordon's Wine Bar. Nearly 50 years later, he recalled his house vividly in his autobiograpy, *Something of Myself*. 'My rooms were small, not over-clean or well-kept, but from my desk I could look out of my window through the fanlight of Gatti's Music-Hall entrance, across the street, almost on to its stage. The Charing Cross trains

Rudyard Kipling's home was already a Villiers Street landmark when this photograph was taken in 1948. Gordon's Wine Bar, next door but one, was then frequented by the novelist Patrick Hamilton and his editor Michael Sadleir, best known for his 1943 novel Fanny By Gaslight.

rumbled through my dreams on one side, the boom of the Strand on the other, while, before my windows, Father Thames under the Shot Tower walked up and down with its traffic.' (There was a shot tower on the other side of the river, near Waterloo Bridge, though Kipling may have been confusing it with the water tower that stood in Victoria Embankment Gardens.)

Glancing out of the window one day, Kipling noticed a man standing in the street below. 'Of a sudden his breast turned dull red like a robin's, and he crumpled,

his work – both in the strong rhythms of his verse and the passionate declarations of his dialogue. Something of the atmosphere of the music halls he frequented around the Strand can be picked up in Peter Ackroyd's 1994 novel *Dan Leno and the Limehouse Golem*. Elizabeth, a sail-maker from the Lambeth Marsh, walks to Craven Street and visits a 'saloon of varieties', with its flickering gas jets, brightly coloured backcloth and its charismatic performer – Dan Leno himself.

*R*ule's in Maiden Lane appears in Graham Greene's The End of the Affair.

The local topography had changed little when Graham Greene wrote *The End of the Affair* in 1950. The narrator, William Bendrix, tracks down and cruelly torments his lover's husband, Henry, in Victoria Embankment Gardens, while 'the fruit-sellers cried like animals in the dusk outside the station'. (The fruit sellers are still there, though in 1976 the tube station changed its name from Charing Cross, the name Greene gives it, to Embankment.) Later in the novel, the third member of the triangle, Sarah, makes an entry in her diary describing a meeting with Bendrix at Rule's in Maiden Lane, on the north side of the Strand. Rule's was one of Greene's favourite restaurants, and for many years a caricature of Greene and his brother Hugh, by the cartoonist Low, hung over their usual table. After leaving Bendrix, Sarah writes, she 'wanted to cry

having cut his throat. In a few minutes – seconds it seemed – a hand-ambulance arrived and took up the body. A pot-boy with a bucket of steaming water sluiced the blood off into the gutter, and what little crowd had collected went its way.' Kipling wrote his first novel, *The Light that Failed* in Villiers Street. In the novel, the rooms where Dick Heldar lives are based on Kipling's.

Kipling's love of the music hall would, in time, exert a strong but almost unconscious influence on unobserved, and I went to the National Portrait Gallery, but it was students' day – there were too many people, so I went back to Maiden Lane and into the church that's always too dark to look at your neighbour'. The church in Maiden Lane is instantly recognizable as Corpus Christi – it is exactly as Sarah describes it.

Bertie Wooster's observations on the Strand, on the other hand, appear to be deliberately misleading. In the story 'Bertie Changes his Mind', PG Wodehouse's young chump is invited to give an address to a girls' school on 'advice which may be helpful to you in after-life'. Without any idea of what he's going to say, Bertie launches into one of those speeches which, once started, take on a horrible momentum of their own:

'I'll tell you something that's often done me a bit of good, and it's a thing not many people know. My old Uncle Henry gave me the tip when I first came to London. "Never forget, my boy," he said, "that, if you stand outside Romano's in the Strand, you can see the clock on the wall of the Law Courts down in Fleet Street. Most people who don't know don't believe it's possible, because there are a couple of churches in the middle of the road, and you would think they would be in the way. But you can, and it's worth knowing. You can win a lot of money betting on it with fellows who haven't found it out." And, by Jove, he was perfectly right, and it's a thing to remember.'

Bertie's nerves seem to have got the better of him: even

allowing for the passage of nearly 80 years, the clock has never been visible from this position, even with binoculars. The spot itself, though, is still readily identifiable. The site of Romano's, at 399 Strand, is now occupied by Stanley Gibbons's stamp showrooms.

When Wodehouse wrote the story in the early 1920s, the opposite side of the Strand was still occupied by the Adelphi, a three-acre residential development built in the late eighteenth century, with a long row of imposing arches facing on to the river. In *David Copperfield*, these arches appear in a scene which, even allowing for Dickens's imaginative genius, has the surreal force of authentic observation. Writing of the Murdstone and Grinby period, Dickens/Copperfield writes: 'I see myself emerging one evening from one of these arches, on a little public-house close to the river, with an open space before it, where some coal-heavers were dancing.'

In the 1860s, Thomas Hardy was studying under the architect Sir Arthur Blomfield in his office at 8 Adelphi Terrace. 'I saw from there the Embankment and Charing Cross Bridge built,' he

Modelled on the architecture of Ancient Rome, the Adelphi Vaults later became a haven for robbers.

recalled. 'The rooms contained fine Adam mantelpieces in white marble, on which we used to sketch caricatures in pencil.' Following his marriage in 1899, Bernard Shaw moved to number 10 Adelphi Terrace. During his 28-year residence he wrote many of his finest plays including *Man and Superman*, *Major Barbara*, *Pygmalion* and *Saint Joan*.

half a crown and pointed him in the direction of the Lyon's Corner House in the Strand.

Another of Barrie's visitors was more successful. In 1890 a nine-year-old girl named Daisy Ashford wrote a novel called *The Young Visiters* (sic), the story of Mr Salteena, 'an elderly man of 42', and his efforts to enter London society ('I am not quite a gentleman but you would hardly notice it but can't be helped anyhow'). When she was in her thirties, Daisy found her old manuscript and showed it to Chatto and Windus, who agreed to publish it, complete with misspellings and grammatical errors. Barrie was approached to write an introduction, but insisted

The Sherlock Holmes pub has been dedicated to Conan Doyle's hero since 1951.

Robert Street formed another part of the Adelphi complex. The plaque on numbers 1–3 commemorates the succession of famous writers who lived there: the satirical poet Thomas Hood, from 1828–30; the novelist John Galsworthy in 1917–18; and JM Barrie, who occupied the top-floor flat from 1911 until his death in 1937. One visitor to the flat was his nine-year-old godson, also called James Barrie. During the visit, Barrie Senior asked his namesake whether he would like to go out for lunch. The boy replied that he would, whereupon the author of *Peter Pan* produced

on meeting the author first to satisfy himself that the book was genuine. The meeting duly took place in 1919, and *The Young Visiters* was an enormous success, though many readers erroneously believed Barrie himself to be the author.

Much of the original Adelphi was pulled down in the 1930s, though some of the newer buildings of the site have retained the Adelphi name. Rose Macaulay's 1950 novel *The World My Wilderness* is set in and around the complex, in the weary, bombed-out London of the immediate post-war period.

In its heyday, the westernmost point of the Strand was marked by the celebrated coaching inn, The Golden Cross. Leaving the inn yard on the roof of a coach, Mr Pickwick and his friends have their first encounter with the rascally Mr Jingle, who delivers a warning in his trademark telegraphese:

> 'Heads, heads – take care of your heads!' cried the loquacious stranger, as they came out under the low archway, which in those days formed the entrance to the coach-yard. 'Terrible place – dangerous work – other day – five children – mother – tall lady, eating sandwiches – forgot the arch – crash – knock – children look round – mother's head off – sandwich in her hand – no mouth to put it in – head of a family off – shocking, shocking!'

The coach on which they are travelling, The Commodore, was the very one which first brought Dickens to London in 1823. In *David Copperfield*, David and Steerforth also stay at The Golden Cross. The hotel is long gone, though its name survives in the form of Golden Cross House, a modern office block. In nearby Duncannon Street is a stylized reclining figure of Oscar Wilde, inscribed with the words from *Lady Windermere's Fan*, 'We are all in the gutter but some of us are looking at the stars'. The statue was unveiled by the actor and writer Stephen Fry, who played the lead role in the film *Wilde*.

Northumberland Street, near Charing Cross, is the site of Hartshorne Lane, where the playwright Benjamin Jonson was born in 1573. Jonson was educated at a school which was held in the church of St Martin-in-the-Fields. His stepfather was a bricklayer, and Jonson followed him into the profession: the pair were among the workmen who built Lincoln's Inn, near Holborn. The Sherlock Holmes pub at 10 Northumberland Street is crammed with mementoes of the famous detective, most of them in an upstairs room which replicates Holmes's study at 221b Baker Street.

A century after his downfall, Oscar Wilde was given a statue in Duncannon Street, opposite Charing Cross Station.

The National Gallery seen from Trafalgar Square. The neighbouring National Portrait Gallery is a treasure-trove of writers' portraits from Coleridge to Virginia Woolf.

*Past the National
Gallery
closed and silent
Where in their frames
Other worlds persist,
the
passions of the artist
Caught like frozen
flames.*

Trafalgar Square's
most prominent building
is the low-slung, neo-
classical National Gallery,
completed in 1838.
Siegfried Sassoon's
comments on the
gallery's visitors in 'In
the National Gallery' echo
MacNeice's similar remarks on the
British Museum:

George Orwell slept rough in Trafalgar Square to gather material for his 1935 novel A Clergyman's Daughter.

The Strand had some of its
thunder stolen in the
1830s, when Trafalgar
Square was laid out at its western
extreme. Henry James was
unimpressed – in one of his travel
essays he writes of 'the grimy
desert of Trafalgar Square'. In
George Orwell's *Nineteen Eighty-
Four* the statue of Nelson has
predictably been replaced by one
of Big Brother, and the area,
renamed Victory Square, is used
to display prisoners of war. In an
earlier novel, *A Clergyman's
Daughter*, Orwell made his first
and last attempt at stylistic
experimentation, in the Joycean
scene where the amnesiac heroine
Dorothy mixes with the down-
and-outs in the square.

In *Autumn Journal* (1938),
Louis MacNeice captures Trafalgar
Square at dusk, shortly before the
outbreak of war:

*Nelson stands on a black
    pillar,
The electric signs go off and
    on –
Distilleries and life insurance
    companies –
The traffic circles, coming
    and gone,*

*Faces irresolute and
    unperplexed,
Unspeculative faces, bored
    and weak,
Cruise past each patient
    victory of technique
Dimly desiring to enjoy the
    next
Yet never finding what they
    seem to seek.*

In Iris Murdoch's novel *The
Bell* (1958), the heroine Dora has
left her husband because she is
afraid of him, only to return to
him for the same reason. She seeks
solace in the National Gallery,
'watching with compassion the
poor visitors armed with guide
books who were peering anxiously
at the masterpieces'. In Julian
Barnes's first novel, *Metroland*
(1980), two precocious school-
boys, the narrator Christopher and
his friend Toni, prowl the National
Gallery with binoculars, observing
the faces of other patrons in the
hope of proving their theory that
'the moment someone perceives a
work of art he is in some way

improved. It seemed quite reasonable to expect that the process could be observed.'

Political marches traditionally converge on Trafalgar Square, sometimes with violent consequences. Bernard Shaw was present in the square on 'Black Sunday' in November 1887, when a socialist demonstration was violently broken up by soldiers. As a student in the 1930s, the American crime writer Ross Macdonald also took part in a political rally, and was chased by a policeman on a horse. In the late 1950s and early 1960s, a group of otherwise disparate writers were briefly united in their support for the Ban the Bomb movement, which held enormous rallies in the Trafalgar Square. Prominent among these activists were John Osborne, Colin Wilson and Bertrand Russell.

THE TEMPLE

The Inner and the Middle Temple, between Fleet Street and Victoria Embankment, are groups of buildings used since the fourteenth century to accommodate barristers and their pupils. Although over the centuries many writers have lived and worked in the Temple, it is still dominated by the legal profession. On summer days the walks, squares and gardens are thronged with barristers in their traditional wigs and black gowns, which accentuate the sense of timeless peace and seclusion. It is the closest London gets to the atmosphere of the colleges of Oxford or Cambridge.

This is certainly how James Boswell saw the Temple when

A scene in the National Gallery in 1905 which seems to belong in a Henry James novel.

he brought a friend here in April 1763. After walking around the City, the pair 'strolled about the Temple, which is a most agreeable place. You quit all the hurry and bustle of the City in Fleet Street and the Strand, and all at once find yourself in a pleasant academical retreat. You see good convenient buildings, handsome walks, and view the silver Thames. You are shaded by venerable trees. Crows are cawing above your head.'

The Temple, an oasis of tranquillity celebrated by Boswell and Trollope among others.

A century later, when the City was an even noisier place, Anthony Trollope was unstinting in his praise of this oasis of calm. 'What a world within a world is the Temple!' he wrote in *The Warden*. 'How quiet are its "entangled walks", as some one has lately called them, and yet how close to the densest concourse of humanity! How gravely respectable its sober alleys, though removed but by a single step from the profanity of the Strand and the low iniquity of Fleet Street!'

The essayist and poet Charles Lamb spent his childhood in the Inner Temple. Lamb was born at 2 Crown Office Row in 1775, where his father was a lawyer's clerk. (His father appears as 'Lovel' in Lamb's 1821 essay 'The Old Benchers of the Inner Temple.') It was at 'cheerful Crown Office Row' that Lamb and his elder sister Mary 'tumbled into a spacious closet of good old English reading, and browsed at will on that fair and wholesome pasturage'. A fountain in Inner Temple Gardens is dedicated to Lamb and quotes his most famous line: 'Lawyers were children once.'

Shakespeare's London locations tend to be generic ('London. A Street.') but in *Henry VI Part I* the various earls repair to the Temple gardens to talk privately. There they pluck red and white roses to represent the warring houses of York and Lancaster.

Shakespeare's dark comedy *Twelfth Night* had its first performance in Middle Temple Hall in 1601 in front of Elizabeth I.

Charles Dickens knew the Temple intimately – probably from the age of 12 when he was working at Warren's Blacking in the Strand. As a novelist, he set some memorable scenes here. In *Martin Chuzzlewit*, Ruth Pinch and her brother Tom regularly meet by the fountain in Fountain Court. One day Ruth is 'a little too soon, or Tom a little too late' and she meets John Westlock instead, because, as Dickens explains: 'The Temple is a public thorough-fare; they may write up on the gates that it is not, but as long as the gates are left open it is, and will be.'

In *Great Expectations*, Philip Pirrip and Herbert Pocket share chambers in Garden Court, by the river, where the convict Magwitch makes his crucial second appearance in Pip's life. In a bizarre short story, 'The Paradise of Bachelors' (1855), Herman Melville made much of the Temple's reputation as an all-male preserve. How the story's outrageous phallic imagery and homosexual innuendo escaped Victorian censorship is one of the mysteries of nineteenth-century literature.

Two great adventure novels of the turn of the century were conceived in the vicinity. As a barrister, Anthony Hope Hawkins had the idea for *The Prisoner of Zenda* as he was walking back to his chambers after winning a case. Published in 1894, the novel was so successful that Hawkins abandoned his legal career to devote himself to writing. The story of *The Scarlet Pimpernel* came to Baroness Orczy while waiting for a tube at Temple Underground Station in 1904.

FLEET STREET

Fleet Street took its name from the Fleet river, a tributary of the Thames. As early as 1290, local monks were complaining about the smell from the Fleet, which was already a foaming brew of sewage, butchers' offal and the by-products of various local tanneries. The Fleet was still reeking in the 1720s, when Alexander Pope dubbed it 'the King of Dykes' with its 'large tribute of dead dogs'.

On the east bank stood the Fleet Prison, in what is now Limeburner Lane. Until its demolition in 1846, several famous authors passed through its gates, including John Donne, who

Michael Frayn, in his comic Fleet Street novel Towards the End of the Morning *(1967), described the offices of the* Telegraph *as a white, imperial slab 'looking more like the Tomb of the Unknown Leader-Writer'.*

The notorious Fleet Prison was built in the Middle Ages and finally closed and demolished in 1846, partly through the efforts of Charles Dickens.

Worde in 1500, until the introduction of desktop publishing in the last quarter of the twentieth century – the name Fleet Street was synonymous with printing and journalism. It was de Worde who first exploited the market for mass-produced literature in the City of London: by the time he died in 1535 his printing works near Shoe Lane had turned out some 800 separate books and pamphlets. Meanwhile, his French-born rival Richard Pynson had set up shop on the corner of Chancery Lane and Fleet Street, where he became the official Printer to the King and produced the first English translation of Sebastian Brant's German classic *The Ship of Fools*. John Hodgets, who had his printing works near the junction with Fetter Lane, specialized in plays, among them Dekker and Webster's *Westward Hoe* (1607), about the adventures of three merry wives in Brentford, John Marston's comedy *The Dutch Courtezan* (1605) and Thomas Heywood's domestic tragedy *A Woman Killed with Kindness* (1607).

was sent there in 1601 after marrying his 16-year-old wife without her father's consent. John Cleland was imprisoned at the Fleet for debt in 1748, and bought his freedom by writing an erotic novel, *Fanny Hill, or Memoirs of a Woman of Pleasure*. The novel made his publisher £10,000, though it brought Cleland only 20 guineas. Charles Dickens's personal experience of the Marshalsea in the Borough gave him a lifelong obsession with prisons. In *The Pickwick Papers* (1836) Mr Pickwick is briefly incarcerated in the Fleet after refusing to pay damages to Mrs Bardell. There he meets a crestfallen Mr Jingle and secures his old enemy's freedom by paying his debts.

For nearly 500 years – from the arrival of Caxton's former assistant Wynkyn de

The first daily newspaper was the *Daily Courant* in 1702. It folded in 1735, but others were to follow. The *Morning Chronicle* appeared for the first time in 1769 and continued for more than a century. Among its contributors were Richard Brinsley Sheridan, Charles Lamb and Charles Dickens, who covered legal and parliamentary stories for the *Chronicle* and gained a reputation as the best reporter in London. In 1846, Dickens set up his own newspaper, the *Daily News*, at 90 Fleet Street, and put his father, John Dickens, in charge of the parliamentary staff. This was probably Dickens's way of keeping an eye on him. Despite the chastening experience of incarceration in a debtor's prison, John Dickens had recently developed a habit of forging his son's name in order to obtain credit. Charles was exasperated, but rather than confront his father head-on he placed advertisements in every major Fleet Street paper announcing that he would not be held responsible for other people's debts. Although a brilliant journalist, Dickens turned out to be only an average editor. He resigned after only 17 issues, but the paper he founded continued, latterly as the *News Chronicle*, until 1960.

One of Dickens's journalists would afterwards describe the atmosphere of the paper's cramped, grimy offices, reeking with the smell of oil and paper and humming with the noise of the steam-powered presses. A century later, the atmosphere of a typical Fleet Street newspaper office had barely changed. In his autobiography *Touched by Angels* (1988), the former *Daily Mirror* editor Derek Jameson describes the pervasive sense of excitement every evening as the massive basement presses would begin to reverberate through the building. Another editor, Arthur Christiansen of the *Daily Express*, would issue brief, penetrating bulletins to his staff several times a week, to ensure that they adhered to the highest standards of journalism – for instance:

Good stories flow like honey. Bad stories stick in the craw. What is a bad story? It is a story that cannot be absorbed on the first time of reading. It is a story that leaves questions unanswered. It is a story that has to be read two or three times before it can be comprehended. And a good story can be turned into a bad story by just one obscure sentence.

It's a homily which many newspaper and magazine editors would do well to memorize. Christiansen left the *Daily Express* in 1957 and later played himself – very badly – in the film *The Day the Earth Caught Fire*. As for the

*T*he stunning art deco Daily Express *building, dubbed 'the Black Lubyanka' by* Private Eye. *The* Express *newspaper magnate Lord Beaverbrook was the model for Lord Ottercove, the central character in William Gerhardie's Fleet Street satire* Doom *(1928).*

The Cock Tavern was the subject of one of Tennyson's lighter poems.

contributor at the age of 87 (frequently spotted on the Docklands Light Railway, on his way to the office). As a young reporter, Deedes was the model for William Boot, the unworldly nature correspondent who is accidentally dispatched to cover a war, in Evelyn Waugh's Fleet Street satire, *Scoop*. Over 40 years later, his friendship with the prime minister's husband Denis Thatcher gave rise to the long-running 'Dear Bill' column in *Private Eye*, consisting of their supposed correspondence.

Heroic alcohol consumption was an intrinsic part of Fleet Street culture. The irregular working hours meant that the local pubs would be crowded soon after opening time – first with reporters and photographers killing time before going out to cover a story; in the afternoon by the same reporters and photographers calling in for a swift one on their way back to the office; and in the evening, by sub-editors and compositors taking a break before putting the paper to bed for the night. When the pubs finally closed towards midnight, many of their customers would move on to the myriad private clubs, many of them run by former journalists, or to the all-night cafés for mixed grills or egg and chips. Even today, long after the newspapers deserted Fleet Street for Wapping and Canary Wharf, the magazine *Private Eye* continues to caricature the archetypal hack as 'Lunchtime O'Booze', whose sozzled, meandering prose invariably ends with a plaintive 'Will this do?' In fact, most Fleet Street editors positively encouraged their staff to visit the local pubs when things were quiet: it was the best way to sniff out new stories and find out what rival papers were up to.

Express, its quality and its circulation figures went into a long decline. Although the paper itself has moved to Blackfriars Road, its old art deco offices, all black glass and chrome, have recently re-emerged from a chrysalis of scaffolding after a lengthy period of restoration. The *Express's* old neighbour the *Daily Telegraph* has moved to the Isle of Dogs, but its fieldstone grey former building survives as Peterborough Court. For old time's sake, the paper's daily selection of topical ephemera continues to be called the Peterborough column. A former editor of the *Telegraph*, William Deedes, was still a regular

A drinking invitation to an editor from a proprietor was quite another matter: the White Hart pub in Fetter Lane was known to *Daily Mirror* employees as the Stab in the Back because of the staff vacancies that were often created there. One former proprietor whom *Mirror* staff would prefer to forget is the late Robert Maxwell, who bought the paper in the 1970s. As well as devoting much of the paper's news space to himself, 'Cap'n Bob', as he was known, had a helicopter pad constructed on the roof in order to make surprise visits to the office, which he humourlessly renamed Maxwell House. A visiting journalist from another paper once watched in appalled fascination as Maxwell emerged from his helicopter, walked to the edge of the building and urinated down into the street.

Samuel Pepys enjoyed an eventful Coronation Day celebration in Fleet Street in 1668. At the Cock Alehouse (opposite the present-day Cock Tavern at 22 Fleet Street), Pepys 'drank and eat a lobster and sang, and [was] mighty merry'. Later the same evening he met up with the actress Mrs Knipp and 'did tocar her corps all over and besar sans fin her, but did not offer algo mas; and so back and led her home'. Another Cock customer was Tennyson, whose poem 'Will Waterproof's Lyrical Monologue' was written at the Cock in 1842:

> *O plump head-waiter*
> *at the Cock,*

> *To which I most resort,*
> *How goes the time? 'Tis five*
> *o'clock.*
> *Go fetch a pint of port.*

A few years after the poem was published, Tennyson's friend (and putative Boswell to his Johnson) William Allingham visited the Cock and asked if the 'plump head waiter' still worked there. He did – and he knew the poem, but he had no idea who among his many customers Tennyson was. Allingham noted in his diary that the waiter was a little aggrieved that he had never actually identified the man who had addressed him so familiarly and so publicly. As the editor of the literary journal the *Criterion*, TS Eliot regularly hosted lunches at the Cock between 1922 and 1939.

The satirical magazine *Punch* was founded in the Punch Tavern at 99 Fleet Street in 1841; the bar is filled with original drawings from the magazine. The most

The Punch Tavern in Fleet Street, where the magazine Punch was born. Its many contributors have included Thomas Hood, William Makepeace Thackeray, Douglas Jerrold, George & Weedon Grossmith, Malcolm Muggeridge and Melvyn Bragg.

Dickens's favourite seat was at the table on the right of the fireplace in the ground-floor bar. Although not a natural frequenter of bars (in his youth he had once fled in terror from a noisy, crowded tavern), WB Yeats was a member of the Rhymers Club, which met at Ye Olde Cheshire Cheese in the 1890s. His poem 'The Grey Rock' is dedicated to the 'Poets with whom I learned my trade, / Companions of the Cheshire Cheese'.

Samuel Pepys was born in Salisbury Court, just off Fleet Street, in 1633 and wrote his famous diary at his home in Seething Lane, about a mile away. By then he was a frequent visitor to the Fountain Tavern at 17 Fleet Street. An upstairs room on the site of the tavern is now used as a permanent exhibition of Pepys memorabilia. The large windows have an excellent view of St Dunstan's Church, which marked the western extent of the Great Fire of London.

Pepys visited Fleet Street in search of other forms of enter-tainment. On 21 December 1663, he went to Shoe Lane to attend

Dickens's favourite seat at Ye Olde Cheshire Cheese is believed to have been this one, on the right of the fireplace.

famous of all the Fleet Street pubs is probably Ye Olde Cheshire Cheese on the corner of Wine Office Court, which retains the atmosphere – and near-darkness – of a seventeenth-century chop house. Since it opened its doors for the first time in 1667, its patrons have included Samuel Johnson, who lived at the end of Wine Office Court in Gough Square, Charles Dickens, Lord Tennyson, Mark Twain, Sir Arthur Conan Doyle and GK Chesterton.

his first cock fight. Pepys was taken aback by the 'strange variety' of people in the audience, which ranged from a former deputy governor of the Tower of London to the 'poorest prentices, bakers, brewers, butchers, draymen, and what not; and all these fellows, one with another, in swearing, cursing, and betting. I soon had enough of it; and yet I would not but have seen it once, it being strange to observe the nature of those poor creatures, how they will fight till they drop down dead upon the table and strike after they are ready to give up the ghost – not offering to run away when they are weary or wounded past doing further.'

Almost exactly a century later, in July 1763, another great diarist, James Boswell, spent an enjoyable quarter of an hour at Mrs Salmon's Waxworks, near Inner Temple Lane. A famous attraction in their day, the Waxworks lasted well into the nineteenth century (Dickens mentions them disparagingly in *David Copperfield*).

On a good day, Fleet Street could induce in Boswell a mood verging on euphoria. After a night of 'sweet repose after the luscious fatigues of the night' with a Covent Garden actress called Louisa, he records how he left the woman still asleep and 'patrolled up and down Fleet Street, thinking on London, the seat of Parliament and the seat of pleasure, and seeming to myself as one of the wits in King Charles the Second's time'.

Fleet Street also has its spiritual side. When he died in 1631, the poet John Donne was both rector of St Dunstan in the West and Dean of St Paul's Cathedral (his was the only memorial in the original cathedral to survive the Great Fire of London in 1666). One of Donne's sidesmen was Izaak Walton, whose much loved *The Compleat Angler* was published in St Dunstan's churchyard in 1653. Samuel Pepys was in St Dunstan's one day in August 1667 when he experienced one of the fits of sexual frenzy which seem to have particularly afflicted him in Fleet Street. Noticing an attractive young woman nearby, the diarist 'did labour to take her by the hand and body; but she would not, but got further and further from me, and at last I could perceive her to take pins out of her pocket to prick me if I should touch her again'. Undaunted, Pepys then 'fell to gaze upon another pretty maid in a pew close to me, and she on me; and I did go about to take her by the hand, which she suffered a little and then withdrew. So the sermon ended, and the church broke up, and my amours ended also.'

Pepys was christened at St Bride's Church, near Salisbury Court. When his brother Tom

Samuel Pepys's long association with Fleet Street is commemorated by the Pepys Exhibition at the Fountain Tavern on Fleet Street.

died in 1664, the church was so full of buried bodies that Pepys had to bribe the sexton sixpence to 'jostle them together' and make more space. Burnt down during the Fire of London, the church was rebuilt by Wren, and later became closely associated with printers and journalists. Most of the pews are dedicated to the memory of Fleet Street reporters and editors. All-night vigils were held here for the journalist John McCarthy during his 1,943-day captivity in the Lebanon, and when the *Observer* journalist Farzad Bazoft was hanged in Iraq in 1990 his memorial service was held at St Bride's.

Pepys, Dryden and Milton all worshipped at St Bride's, now known as the journalists' church.

St Dunstan in the West, where Pepys once propositioned two women during morning service.

However, Fleet Street's most graceful tribute to one of its own can be found not in a church but on a wall on the corner of Fleet Street and Ludgate Circus. Edgar Wallace is now seldom read, but in the first three decades of the twentieth century he was Britain's most popular thriller writer. (He was also one of the most prolific, writing a complete novel in a matter of days; his most popular play *On the Spot* was written over a weekend.) When he was writing he would drink endless cups of sweet tea. His method of regulating his output was singular: he would touch his massive bald head and if it was hot he would finish work for the day. Wallace began his career as an 11-year-old, playing truant to sell newspapers in Ludgate Circus, a few yards away from the bronze plaque which commemorates him. The plaque is inscribed to 'Edgar Wallace, reporter': 'He knew wealth and poverty, yet had walked with kings and kept his bearing. Of his talents, he gave lavishly to authorship – but to Fleet Street he gave his heart.' He died in Hollywood in 1932, while working on the script for *King Kong*.

In 1818, Samuel Taylor Coleridge and William Hazlitt were invited, quite independently of each other, to deliver a series of lectures in Fleet Street. Coleridge's lectures were to be on European literature and were held at the Philosophical Society in Fleur-de-Lis-Court, just off Fleet Street near Fetter Lane. Hazlitt's lectures, on English poetry, were delivered at the Surrey Institution in Blackfriars Road.

The relationship between the two men was an odd, intense one.

As a 17-year-old, Hazlitt had idolized Coleridge and other members of the Romantic movement. Coleridge befriended the shy young man, and encouraged him when he became a writer. By 1818 Hazlitt, now a confident, successful literary critic, had inexplicably turned on his former mentor, writing vicious reviews of his poem 'Christabel' and his philosophical work *Biographia Literaria*. Coleridge was hurt and bewildered by Hazlitt's disloyalty and waited nervously for the attack to be renewed in his lectures. Hazlitt duly obliged, dismissing Coleridge's journalism as 'dreary trash', his plays as 'drawling sentiment', and most of his poetry as unworthy of his talents. 'But,' said Hazlitt, suddenly changing tack, 'I may say of him here that he is the only person I ever knew who answered to the idea of a man of genius. He is the only person from whom I ever learnt anything. He was the first poet I ever knew. His genius at that time had angelic wings, and fed on manna. He talked on for ever; and you wished him to talk on for ever.' But what of the middle-aged Coleridge, still talking less than half a mile away in Fleet Street? Here, Hazlitt delivered his *coup de grâce*. 'Shall I, who heard him then, listen to him now? Not I! ... But still the recollection comes rushing by with thoughts of long-past years, and rings in my ears with never-dying sound.'

The house at 17 Gough Square is the only one among Dr Johnson's half-dozen or more London addresses to have survived. Johnson moved to 'Goff Square', as he called it, in 1746. Soon afterwards, he and his six assistants began work on the *Dictionary of the English Language*. It took nine years to complete, though Johnson later confided to James Boswell that if had applied himself more he could have done it in three. As a 'relief' from the *Dictionary*, Johnson founded a new review, the *Rambler*. It appeared twice a week for two years (March 1750–March 1752) and, with the exception of five articles, was written entirely by Johnson. Always prone to depression, Johnson

Gough Square commemorates not only Johnson's home (below) but also his cat, Hodge (left).

was devastated by the death of his wife Elizabeth (whom he called Tetty) in 1752, apparently from an overdose of opium. Her blind friend Anna Williams, who had lived in the house with them, continued to live with him at Gough Square. James Boswell later noted that 'Miss Williams is supported chiefly by Mr Johnson's generosity, and I believe nobody has ever had the folly or the malice to suspect anything criminal between them.' In fact, Johnson had another dependant, an

Johnson Court off Fleet Street, where Dickens delivered his first manuscript at the age of 21 to the offices of the Monthly Magazine.

impoverished doctor named Robert Levett who also shared his home. Levett's death in 1782 occasioned Johnson's moving elegy, beginning 'His virtues walked their narrow round'.

While the *Dictionary* made Johnson's reputation, it did not make his fortune. In 1758 he was arrested for debt (Samuel Richardson helped out with a gift of six guineas), and the following year Johnson moved out of Gough Square, in favour of more modest lodgings in Staple Inn. In 1914, 17 Gough Square was opened to the public. Among the exhibits are one of

the chairs from the original Cock Tavern, and a first edition of the *Dictionary*.

Johnson's Court, at the western end of Gough Square, takes its name not from Samuel Johnson, but from a tailor who lived there in the sixteenth century. Dr Johnson did live there, however: he spent 11 years at number 7, before moving to his last home, in Bolt Court, where he died in 1784. The offices of the *Monthly Magazine* were in Johnson's Court in 1833, when a nervous young journalist named Charles Dickens came to deliver his very first article ('Mr Minns and His Cousin'), 'stealthily one evening at twilight, with fear and trembling, into a dark letter-box, in a dark office, up a dark court in Fleet Street'.

The departure of the newspapers in the 1980s and 1990s was generally seen as the death of Fleet Street, and it is true that it has been a quieter place ever since. But the 'Street of Shame' has been written off before. More than a century ago, Anthony Trollope was mourning the passing of the Fleet Street that Boswell, Johnson and Pepys knew, and predicting worse to come. Writing in 1854, he breaks off from the narrative of *The Warden* (the first of the Barsetshire novels) to deliver a combined eulogy and prediction. The original St Dunstan's Church had been pulled down and rebuilt, the 'ancient shops with their faces full of pleasant history' were disappearing, 'the Bar itself is to go ... [and] rumour tells us of some huge building that is to appear in these latitudes dedicated to law'. Trollope's information was accurate. Temple Bar, which marked the boundary between the cities of Westminster and London, and where Boswell and Johnson used to part at the end of their walks, was pulled down in 1878 because it was in the way of the traffic; and in 1882, the year of Trollope's death, the Royal Courts of Justice were opened, close to where Temple Bar had stood at the western end of Fleet Street.

LONDON BRIDGE, BANK OF ENGLAND AND THE MONUMENT

Unreal City,
Under the brown fog of a
winter dawn,
A crowd flowed over London
Bridge, so many,
I had not thought death had
undone so many.
Sighs, short and infrequent,
were exhaled,
And each man fixed his eyes
before his feet.
Flowed up the hill and down
King William Street,
To where Saint Mary
Woolnoth kept the hours
With a dead sound on the
final stroke of nine.

Almost 80 years after it was published, TS Eliot's *The Waste Land* still offers a defining image of the modern City. Every morning, commuters stream into the City across London Bridge, and the clock of St Mary Woolnoth still extends high over Lombard Street.

Even at the time, Eliot's critics and literary friends found it hard to reconcile the writer of dense, visionary works like *The Waste Land* and *The Hollow Men* with the immaculately dressed figure

(complete with rolled umbrella and display handkerchief) who worked in the City at Lloyd's Bank from 1917–25. The reason was largely practical: he needed the money, and the regular hours limited the time he would otherwise have had to spend with his mentally unstable wife, Vivien. Another poet and critic, IA Richards, once visited Eliot in Cornhill and found him in his basement office, 'stooping, very like a dark bird in a feeder, over a big table covered with all sorts and sizes of foreign correspondence. The big table almost entirely filled a little room under the street. Within a foot of our heads when we stood were the thick, green glass squares of the pavement on which hammered all but incessantly the heels of the passers-by.'

E liot is not the only writer to have found life in a bank unexpectedly congenial. The author of *The Wind in the Willows*, Kenneth Grahame, had been looking forward to going to Oxford, but just as he was about to leave school his family's finances took a turn for the worse and a position was found for him at the Bank of England, in Threadneedle Street, as a 'pale-faced quill-driver'. For a

M orning commuters pour across London Bridge (above), while the clock of St Mary Woolnoth sounds 'the final stroke of nine' (below).

man of Grahame's artistic sensibilities, the 'Old Lady of Threadneedle Street', as Sheridan had dubbed it, was not such a bad place to be in the early 1880s. The Bank rather encouraged creativity among its staff, and Grahame wrote a series of articles on paganism and the English countryside. A friend, the ebullient writer and editor WE Henley (the inspiration for Long John Silver in Robert Louis Stevenson's *Treasure Island*) tried to persuade him to give up work in the Bank and devote himself to writing, but Grahame could not pull himself away from the certainties of a salaried existence. Something of the inner struggle between the two modes of existence can be seen in *The Wind in the Willows*, where Rat allows himself to be talked out of the leaving the river and seeking his fortune like the Sea Rat. Despite being held up by an armed robber in 1903, Grahame remained at the Bank for 18 years, latterly as Secretary, until his retirement in 1908, shortly before the publication of *The Wind in the Willows*.

The Bank of England where Kenneth Grahame worked.

PG Wodehouse, on the other hand, bailed out of his City job at the earliest possible opportunity. Having been ordered by his father,

a former judge in Hong Kong, to find a steady job before attempting to make a living as a writer, Wodehouse spent two years (1900–2) at the Hong Kong and Shanghai Bank in Gracechurch Street, but resigned before he could be sent East, where his brothers spent their working lives. Wodehouse's experiences at the Hong Kong and Shanghai formed the basis of one of his funniest novels, *Psmith in the City* (1910), in which the genial young cricketer Mike and his friend Psmith, a monocled old Etonian with verbal diarrhoea, take up junior positions at the 'New Asiatic Bank' somewhere in the vicinity of Mansion House. Even allowing for exaggeration, the novel offers some insight into the relaxed, gentlemanly world of commerce in an era that knew nothing of stress in the workplace. Here is Mike's working day:

He would arrive in the morning just in time to sign his name in the attendance book before it was removed to the accountant's room. That was at ten o'clock. From ten to eleven he would potter... From eleven to half past twelve he would put in a little gentle work. Lunch... could be spun out from half past twelve to two. More work from two till half past three. From half past three till half past four, tea in the tea-room, with a novel. And from half past four till five either a little more work or more pottering, according to whether there was any work to do or not. It was by no means an unpleasant mode of spending a late January day.

The City as described by Iain Sinclair at the other end of the twentieth century is completely different to Wodehouse's picture, apart from a few stray churches which have somehow survived the Blitz. Oblivious to their surroundings, its worker ants willingly deny themselves the basic human pleasures:

These days businessmen take the cellphones out for lunch, instead of their mistresses. No booze. No hanks of bloody meat. Elegant blue bottles of carbonated water. Tables that seem to have been laid out for a perfume launch... They start early and drink late. You have to be able to out-breakfast the opposition.

In the mid-1930s, Ian Fleming was working for Rowe and Pitman, a firm of stockbrokers, in Bishopsgate. Years later, when the James Bond novels had made him rich and famous, Fleming cheerfully admitted to having been 'the world's worst stockbroker', but there was more to the job than met the eye. One of the senior partners, Lancelot Hugh Smith, was a talent spotter for Naval Intelligence, and when war broke out in 1939, Fleming was co-opted into the intelligence division of the Royal Naval Volunteer Reserve. The notion of a respectable firm acting as a front for Secret Service agents was still in Fleming's mind when he conceived 007: Bond and his boss 'M' are theoretically employees of a firm called Universal Export.

The heart of City banking is generally held to be Lombard Street, where

Barclay's, Lloyd's and Martin's banks once had their head offices. Charles Dickens's first love, Maria Beadnell, was living at 2 Lombard Street (her father was the manager of the bank next door) when the 18-year-old Dickens met her in 1830. In *David Copperfield* she appears as Dora Spenlow, whose 'captive and slave' David becomes. In the novel, David marries Dora, but comes to realize that he and his 'child-wife' are incompatible. In real life, Maria spurned Dickens before he had the chance to propose, though towards the end of their relationship the infatuated young man was walking all the way from Westminster to Lombard Street just to gaze up at her window.

His love for Maria had a poignant coda. One evening, Dickens was glancing through some letters which had just arrived when he realized that something had inexplicably disturbed him. When he looked more closely at the letters, he realized why: he now registered that the handwriting on one of them was that of Maria Beadnell, whom he hadn't seen for 20 years. He replied to her letter and arranged to meet her – only to discover

Lombard Street was already London's banking quarter when Alexander Pope was born here in 1688.

London, the crouching monster, like every other monster has to breathe, and breathe it does in its own obscure, malignant way. Its vital oxygen is composed of suburban working men and women of all kinds, who every morning are sucked up through an infinitely complicated respiratory apparatus of trains and termini into the mightily congested lungs, held there for a number of hours, and then, in the evening, exhaled violently through the same channels.
Patrick Hamilton, *The Slaves of Solitude*, 1947.

that the pretty flirtatious girl he had loved had become a fat, garrulous, silly woman. The encounter with Maria was to find its way into another novel, *Little Dorrit*, in the scene where Arthur Clennam meets his first love, Flora Finching, for the first time in many years, and experiences a similar disillusionment. It is through Arthur Clennam that Dickens writes what is perhaps his most vivid, and melancholy, City scene, where Clennam, newly returned to London after many years abroad, sits in a coffee house on Ludgate Hill, on a grey City Sunday evening, listening to the City church bells and putting off the moment when he must go to his mother's dark, loveless house by the river. No passage in literature conveys so accurately the mournful quality of the City on a Sunday; unlike so much of Dickens's London, the scene is still true today.

Dickens's earlier novel *The Pickwick Papers* is more cheerful. The best place in the City to retread the steps of Mr Pickwick and Sam Weller is the George and Vulture Inn, in Bengal Court (off Lombard Street). The pub has changed little since the pair came here to drown their sorrows while the case of Bardell v. Pickwick was heard at the Guildhall.

The Monument, on the corner of Monument Street and

Fish Street Hill, was built between 1671 and 1677 to commemorate the Great Fire of London, and is another City location which can be experienced in much the same way now as when it was new. A Catholic, Alexander Pope took great exception to an inscription (since removed) on the Monument's base which blamed the Fire on a Popish plot. 'London's column, pointing at the skies, / Like a tall bully, lifts the head and lies' was his comment in *Moral Essays*. One wonders what Pope would have made of the National Westminster Tower, which soars 600 feet into the air (three times as high as the Monument) less than a quarter of a mile from Pope's birthplace in Lombard Street.

On 2 April 1763, James Boswell strolled across London Bridge, admiring 'the Thames's silver expanse and the springy bosom of the surrounding fields'. Then, somewhat against his better judgement, he climbed to the top of the Monument:

This is a most amazing building. It is a pillar two hundred feet high. In the inside, a turnpike stair runs up all the way. When I was about half way up, I grew frightened. I would have come down again, but thought I would despise myself for my timidity. Thus does the spirit of pride get the better of fear. I mounted to the top and got upon the balcony. It was horrid to find myself so monstrous a way up in the air, so far above London and all its spires. I durst not look round me. There is no real danger, as there is a strong rail both on the stair and the *balcony. But I shuddered, and as every heavy wagon passed down Gracechurch Street, dreaded that the shaking of the earth would make the tremendous pile tumble to the foundation.*

In fact, the 'strong rail' was not completely fail-safe. Until 1842, when the balcony was completely railed in, the Monument was a favourite spot for suicides.

The most arrogant building in the City, the Nat West Tower was also the tallest in Europe until it was eclipsed by the Canary Wharf Tower.

Samuel Taylor Coleridge had his first experience of opium while still a pupil at Christ's Hospital.

CHRIST'S HOSPITAL, OLD BAILEY AND NEWGATE STREET

When the rector of the Devon village of Ottery St Mary, John Coleridge, died suddenly from a heart attack in 1781, the family agreed that his youngest son, nine-year-old Samuel Taylor Coleridge, should be sent to London to attend Christ's Hospital, a school in Newgate Street which had been set up to educate the sons of poor clergymen. Coleridge duly arrived for the autumn term in September 1782, clad in the traditional Christ's Hospital uniform of a blue coat and yellow stockings – the latter chosen by the school authorities as the most effective colour for preventing rats from nipping the boys'

Christ's Hospital was also known as the Bluecoat School, after its distinctive uniform. As well as Coleridge and Lamb, its pupils have included Leigh Hunt and Thomas Barnes, the first great editor of The Times.

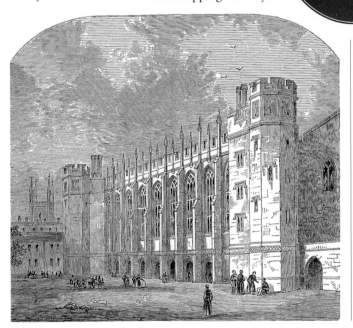

ankles. Another new boy was Charles Lamb. In his 1820 essay 'Christ's Hospital Five-and-Thirty Years Ago' Lamb painted a vivid picture of Coleridge as a schoolboy – alternately desperately homesick, reading voraciously and, above all, *talking*, incessantly and brilliantly, to his schoolmates. When he wanted peace and quiet, Coleridge would climb onto the school roof – a habit which he probably had in mind when he wrote, in his poem 'Frost at Midnight', that

*...I was reared
In the great city,
pent 'mid
cloisters dim,
And saw
nought lovely
but the sky and
stars.*

He was also experiencing what his biographer Richard Holmes has described as his 'epic daydreams'. One day he fancied he was Leander crossing the Hellespont and walked down Cheapside making swimming movements with his hands. When he accidentally hit a passer-by, the man angrily accused him of trying to pick his pocket. Coleridge explained that he was merely re-enacting the story of Hero and Leander and the man, realizing that the boy's explanation was so preposterous it had to be true, arranged for him to become a member of the library in nearby King Street. On another out-of-bounds expedition, Coleridge went swimming in the New River in the East End and contracted rheumatic fever for which he was treated, ominously, with opium.

Coleridge marked his departure from Christ's Hospital with a sonnet, 'On Quitting School for College'. As a Cambridge undergraduate he and his Oxford friend Robert Southey drew up plans for a new, utopian way of living – Pantisocracy – which would involve setting up a commune on the banks of the Susquehanna river in Pennsylvania. During college vacations he took lodgings at the Salutation and Cat tavern, opposite his old school in Newgate Street, where he tried to persuade members of the 'Grecians' – Christ's Hospital boys earmarked for Oxford and Cambridge – to join the movement. Charles Lamb looked back fondly on these evenings with Coleridge and Southey, when they would talk over Welsh rarebit and egg-flip, and smoke fragrant Virginia tobacco. The commune by the Susquehanna never happened (mainly because Southey's enthusiasm was waning), but the friendship between Lamb and Coleridge endured. In middle age, Lamb described his friend as 'an archangel, a little damaged'. A plaque on the wall of St Sepulchre's Church in Giltspur Street commemorates Lamb, as 'Perhaps the most loved name in English literature, who was a Bluecoat Boy here for seven years.'

Until 1902, Newgate Street was dominated by Newgate Prison, which stood on the corner of Old Bailey, directly opposite the Viaduct Tavern. The prison was pulled down and rebuilt several times, though the conditions did not improve until the second half of the nineteenth century. The poet Sir Thomas Malory, author of the

The exercise room of the Newgate Prison. Henry Fielding described the prison as a 'prototype of hell' – with good reason: the sanitation was appalling, disease was rife, and the warders famed for their corruption and sadism. When Elizabeth Fry visited the jail in 1813 she was so appalled by the conditions that she devoted the rest of her life to penal reform.

Arthurian cycle *Le Morte D'Arthur* (1470), is believed to have been an inmate at Newgate, possibly for murder. The playwright Ben Jonson was imprisoned here in 1598 after killing the actor Gabriel Spencer (see Shoreditch).

In June 1780, Newgate was at the centre of the worst rioting the City has ever seen. An anti-Catholic march led by Lord George Gordon, an MP and leader of the Protestant Association, had got out of control, and after rampaging through Soho and Covent Garden the mob poured down Holborn and into the City. The poets George Crabbe and William Blake were both onlookers in the crowd as the mob broke down the gates of the Newgate, smashed the windows and then piled up all the flammable material they could find in order to set fire to the prison. Some of the prisoners were burnt to death; others were freed by the rioters, who pulled them up through the roof, still with their

The Viaduct Tavern near the Old Bailey is one of the stops on an epic City pub crawl in Iris Murdoch's novel Under the Net.

'nothing but ribaldry, debauchery, levity, drunkenness and flaunting vice in fifty other shapes. I should have deemed it impossible that I could have felt any large assemblage of my fellow creatures to be so odious.'

Yet there was an element of special pleading here: Dickens seems to have been guiltily fascinated by executions and on this occasion went to considerable lengths to secure a good view of the proceedings (from the upper window of somebody's house).

When the prison was finally demolished in 1902, the site was used to extend the Central Criminal Court, in the street called Old Bailey. The court itself has been known as the Old Bailey for centuries – the notorious Judge Jeffreys was the Recorder, or senior law officer, here in the 1670s. It was at the Old Bailey that the destruction of Oscar Wilde took place in 1895.

In happier times, Wilde had worked just a stone's throw from the Old Bailey, as the editor of the *Woman's World* magazine on Ludgate Hill. (Wilde never stayed in the office for more than a few hours at a time because the publishers had a no-smoking rule.) But even then, Wilde was sowing the seeds of his own destruction. At a time when it was a criminal offence to be a practising homosexual, he was, to use his own phrase, 'feasting with panthers' – consorting with working-class young men in expensive London hotels and paying them for their time. They would then systematically blackmail him. But it was his affair with Lord Alfred Douglas ('Bosie') that would lead him back to the Old Bailey.

manacles attached. Crabbe wrote that he 'never saw anything so dreadful ... you have no conception of the frenzy of the multitude'. Dickens wrote an account of the rioting in *Barnaby Rudge*, and included a sharp vignette of the rebuilt prison in *Great Expectations*, where young Pip passes the prison wall and finds 'the roadway covered with straw to deaden the noise of passing vehicles; and from this, and from the quantity of people standing about, smelling strongly of spirits and beer, I inferred that the trials were on'.

Dickens visited Newgate several times to witness public hangings. Of one such execution, in 1840, he described the mob that gathered to witness the occasion as

After provocation from the Marquess of Queensbury, Wilde had no choice but to sue him for libel (see Mayfair).

When the hearing began in April 1895, Wilde dominated the proceedings with his customary wit and charm. At one point, Queensberry's counsel, Edward Carson, read out a passage from Wilde's novel *The Picture of Dorian Grey* and demanded to know whether Wilde was the author. Wilde replied that he was. Carson then recited some lines of verse from an article Wilde had written. 'And I suppose you wrote that also, Mr Wilde?' Carson sneered. Wilde paused until the court was completely hushed, then said quietly, 'Ah no, Mr Carson. Shakespeare wrote that.' Carson blushed and read out another line of verse. 'And I suppose Shakespeare wrote that also, Mr Wilde?' 'Not as you read it, Mr Carson,' Wilde replied. The court rang with laughter.

Later, Carson questioned Wilde about one of the young men, a servant, whom he had entertained in the West End. 'Did you ever kiss him?' Carson asked. 'Oh dear, no,' Wilde replied. 'He was a peculiarly plain boy. He was, unfortunately, extremely ugly. I pitied him for it.'

He had gone too far and he knew it. This time his opponent pounced, demanding to know whether Wilde was in the habit of kissing young men if they were *not* ugly. Wilde was reduced to blustering humility: 'You sting me and insult me and try to unnerve me; and at times one

says things flippantly when one ought to speak more seriously.' The judge instructed the jury to rule in Queensberry's favour, thereby branding Wilde a sodomite.

A second, criminal trial was now inevitable. Wilde was duly convicted of indecency and sodomy and sentenced to two years' hard labour – the harshest sentence the law could impose. On his release, with his health broken and his reputation ruined, he moved to Paris, where he died penniless in November 1900. In his 1987 biography *Oscar Wilde*, Richard Ellmann points out that with Wilde's downfall 'the nineties' ended, for all intents and purposes, not in 1899 but in 1895.

The scene of Wilde's destruction continued to play a part in popular literature. In the novel *London Belongs to Me* (1945), Norman Collins cuts the building itself down to size – 'It is just a large bleak factory of the Criminal Law with an enormous gilt doll,

Newgate Prison was burnt down during the Great Fire of London (1666) and the Gordon Riots (1780) but rebuilt each time.

In 'Homage to Wren (a memory of 1941)', Louis MacNeice writes from the point of view of a fire-watcher in the cathedral during the Blitz:

> *At sea in the dome of St Paul's*
> *Riding the firefull night,*
> *Fountains of sparks like a funfair,*
> *We patrolled between the inner and outer walls,*
> *Saw that all hatches were screwed down tight*
> *And felt that Sir Christopher Wren had made*
> *everything shipshape.*
>
> *Then went on deck with the spray*
> *Of bombs in our ears...*

After the raid, the watcher surveys the desolation:

> *Then the storm subsided and it was dawn,*
> * it was cold,*
> *I climbed to the crow's nest for one last look at*
> * the roaring foam,*
> *League upon league of scarlet and gold,*
> *But it was so cold I stretched out my hands*
> * from the drunken mast*
> *And warmed my hands at London and*
> * went home.*

dressed up as Justice, standing on top of the dome.' In Iris Murdoch's *Under the Net* (1954) Jake Donaghue and his friends spend a summer evening searching the City for the philosopher Hugo Belfounder, beginning their quest at the Viaduct Tavern, opposite the Old Bailey. Fictional Old Bailey cases were fought in Agatha Christie's play *Witness for the Prosecution* (1953) and in John Mortimer's long-running series of novels and stories featuring Rumpole of the Bailey. The Old Bailey itself was the setting for another famous literary *cause célèbre* in 1960, when Penguin Books were prosecuted for obscenity after publishing DH Lawrence's *Lady Chatterley's Lover,* unexpurgated. Among the distinguished witnesses who defended the novel's literary merits was EM Forster, then 81, who appeared in a raincoat, declined the offer of a chair, and praised his old friend Lawrence as 'the greatest imaginative writer of his generation'. He did, however, concede that Lawrence's greatest work was probably not *Lady Chatterley* but *Sons and Lovers.*

ST PAUL'S AND CHEAPSIDE

Old St Paul's Cathedral was the burial place of the Elizabethan poet and soldier Sir Philip Sidney, who died from an infected thigh wound at the Battle of Zutphen in 1586. The poet and preacher John Donne later became Dean of St Paul's. His memorial, showing him in a shroud and rising from death at the Last Judgement, was the only monument in the cathedral to survive the Fire in 1666, which also spelt financial ruin for the booksellers who traditionally conducted their business from St Paul's churchyard. Samuel Pepys had a regular contract with one of these dealers. On 23 July 1664 he records coming here to buy books, presumably as a form of intellectual penance, after an afternoon's sexual adventuring in Fleet Street.

Wren's masterpiece, the present St Paul's Cathedral, was built between 1675 and 1710. From certain angles it seems to be floating above the City, especially when seen unexpectedly at night from the riverside or from the foot of Ludgate Hill. The sight of St Paul's riding calmly above the flames while Hitler's bombs showered around it inspired two vivid poems. In 'Epilogue to a Human Drama' Stephen Spender recalled how the other City churches

> *Which had glittered emptily*
> *in gold and silk,*
> *Stood near the crowning dome*
> *of the cathedral*
> *Like courtiers round the*
> *Royal Martyr.*
> *August shadows of night*
> *And bursting days of*
> *concentrated light*
> *Dropped from the skies to*
> *paint a final scene –*
> *Illuminated agony of*
> *frowning stone.*

For more than a decade after the war, the City was a strange landscape of empty spaces, bomb-blasted ruins, and unexpected vistas ending abruptly at buildings that had miraculously escaped the

bombing. The epic pub crawl in Iris Murdoch's *Under the Net* takes place in a City that is only beginning to recover from the onslaught. The church she mentions here, St Nicholas Cole, was still a semi-ruin in 1954, though modern buildings have since concealed it from anyone standing in Cheapside:

> *The evening was by now well advanced. The darkness hung in the air but spread out in a suspended powder which only made the vanishing colours more vivid. The zenith was a strong blue, the horizon a radiant amethyst. From the darkness and shade of St Paul's Churchyard we came into Cheapside as into a bright arena, and saw framed in the gap of a ruin the pale neat rectangles of St Nicholas Cole Abbey, standing alone away to the south of us on the other side of Cannon Street. In between, the willow herb waved over what remained of streets. In this desolation the coloured shells of houses still raised up filled and blank squares of wall and window. The declining sun struck on glowing bricks and flashing tiles and warmed the stone of an occasional fallen pillar.*

When the City was rebuilt, there was widespread condemnation of the architects who hemmed in St Paul's with unimaginatively designed tower blocks. Iain Sinclair,

St Mary Woolnoth was designed by the architect Nicholas Hawksmoor, whose namesake is a character in Peter Ackroyd's best-known novel.

however, finds even shrunken, modern-day St Paul's excessive. In *Lights Out for the Territory* he complains that 'the humpbacked dowager is too grandiose and self-satisfied, dominating the heights of Ludgate Hill like a baroque power-point'.

Other writers have found a rich source of material in the City's churches. In *Summoned by Bells*, John Betjeman describes how, at the age of about 12, he began to explore 'St Botoloph this, St Mary that' during day-long excursions from the family home in Chelsea. His love of these churches, with their 'high box pews' and 'ticking gallery clock, and charity bench' was motivated less by the love of God than by a longing for the past and a quiet sense of superiority over those who were not in on the secret:

Cheapside was once renowned for its pillory, its public executions and its riotous apprentices.

*How trivial used to seem the
Underground,
How worldly looked the over-
lighted west,
How different and smug and
wise I felt
When from the east I made
my journey home!*

Peter Ackroyd's novel *Hawksmoor* (1985) offers a less comforting view of the City churches. In the novel, Detective Chief Superintendent Nicholas Hawksmoor examines the body of a boy on the steps of St Mary Woolnoth in Lombard Street, then enters the church to rinse his face in the font.

From medieval times, Cheapside had a reputation as the noisiest, bawdiest, and frequently the most violent part of the City. The local apprentices were particularly renowned for their drinking and fighting. In Chaucer's *Canterbury Tales*, the Cook tells of a Cheapside apprentice who 'loved bet the taverne than the shoppe'

*For whan ther any riding
[procession] was in Chepe,
Out of the shoppe
thider would he lepe.*

Thomas Middleton's comedy *A Chaste Maid in Cheapside* (1613) is the raunchy tale of Sir Walter Whorehound and his scheme to marry off his mistress to the rich but stupid son of Yellowhammer the goldsmith.

Many of the streets off Cheapside are named after the markets that were held there. The Mermaid Tavern in Bread Street was where Sir Walter Ralegh established one of the first literary clubs, the Friday Street Club, around 1603. Regulars included Marlowe, Shakespeare, Donne, who was born in Bread Street, and Beaumont, who celebrated the Mermaid in a poem addressed to Ben Jonson:

*What things
have we seen
Done at the
Mermaid! heard
   words that have
   been
So nimble, and so
full of subtle
   flame,
As if that every
one from
   whence they
   came
Had meant to
put his whole
   wit in a jest,
And had resolved
to live a fool
   the rest
Of his dull life.*

The line about 'subtle flame' was prophetic – the Mermaid was burnt down during the Great Fire of London. John Keats shared lodgings with his brothers George and Tom at 76 Cheapside while working across the river at Guy's Hospital. His poem 'Lines on the Mermaid Tavern' paid tribute to his Elizabethan predecessors:

*Souls of poets dead and gone,
What Elysium have ye known,
Happy field or mossy cavern,
Choicer than the Mermaid
Tavern?*

Another Romantic poet, Wordsworth, found inspiration in nearby Wood Street. 'The Reverie of Poor Susan' recalls the time when the City was still dotted with patches of woodland and singing thrushes could be heard in the trees.

When he was ten, Charles Dickens travelled on a coach from Chatham to the City, to join his parents who were living in

Camden Town. He wrote in *The Uncommercial Traveller*: 'Through all the years that have since passed, have I ever lost the smell of the damp straw in which I was packed – like game – and forwarded, carriage paid, to the Cross Keys, Wood Street, Cheapside, London?'

CORNHILL TO ALDGATE

Modern buildings have obscured Cornhill's once commanding position as the highest hill in the City of London. Its prominent position and busy traffic made it the obvious place to instal a public pillory, where Daniel Defoe a Cornhill hosier, was put in 1703, after writing a satirical

Mansion House, Cheapside mentioned in 'Gone Astray' by Dickens. The narrator is peering through the kitchen window watching dinner being prepared when his heart 'began to beat with hope that the Lord Mayor, and the Lady Mayoress, and one of the young Princesses their daughters, would look out of an upper appartment and direct me to be taken in.'

Daniel Defoe's defiant appearance in the Cornhill pillory, depicted here by Eyre Crowe, is now part of City folklore.

pamphlet, 'The Shortest Way with Dissenters'. Satire was a dangerous profession in the early eighteenth century: although Defoe was himself a dissenter, and his catalogue of suggested punishments was meant to be ironic, the government took him seriously and ordered him to be arrested. By then, Defoe had gone to ground, and he subsequently became one of the few authors whose appearance is known chiefly through his description in the *Police Gazette*. City watchmen were warned to be on the look out for 'a middle-sized spare man, about forty years old, of a brown complexion and dark brown coloured hair, but wears a wig; a hooked nose, a sharp chin, grey eyes and a large mole near his mouth'. Subsequently arrested and tried at the Old Bailey, Defoe was fined 200 marks, ordered to stand three times in the pillory, imprisoned during the queen's pleasure and bound over for the next seven years.

Defoe duly stood in the Cornhill pillory for three days (29, 30 and 31 July 1703) but, morally if not financially, he had the last laugh. His fame had spread, and when he arrived for his punishment local people formed a guard, covered the pillory with flowers and drank his health. In return, Defoe wrote a poem, 'Hymn to the Pillory' which was sold in large numbers and which ridiculed the legal authorities:

> *Tell them the men who placed*
> *him here*
> *Are scandals to the times;*
> *Are at a loss to find his guilt,*
> *And can't commit his crimes.*

In 1848 the publishers Smith & Elder had their offices at 65 (now 32) Cornhill where two of their authors, Anne and Charlotte Brontë, paid them a surprise visit – surprising in more ways than one, as the company had been under the impression that they had been dealing with two gentlemen named Acton and Currer Bell. In 1860, Charlotte's literary hero William Makepeace Thackeray became the first editor of the *Cornhill Magazine*. In its early days the *Cornhill* specialized in serializing novels, among them Thackeray's *The Adventures of Philip* and *Denis Duval*, Trollope's *Framley Parsonage* and Elizabeth Gaskell's *Wives and Daughters*. The magazine continued until as recently as 1975.

East India House once stood on the corner of Lime Street and Leadenhall Street. One of its employees was Charles Lamb, who was taken on as a clerk at the age of 17 and remained there for 33 years: 'I have left the d–d India House for good,' he wrote exultantly to a friend on his retirement in 1825. Another employee was Thomas Love Peacock, whose hilarious, unclassifiable novels (among them *Melincourt, Nightmare Abbey* and *Crotchet Castle*) are peopled by caricatures of the leading intellectuals of the day, among them Coleridge, Byron and Peacock's close friend Shelley.

The son of a prosperous City wine merchant, Geoffrey Chaucer spent much of his early life on the continent, as a soldier and later a diplomat in the service of Edward III, who rewarded him in 1374 with a daily pitcher of wine. In the same year, Chaucer became Comptroller of Customs and Subsidy of Wools, Skins and Tanned Hides in the Port of London, and moved into rent-free accommodation directly above one of the City gates, Aldgate (removed in the eighteenth century). Although he continued to travel extensively on court business, Chaucer retained the house until 1388. By then he had begun his most famous work, the *Canterbury Tales*, which were left unfinished on his death in 1400.

Daniel Defoe's *Journal of the Plague Year*, published in 1722, was a revolutionary exercise in documentary-style realism. It purports to be the diary of an Aldgate saddler during the plague of 1665, and was praised by Hazlitt for its 'epic grandeur, as well as heart-breaking familiarity'.

BLACKFRIARS TO THE TOWER OF LONDON

In 1596, the actor James Burbage bought part of the site of the former Blackfriars Monastery, intending to convert it into a new theatre, to be called the Blackfriars Playhouse. Burbage died the following year, and the theatre was leased to one of the then popular troupes of boy

Parts of the City, such as Simpson's in Ball Court, and the George and Vulture in Birchin Lane, would still be recognized by Dickens and Thackeray.

the winter. In 1613, Shakespeare bought a house in Blackfriars, close to the theatre in the old monastery gatehouse. The title deed, which records that the house was sold for £140, with Shakespeare putting up £80 in cash, is on display in the Guildhall Library.

The theatre itself was later closed down by the Puritans, and demolished in 1655. When the Mermaid Theatre was opened a few hundred yards away, in Puddle Dock, in 1959, it was the first new theatre to be built in the City of London for over 300 years.

Upper Thames Street hugs the river between Puddle Dock and London Bridge, with its continuation, Lower Thames Street, extending almost to the Tower. Much of the street was destroyed during the Fire of London. In March 1668, Samuel Pepys recorded that he 'walked all along Thames Street, which I have not done since it was burned ... and there do see a brave street likely to be, many brave houses being built ... The raising of the street will make it mighty fine.' Fine it was, for a while, but in the nineteenth century the area went into a long decline. In *Little Dorrit* (1855), Arthur Clennam visits his mother at her house there, passing on the way 'silent warehouses and wharves, and here and there a narrow alley leading to the river, where a wretched little bill, FOUND DROWNED, was weeping on the wet wall'.

The Upper Thames Street waterfront had changed little in the early 1950s, when Iris Murdoch's peripatetic hero Jake Donaghue and his friends came here at three o'clock on a summer morning for an illegal swim in the

Geoffrey Chaucer, the first great poet to write in English, spent much of his early life in the service of Edward III. In 1374 he became Comptroller of Customs and Subsidy of Wools, Skins and Tanned Hides and moved into rent-free accomodation above the old Aldgate.

actors. Shakespeare's bitter dislike of these child performers can be seen in a famous exchange, in which Rosencrantz tells an incredulous Hamlet that

There is, sir, an eyrie of children, little eyases [young hawks] that cry out on the top of question, and are most tyrranically clapped for't: these are now the fashion, and so berattle the common stages – so they call them – that many wearing rapiers are afraid of goose-quills, and dare scarce come hither.

In 1608, the playhouse was taken over by James Burbage's son Richard, and Shakespeare became one of the shareholders. Unlike Burbage's other theatre, the Globe, the Blackfriars was an indoor venue. From then on, Burbage's company alternated between the Globe, in the summer, and the Blackfriars in

Thames. The scene demonstrates Iris Murdoch's love of swimming, which would surface in other novels such as *The Philosopher's Pupil*, and which her husband John Bayley would recollect so fondly in his memoir, *Iris*. Jake's invigorating dip in the Thames (when the water was considerably more polluted than it is now) is perhaps the most sensuous passage she ever wrote:

> *The night air touched my body with a touch which was neither warm nor cold, only very soft and unexpected. My blood buzzed behind my skin with a nervous beat ... Then the water was about my neck and I shot out into the open river.*
> *The sky opened out above me like an unfurled banner, cascading with stars and blanched by the moon. The black hulls of barges darkened the water behind me and murky towers and pinnacles rose indistinctly on the other bank. I swam well out into the river. It seemed enormously wide; and as I looked up and down stream I could see on one side the dark pools under Blackfriars Bridge, and on the other the pillars of Southwark Bridge glistening under the moon. The whole expanse of water was running with light. It was like swimming in quicksilver.*

Lower Thames Street makes an appearance in TS Eliot's *The Waste Land*:

> *O City city, I can sometimes hear*
> *Beside a public bar in Lower*

> *Thames Street,*
> *The pleasant whining of a mandoline*
> *And a clatter and a chatter from within*
> *Where fish men lounge at noon: where the walls*
> *Of Magnus Martyr hold Inexplicable splendour of Ionian white and gold.*

The 'fish men' will have come from Billingsgate market, opened before the invasion of William the Conqueror and moved to the Isle of Dogs in 1982. The beautiful interior of the church of St Magnus Martyr is still a calm counterpoint to the incessant

The church of St Magnus Martyr in Lower Thames Street, mentioned by TS Eliot in The Waste Land.

131

The Guildhall, scene of the famous action of Bardell v. Pickwick in The Pickwick Papers, *in which Mr Pickwick is sued for breach of promise by his landlady.*

under Charles II.

Although the diary is crammed with familiar London locations, Pepys sometimes seems to speak from another world, now unreachable across the centuries. He refers casually to the limbs of traitors being displayed on the Aldersgate ('a sad sight to see' is his only comment); he takes a barge to Woolwich to look at a sunken galleon; he thrashes his servant so hard that his arm aches for the rest of the night; he sits on his roof to take in the night air but is driven down when his neighbour Sir William Penn empties a smelly 'shitten pot' next door.

And yet, in many ways the minutiae of Pepys's domestic life would be familiar to any suburban husband in the early years of the twenty-first century. We read about Pepys dragging himself to work with a raging hangover and throwing up when he gets to the office. We learn that he likes to be seen as one of the lads when some workmen come to do up his house, 'it being my luck to meet with a sort of Drolling Workmen upon all occasions'. He also worries about what the neighbours think. Arriving home from work, Pepys discovers the front door has been left open by Luce the cookmaid:

traffic outside. The white and gold to which Eliot refers comes not only from the decoration, but from the daylight which streams through the windows.

Samuel Pepys wrote most of his diary at his house in Seething Lane, practically next door to the Navy Office where he worked.

It is often forgotten that he was a young man when he wrote his diary: not yet 27 when he started it on New Year's Day 1660, and only 32 when he made his last entry on 31 May 1669. Written secretly and in code, Pepys's diary is the best account we have of what it was like to live in London in the seventeenth century – at a time of plague, fire and political upheaval. Pepys had been in the crowd when Charles I was beheaded in 1649, and the early part of the diary is dominated by the restoration of the monarchy

which so vexed me, that I did give her a kick in our entry and offered a blow at her, and was seen so doing by Sir W Penn's footboy, which did vex me to the heart because I know he will be telling their family of it, though I did put on presently a very pleasant face to the boy and spoke kindly to him as one without passion, so as it may be he might not think I was angry.

Even Pepys's decision to buy a periwig has a modern ring to it. After noticing one day that 'the King is mighty grey' and hearing a rumour that he intends to wear a periwig, Pepys rushes out and buys one himself. He is, however, self-conscious about wearing his new wig to church, and is quietly relieved when nobody laughs.

Like many unfaithful husbands (and his appetite for casual philandering was gargantuan, even by the standards of the day), Pepys was not immune to sexual jealousy. His behaviour in Seething Lane on 26 May 1663 has a peculiarly timeless quality. Suspicious of the dancing teacher, Mr Pembleton, who is giving his wife lessons while he is at work, Pepys cannot concentrate at the office and goes home early. Finding Mr Pembleton and his wife alone in the house, Pepys avoids making a scene, but stomps upstairs to his study, quietly slipping on to the landing to check the beds for signs of recent use. No such evidence is to be found, but Pepys spends the rest of the night in a sulk. Finally, at three o'clock in the morning

he 'accidentally' wakes his wife (by peeing noisily into his chamber pot) to have the matter out. By breakfast, the matter is happily resolved with Pepys now satisfied that there has been 'no evil intent'.

Pepys's own sexual exploits continued unabated, usually at a safe distance from home, in

fleshpots such as Lambeth Marsh. But his luck finally ran out one Sunday morning in October 1668, when his wife, Elizabeth, caught him *in flagrante delicto* with one of her maids, Deb Willet. Pepys's account of the scenes that followed – his wife's tearful rage, his guilt and remorse, and his increasingly desperate attempts to catch a glimpse of

The Tower of London, built in the eleventh century, is anachronistically referred to in Mark Twain's A Connecticut Yankee in King Arthur's Court (1889), which is set in sixth-century Arthurian England.

Unwilling guests at the Tower of London include Sir Walter Ralegh. (left) and Pepys.

Smithfield Market, as seen from Little Britain where the lawyer Jaggers has his offices in Great Expectations.

From the roof of his house at Seething Lane, Pepys watched the celebrations on the night Charles II was restored to the throne. 'The City had a light like a glory round about it, with bonfires,' he wrote. Seething Lane was only a few minutes' walk from the Tower of London, where at the height of the Great Fire of London he watched 'the practice of blowing up of houses in Tower Street, those next the Tower, which at first did frighten people more than anything; but it stop[ped] the fire where it was done'. This wasn't the last unsettling experience Pepys would have at the Tower. Some months later, in December 1666, he was on his way home from Whitehall when he came across a crowd of some 400 militant seamen on Tower Hill. The sailors were angry that they hadn't been paid, and when their ringleader stood up on a pile of bricks and began to make a fiery speech, Pepys – a senior official in the Navy Office – grew alarmed and hurried home, half expecting his house to be attacked. Then, in 1679, Pepys found himself a prisoner in the Tower, after he was accused of selling naval secrets to the French.

Deb after she has been dismissed – is related with unflinching honesty and novelistic intensity.

Pepys ended his diary the following May: he was suffering from painful eye-strain and feared, wrongly as it turned out, that he was going blind. Six months later Elizabeth died at the age of 29, from a fever contracted on a tour of the Low Countries. Grief stricken (and no doubt guilt stricken too), Pepys arranged for a marble monument to his wife to be placed in the church they had attended together (St Olave's in Seething Lane), on the north wall of the Sanctuary where Pepys could see it from his pew.

It can have been of little comfort to Pepys that he was in good literary company. Almost within living memory, Sir Walter Ralegh had had the dubious distinction of being imprisoned in the Tower by two consecutive monarchs – first by Elizabeth I, when he had the temerity to marry one of her ladies-in-waiting without troubling to seek royal permission first, then under James I, under trumped-up charges of treason. After many years in prison, Ralegh was finally beheaded in 1618. Earlier, Thomas More, the courtier and author of *Utopia*, had been incarcerated and subsequently beheaded at the Tower for refusing to sanction Henry VIII's divorce from Catherine of Aragon, and More's contemporary, the poet Thomas Wyatt, was imprisoned there twice – first for having an affair with Anne Boleyn, then for being an ally of Thomas Cromwell.

Pepys himself fared rather better. The charges against him were quickly dropped and he was released from the Tower after just six weeks. He almost immediately moved away from the area, first to Buckingham Street, off the Strand, and finally to Clapham. On his death in 1703 Pepys's body was brought back to Seething Lane. He is buried, close to his wife, at St Olave's.

SMITHFIELD

In the Middle Ages, Smithfield (then 'Smoothfield') was a grassy area just outside the City walls, used as a horse market. Later it was used for jousting, and then as an execution ground where witches, heretics and common criminals were burnt or boiled alive in front of huge, unruly crowds. The executions eventually moved to Tyburn, in west London, but Smithfield's violent reputation continued, mainly because of the famously rowdy Bartholomew Fair, which was held every August on Bartholomew's Day. Ben Jonson's most vivid 'London' play, *Bartholomew Fair* (1614), gives a fair idea of the robbery and trickery that went on there. Justice Adam Overdo and the puritan Zeal-of-the-Land Busy, go to the fair in order to be

shocked at the iniquities and are eventually put in the stocks. In 1668 Samuel Pepys went to the fair, with his wife and her servant Deb Willet, and saw 'the dancing of the ropes and nothing else, it being late'. A few days later Pepys attended a puppet version of Jonson's play and 'loved the wit of it', though he also complained that Jonson's sending up of the Puritans 'begins to grow stale, and of no use, they being the people that at last will be found the wisest'. A century and a half later, Wordsworth visited the fair accompanied by his sister Dorothy and his London friend Charles Lamb. Wandering among the fairground booths, performing animals, contortionists and freak shows, Wordsworth describes the experience in *The Prelude* (Book 7) as

> a hell
> For eyes and ears!
> what
> anarchy and din
> Barbarian and
> infernal! 'tis
> a dream,
> Monstrous in colour,
> motion,
> shape, sight, sound.

Warming to his theme, the

their cattle to the daily market frequently arrived drunk and deliberately stampeded their animals through the narrow City streets before handing them over for slaughter in the market. Drainage and sanitation were practically non-existent and the surrounding streets literally ran with blood. Dickens described the scene in *Oliver Twist* (1837): 'The ground was covered, nearly ankle deep, with filth and mire; a thick stream perpetually arising from the reeking bodies of the cattle.' In *Great Expectations* (1861) Pip crosses through the market on his way to the lawyer Jaggers's offices in nearby Little Britain, and finds it a 'shameful place, being all asmear with filth and fat and blood and foam'. In the 1860s the market was cleaned up and put under cover, where it continues today, the sole survivor of the great City markets. In *Imperial Palace* (1930), Arnold Bennett described the tamed and sanitized market with its four predominant colours: 'bright blue of the painted constructional ironwork, all columns and arches; red-pink ivories of meat; white of the salesmen's long coats; and yellow of electricity'.

Smithfield's other great institution is St Bartholomew's Hospital, founded in 1123 and the oldest hospital in the capital. The poet Robert Bridges came here to study medicine in 1869, and after qualifying he continued to practise in the hospital for some years. He was later appointed Poet Laureate. St Bartholomew's is well known to Sherlock Holmes aficionados as the scene of the first meeting between Holmes and Dr Watson. In *A Study in Scarlet* (1887), the pair meet in the hospital's chemical laboratory, where – fittingly, given the area's history –

St Bartholomew's Hospital, the oldest in the city, was originally part of an Augustinian priory. Over the main gate stands a statue of Henry VIII, who destroyed the priory during the dissolution of the monasteries, but later reopened the hospital. The hospital is where Arthur Conan Doyle chose to set the scene of the first meeting between Sherlock Holmes and Dr Watson.

country-dwelling Wordsworth sees the anarchy and confusion of the Fair as a microcosmic version

Of what the mighty City is
*   itself*
To all except a straggler here
*   and there,*
To the whole swarm of its
*   inhabitants.*

The City authorities seem to have taken the same view as Wordsworth, seeing the fair as an annual threat to public order. It was closed down in 1855.

Smithfield's reputation for rowdiness and disorder was not, however, confined to the annual fair. The farmers who brought

Holmes has just discovered 'an infallible test for blood stains'. Located in the grounds of the hospital, but accessible to all, the cool, quiet church of St Bartholomew the Less has a plaque depicting the fifteenth-century scribe John Shirley and his wife dressed as pilgrims.

Another future Poet Laureate, John Betjeman, moved into 43 Cloth Fair in 1955 and lived there for over 20 years, though he was eventually driven out by the incessant stream of articulated lorries coming in and out of the market. The journalist and reviewer Graham Lord met him there several times over the years:

The first time, in 1966, he was 60 and I was 23 and extremely nervous – he was the first author I ever interviewed – but he made me feel instantly as if we were friends. He sprawled chubbily on the bed at his cosy London flat in the medieval street of Cloth Fair, near Smithfield Market, legs crossed, waving a nonchalant glass of vodka, and his constant laughter was irresistible: he would throw back his head, open his mouth wide and bleat like some demented sheep. It was simply impossible to be overawed by a man who still talked to his childhood teddy-bear, Archibald Ormsby-Gore ('he's my gloomy, Calvinistic, leisure-hating conscience'), as it squatted horribly bald and blind on a shelf in the corner. Who called me 'dear boy' and begged me to smoke ('I'm longing for you to smoke, please blow it in my direction') even though he had once again just given up. Indeed, when he was laughing

he looked so vulnerable – with his spaniel eyes so defensive and easily hurt – that I felt I should be protecting him. After lunch, on the way to show me the Hogarth staircase at his favourite hospital, Bart's, he froze bewildered in the path of a car – he hated them all – and flapped his arms helplessly at the driver.

Hosier Lane, on the south side of Smithfield Square was described by the seventeenth-century historian John Strype as 'of great resort during the time of St Bartholomew's Fair, all the houses generally being made public for tippling and lewd sort of people'. This may explain why Samuel Pepys chose 'a little blind alehouse within the walls' in Hosier Lane for a surreptitious meeting with Deb Willet, after his wife had discovered their affair. Pepys found Deb to be 'mighty coy' on this occasion, though he did prevail upon her to 'tocar mi thing' in the semi-darkness.

Little Britain, the narrow street which zig-zags between West Smithfield and Aldersgate Street, was once famous for its booksellers. John Milton lived here briefly in 1662, and in 1712 the three-year-old Samuel Johnson lodged in the street with his mother. The pair had travelled to London so that Samuel could be touched by Queen Anne and cured of the scrofula which disfigured his face. He was indeed touched by the Queen and retained a dim memory of 'a lady in diamonds, and a long black hood'. In 'An Account of the Life of Samuel Johnson, from his Birth to his

Horace Walpole was among the hundreds of people who came to witness the ghostly goings-on at 33 Cock Lane.

Hogarth's print 'The Distrest Poet' shows the contrast between the exalted but vain and foolish aspirations of a Grub Street poet, and the dreariness and distress which these aspirations create.

Eleventh Year; Written by Himself", Johnson recalled that during the visit, his mother bought him a small silver cup and spoon. 'The cup,' he added, 'was one of the last pieces of plate which dear Tetty sold, in our distress. I have now the spoon.'

In 1762, Johnson became involved in the strange affair of the Cock Lane Ghost. An 11-year-old girl who lived at 33 Cock Lane (parallel to Hosier Lane) claimed to have heard ghostly knocking and scratching as she lay in bed at night, and as word spread, crowds gathered in the street hoping to experience the phenomenon. The rector of the nearby church of St John's took the girl into his care and invited a group of eminent men, including Johnson, to investigate the haunting. In his 'Account of the Detection of the Imposture in Cock Lane', published in the *Gentleman's Magazine*, Johnson concluded the affair had been a hoax, perpetrated by the girl and her father, a clerk at the church of St Sepulchre.

MOORGATE

This area on the City's northern boundary takes its name from the postern gate which once led out to the moor on the other side of the London Wall. The gate was removed in 1762, and the moor which once lay on the other side is now dominated by the airport-like Barbican

Centre, opened in 1982, which contains several theatres, cinemas and a concert hall. In Nicholas Royle's 1995 short story 'London Wall' the narrator complains that 'it would be nice to see a section of the original wall just standing there without any support from Britain's heritage industry, with its cancer of brown signs'.

In the late eighteenth century Moorgate was a busy place, with constant traffic coming into the City from the growing suburbs of north-east London, such as Bethnal Green, Hackney and Walthamstow. John Keats's father, Thomas, ran a successful local inn. The Swan and Hoop, at 24 The Pavement (now an unremarkable pub, The John Keats, at 85 Moorgate) had a spectacular 117-foot-long façade, two coach-houses and stabling for 50 horses. John Keats lived there with his family until he was sent to boarding school in Enfield. Months later, when Keats was eight, his father was thrown from his horse and killed, just outside the gates of Bunhill Fields, in City Road. Thomas died without making a will, and when Keats's mother Frances remarried a year later her new husband took over the inn. When the marriage broke down, Keats's mother no longer

The Barbican formed part of the City wall, where John Milton had a house from 1645–49.

had any control over the family business, consigning Keats and his siblings to a lifetime of financial insecurity.

Bunhill Row was the last home of John Milton, who lived there from 1662 and completed *Paradise Lost* there the following year. He and his third wife moved briefly to Chalfont St Giles to escape the plague of 1665, but he returned to Bunhill Row to oversee the publication of *Paradise Lost* (it made him just £10) and write its sequel *Paradise Regained*. Nearby Milton Street is named not after him but a local landlord of the same name. Under its former name, Grub Street, it was synonymous with the overworked, penurious hack writers who lived there in the eighteenth century. The term was revived by George Gissing in his 1891 novel *New Grub Street*, set mainly in Fitzrovia and Marylebone and still sobering reading for anyone contemplating a career as a freelance writer.

Daniel Defoe died at his lodgings in Ropemaker Street in 1731, at the age of 71, and was buried at Bunhill Fields, the traditional burial ground for nonconformists, who could be buried here without recourse to the *Book of Common Prayer*. In 1870 Defoe's simple grave was augmented by a marble obelisk, after a newspaper appeal to children who had enjoyed *Robinson Crusoe*. Also buried here is John Bunyan, whose tomb depicts a pilgrim labouring under a burden, with the recumbent figure of the author on the top. William Blake is buried nearby, close to his wife Catherine. Movingly, flowers are still being left on his grave.

The cemetery at Bunhill Fields contains the graves of Bunyan (above), Defoe (left) and Blake and his wife. The churchyard was opened in 1665, initially for victims of the plague.

CHAPTER 2

NORTH LONDON

◆

REGENT'S PARK AND PRIMROSE HILL

One of the scattered areas of greenery that once formed the ancient Forest of Middlesex, Regent's Park was formally laid out by the architect John Nash and named after his patron, the Prince Regent. Nash's imaginative plans included the glittering white terraces that line the Outer Circle, which forms the circumference to the park, and the much smaller Inner Circle, a stucco wheel within a wheel, near the long, tapering boating lake. The Open Air Theatre in Queen Mary's Gardens was opened in 1900 and specializes in performances of Shakespeare's 'outdoor' comedies, such as *As You Like It* and *A Midsummer Night's Dream*.

The Zoological Gardens opened in 1828, on the north side of the park. In 1831, the 19-year-old Edward Lear was appointed official draughtsman to the Zoological Society (he took lodgings not far from the park, at 30 Seymour Street). One of Lear's first commissions was to draw the zoo's parrots for an ornithological guide, *Illustrations of the Family of the Psittacidae*. The illustrations came to the attention of the Earl of Derby, who asked him to paint his own private menagerie at Knowsley Hall, near Liverpool. Lear wrote *A Book of Nonsense* for the Earl's grandchildren while he was working at Knowsley Hall. Writing in *Punch* in 1846, with his tongue firmly in his cheek, William Makepeace Thackeray described a visit to London Zoo:

Fancy my feelings, Sir, when I saw in these gardens – in these gardens frequented by nursery-maids, mothers, and children – an immense brute of an elephant, about a hundred feet high, rushing about with a wretched little child on his back, and a single man vainly endeavouring to keep him back! I uttered a shriek;

Regent's Park was once deer-hunting ground for Henry VIII.

An illustration from A Book Of Nonsense *(above) by Edward Lear who worked at the Zoological Gardens (below).*

I called my dear children about me. And I am not ashamed to confess it, Sir, I ran. I ran for refuge into a building hard by, where I saw – ah, Sir, an immense boa constrictor swallowing a live rabbit – swallowing a live rabbit, Sir, and looking as if he would have swallowed one of my little boys afterwards. Good heavens! Sir, do we live in a Christian country, and are parents and children to be subjected to sights like these?

Louis MacNeice was living in Primrose Hill in 1938, when he wrote his long poem *Autumn Journal.* In it he writes of

...a rustle
Of leaves in Regent's Park
And suddenly from the Zoo I
* hear a sea-lion*
Confidently bark.

Ted Hughes and Sylvia Plath were also kept awake by the animals when they moved to a second-floor flat at 3 Chalcot Square in 1960. Hughes speaks of wolves consoling them in his poem 'Life after Death' from *Birthday Letters* (1998).

After the couple separated, Plath moved, with her two small children, into the two top rooms at 23 Fitzroy Road, just around the corner from Chalcot Square. The address attracted her because WB Yeats had lived in the house as a child. Plath spent the freezing winter of 1962–3 there, writing some of the poems which would appear in her final collection, *Ariel.* In January 1963 her only

novel, *The Bell Jar*, was published. A month later, Plath gassed herself in the kitchen as her children slept in the next room.

Plath's last poem 'Edge', written a week before her death, begins ominously:

The woman is perfected.
Her dead

Body wears the smile of
* accomplishment,*
The illusion of a Greek
* necessity*

Flows in the scrolls of her toga,
Her bare

Feet seem to be saying:
We have come so far, it is over.

Plath's final journal, which she kept until three days before her death, was destroyed by Hughes; another, from late 1959 to 1961, was left unaccounted for after Hughes's death in 1998.

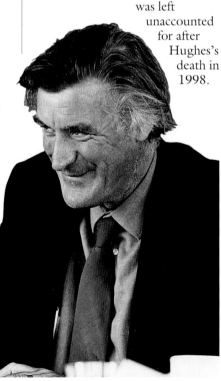

T̲ed Hughes (1930–98) was made Poet Laureate in 1984 and ended his career with two of his finest works: Birthday Letters, *a poetic memoir to Sylvia Plath, and* Tales from Ovid.

A new edition of her surviving journals, covering the period 1950–59 and part of 1962 was published in April 2000. The following July, English Heritage attached a plaque to her earlier home in Chalcot Square, in a low-key ceremony attended by the couple's daughter Frieda (now a published poet herself) and son Nicholas Hughes.

In 1962 the novelist Angus Wilson, who had a peculiar fascination for zoos, moved to a second-floor (later a top-floor) flat at 2 Regent's Park Terrace. A regular guest was the eccentric (and occasionally deranged) Dutch poet Gerard Kornelis van het Reve, whose party trick of collecting his farts in a jar and igniting them eventually found its way into Wilson's novel *As If by Magic*.

The flat was a few minutes' walk from London Zoo, where Wilson had set his 1961 novel *The Old Men at the Zoo*. Set just before the outbreak of the Third World War, the story is told by the zoo's secretary, Simon Carter, who is charged with the evacuation of the zoo animals to the countryside. This had indeed happened in 1939 (though the more dangerous animals, including the snakes, had been slaughtered and used for meat), but Wilson derived much of the detail from the temporary removal of British Museum exhibits, in which he had been closely involved (see Bloomsbury).

Three or four of the most memorable scenes in fiction take place in or near Regent's Park. In George Gissing's *New Grub Street* (1891), the struggling novelist Edwin Reardon is first seen in his top-floor flat on the edge of Regent's Park. Reardon has a fine view:

The green ridge from Hampstead to Highgate, with Primrose Hill and the foliage of Regent's Park in the foreground; the suburban spaces of St John's Wood, Maida Vale, Kilburn; Westminster Abbey and the Houses of Parliament, lying low by the side of the hidden river, and a glassy

George Eliot's home, the Priory, near Regent's Park. (The site has since been demolished). After moving in to her new home, she discovered that the removal men had stolen her purse.

gleam on far-off hills which meant the Crystal Palace; then the clouded majesty of eastern London, crowned by St Paul's dome.

Yet Reardon's home is the very antithesis of an ivory tower. Instead, he is driven to the verge of madness by poverty and his inability to write anything that is artistically worthy or financially viable. On this occasion, near the beginning of the novel, he goes for a solitary walk 'in the darkness round the Outer Circle of Regent's Park, racking his fagged brain in a hopeless search of characters, situations, motives'.

*The night is damp and still
And I hear dull blows on
    wood outside my window;
They are cutting down the
    trees on Primrose Hill.
The wood is white like the
    roast flesh of chicken,
Each tree falling like a closing
    fan;
No more looking at the view
    from seats beneath the
    branches,
Everything is going to plan;
They want the crest of this hill
    for anti-aircraft,
The guns will take the view
And searchlights probe the
    heavens for bacilli
With narrow wands of blue.*

The Gloucester Gate, in the Outer Circle of Regent's Park where the ambitious, cynical journalist Jasper Milvain meets his fiancée Marian Yule in order to break off their engagement once he discovers she no longer has a dowry in George Gissing's New Grub Street.

In Patrick Hamilton's *Twenty Thousand Streets under the Sky* (1935), the barmaid Ella reluctantly agrees to take a night-time stroll in the park with her appalling suitor Mr Eccles, who single-mindedly propels her to a remote spot under some trees for an unwelcome kissing session. William Masen, the narrator of John Wyndham's occasionally ludicrous *The Day of the Triffids*, drives to Regent's Park one day and finds 'groups of triffids lurching southwards. Somehow or other they had contrived to pull up their stakes and were dragging them along behind them on their chains.'

Primrose Hill overlooks Regent's Park on the other side of Prince Albert Road. Until the reign of Elizabeth I, it was thickly forested and a popular place for hunting boars and stags. An oak tree at the foot of the hill was planted in 1964 to comemorate the 400th anniversary of Shakespeare's birth.

In *Autumn Journal*, Louis MacNeice records evenings at his home in Primrose Hill, as London prepares for war:

Aldous Huxley's wartime novel *Time Must Have a Stop* (1944) describes the same anti-aircraft battery in action: in one scene, a man meditates in his flat during an air raid, while 'the guns on Primrose Hill were banging away in a kind of frenzy'. After the war the guns were removed (though traces remain) and the benches returned. In Dodie Smith's much loved children's novel *The Hundred and One Dalmations* (1956) Pongo and his wife Missis stand on the summit of the hill and bark out a message across London asking for help in tracing their missing puppies.

Primrose Hill's main thoroughfare, Regent's Park Road, was home, in their final years, to both Friedrich Engels (Number 121) and Kingsley Amis (Number 194), though a hundred years separates their tenure. Engels spent his years here translating the second and third volumes of *Das Kapital* after Marx's death. For Amis they were years of drinking and writing. His local was the Queens on Regent's Park Road. His 1990 novel *The Folks That Live On the Hill* is set in the area.

SOMERS TOWN

Overshadowed by three massive railway termini, Euston, St Pancras and King's Cross, Somers Town forms a harsh contrast to the leafy acres of Regent's Park and Primrose Hill. Its acres of slum housing, originally intended for railway employees, were among the worst in London until they were finally cleared away shortly before the Second World War. In Gerald Kersh's *Night and the City* (1938), Adam, the Soho clip-joint waiter who wants to be a sculptor, walks through Somers Town on his way to Harry Fabian's wrestling gym:

> He walked fast, through Euston Road and past King's Cross; faster and faster, and deeper and deeper into the sombre, rumbling gut of north-west London – nightmare-land of blank, black walls eroded by the acrid breath of the railways.

The area remains a grimly picturesque north London back-water, criss-crossed by railway lines and canals and dotted with stark, desolate disused gas-works – a landscape evoked in John Healy's *The Grass Arena* (1988) and more dreamily in Aidan Andrew Dun's long poem *Vale Royal* (1995).

In *Lights Out for the Territory* (1997), Iain Sinclair's extended essay 'X Marks the Spot' is a paean to the area's little-known literary heritage, particularly around St Pancras Church in Pancras Road – 'an island shaded in torpor, heavy with melancholy, the drowned dead'. Percy Bysshe Shelley was living nearby (in a house long since obliterated by the Midland Railway) when he saw and fell in love with Mary Godwin in the churchyard, where she was visiting the grave of her mother, Mary Wollstonecraft. As an architectural student in the 1860s, Thomas Hardy was responsible for removing graves from the churchyard to accommodate the railway. He found the work traumatic, as his poem 'The Levelled Churchyard' recalls:

> O Passenger, pray list and catch
> Our sighs and piteous groans,
> Half-stifled in this jumbled patch
> Of wrenched memorial stones!

Mary Shelley (1797–1851). Her most famous work, Frankenstein, or the Modern Prometheus, *was conceived during a holiday in Switzerland in 1816.*

The gasworks and desolate landscape of Somers Town evoked in John Healey's The Grass Arena *and Aidan Andrew Dun's* Vale Royal.

*We late-lamented, resting here
Are mixed to human jam,
And each to each exclaims in fear,
'I know not which I am!'*

In *Lights Out for the Territory*, Iain Sinclair describes a summer evening walk in Somers Town, 'the sun on the horizon catching the skeletal gasholder crowns, the fantastic mustard hotel of St Pancras railway station, its windows and pinnacles and red brick balconies'.

Oscar Wilde booked two rooms at the hotel (the Midland Grand) in May 1895, immediately after losing his libel action against Lord Queensberry. With a criminal trial now imminent, the exhausted Wilde was hoping to stay anonymously at the hotel for a few days, but as he was sitting down to dinner the manager approached and ordered him to leave: a group of thugs had been dispatched by Queensberry to follow him to the hotel and threaten to attack the building unless Wilde was thrown out. The humiliation was repeated at another London hotel, and Wilde eventually sought sanctuary at his brother's house in Chelsea where, as Willie Wilde later remembered, he 'fell down on my threshold like a wounded stag'.

The Midland Grand closed in the 1930s but was spared from demolition through the efforts of, among others, John Betjeman. Appropriately, Betjeman's last public appearance, in June 1983, was at St Pancras Station itself, to name a locomotive after himself.

In JK Rowling's *Harry Potter and the Philosopher's Stone* (1997), Harry departs for his first term at Hogwarts School of Witchcraft and Wizardry from 'platform nine and three quarters' at King's Cross Station.

The British Library in Euston Road is probably the most controversial building to have appeared in London for the last 25 years. Mooted in 1962, the building finally opened in 1998, at a cost of £520 million – more than four times its original budget. In the meantime, the design was likened by Prince Charles to 'an assembly hall for an academy of secret police', and the library's public image was not improved when a slide display beamed a three-foot slogan, 'The British Library. For the nation's written heretage [sic]' against the building for an entire weekend in 1998. The library's collection is, however, impressive: some 17 million books, newspapers and periodicals and 300,000 manuscripts, housed on 267 miles

of shelving, and visited by almost half a million people every year.

CAMDEN TOWN

Originally a country village, Camden Town began to expand in the early nineteenth century with the construction of the Regent's Canal. When he was ten, Charles Dickens moved with his parents to a terraced house at 16 Bayham Street. Camden Town was then in a state of limbo: still surrounded by fields and market gardens, but within sight of the dome of St Paul's. In Dickens's lifetime, Camden Town would be fully absorbed into the City. In *David Copperfield*, David's bedroom at Mr Micawber's house in Windsor Terrace – a 'close chamber... very scantily furnished' – was based on Dickens's bedroom in Bayham Street, in a tiny garret at the back of the house. The family moved to Gower Street in 1824, shortly before John Dickens was arrested for debt and Charles was put to work at the blacking factory. The house in Bayham Street has not survived, though the site is marked by a plaque at number 141.

When Dickens ended his marriage in the late 1850s, his wife Catherine was summarily removed to a house at 70 Gloucester Crescent, only a few streets away from Dickens's childhood home. Catherine lived an increasingly lonely life, effectively banished from her family: only her eldest son, Charley, elected to live with her rather than his father. When her eldest daughter Katie married Wilkie Collins's younger brother

Charles in the summer of 1860, the wedding took place near Dickens's home, Gad's Hill Place, near Chatham.

Catherine spent the day alone at Gloucester Crescent. At one time, Katie and her sisters were having music lessons in a house opposite their mother's in Gloucester Crescent, but never dared to visit her because they knew it would annoy their father. Late in life, Katie told an interviewer: 'We were all *very* wicked not to take her part; Harry [a brother] does not take this view, but he was only a boy at the time, and does not realize the grief it was to our mother, after

Catherine Dickens (left), whose house (above) in Gloucester Crescent is concealed from the public gaze – much as she was in her lifetime.

The attic in 16 Bayham Street. Dickens remembered his childhood home as 'a mean, small tenement, with a wretched little back-garden abutting on a squalid court'.

The 'mole hunt' in John Le Carré's Tinker Tailor Soldier Spy *ends by the Regent's Canal in Camden Town.*

having all her children, to go away and leave us. My mother never rebuked me. I never saw her in a temper. We like to think of our geniuses as great characters – but we can't.'

Much of George Gissing's novel *New Grub Street* (1891) concerns the travails of men who marry above, or beneath, themselves – a problem of which Gissing had considerable personal experience (see Marylebone). The bitter, unsuccessful literary critic Alfred Yule is a member of 'the well-defined category of men with unpresentable wives'. He and his family live in St Paul's Crescent, which Gissing describes as 'a poor house in an obscure quarter'. More than a century later, the description is still entirely accurate.

In a memorable scene towards the end of the novel, Yule leaves the house early one freezing morning, after a furious argument with his wife and daughter, and goes for a walk in an attempt to

assuage 'the nightmare of his rage and hopelessness'.

When he reached Camden Town railway station he was attracted by a coffee stall; a draught of the steaming liquid, no matter its quality, would help his blood to circulate. He laid down his penny, and first warmed his hands by holding them round the cup. Whilst standing thus he noticed that the objects at which he looked had a blurred appearance; his eyesight seemed to have become worse this morning. Only a result of his insufficient sleep perhaps. He took up a scrap of newspaper that lay on the stall; he could read it, but one of his eyes was certainly weaker than the other; trying to see with that one alone, he found that everything became misty.

Yule buys a cup of coffee for a shabbily dressed man standing nearby, who turns out to be a former surgeon, and accompanies the man to his lodging, 'the poorest possible kind of bed-chamber', where he has his eyes

tested. He is going blind and must soon become 'a useless old man, a burden and annoyance to whosoever had pity on him'. With nothing else to do, he returns meekly to St Paul's Crescent to make up with his family.

Dylan Thomas's last London home was the basement flat at 54 Delancey Street, where he and his wife Caitlin moved during the winter of 1951. The house belonged to a friend, Margaret Taylor. She was then married to the historian AJP Taylor, who loathed Thomas and resented his wife's pandering to him. Despite Alan Taylor's hostility, the Thomases had frequently stayed at the Taylors' home in South Leigh, near Oxford, where Margaret acquired a gypsy caravan for Dylan to work in peace. (This wasn't always achieved: on one occasion the fiery Caitlin tipped the caravan over with Dylan inside.) For old time's sake, Margaret had the caravan towed to Delancey Street, where it was parked in the garden.

John Betjeman's poem 'Business Girls' manages to convey the essence of Camden Town with a few well-chosen words:

From the geyser ventilators
Autumn winds are blowing
* down*
On a thousand business
* women*
Having baths in Camden
Town.

Waste pipes chuckle into
* runnels,*
Steam's escaping here and
* there,*
Morning trains through
* Camden cutting*
Shake the Crescent and the
* Square.*

John Le Carré's espionage novel, *Tinker Tailor Soldier Spy* (1974) has its climax in a house in a very ordinary Camden residential street. 'Lock Gardens' does not appear in the *A-Z*, but is typical of its kind: 'a terrace of four flat-fronted nineteenth-century houses built at the centre of a crescent, each with three floors and a basement and a strip of walled back garden running down to the Regent's Canal'. George Smiley lures the MI6 'mole' to the house and sits waiting for him in the kitchen, while his colleague, Guillam, waits on the canal towpath behind the house, his nerves so taut that 'for a moment he saw the whole architecture of that night in apocalyptic terms: the signals of the railway bridge turned to gallows, the Victorian warehouses to gigantic prisons, their windows barred and arched against the misty sky'. The trap set, Guillam races along the towpath and climbs a steel stairway which zig-zags up to Gloucester Avenue, to rendezvous with another watcher on the corner of Princess Road.

The playwright Alan Bennett has lived in Camden Town since the early 1960s. His long essay (later a play) *The Lady in the Van* is about Miss Shepherd, an elderly, eccentric woman who lived in a succession of vans near Bennett's house in Gloucester Crescent. To Bennett and his neighbours she became a familiar sight, 'moving slowly around her

'A quiet byway, called St Paul's Crescent, consisting of small, decent houses.' George Gissing: New Grub Street, *1891.*

immobile home, thoughtfully touching up the rust from a tiny tin of primrose paint, looking, in her long dress and sunhat, much as Vanessa Bell would have looked had she gone in for painting Bedford vans'. Alarmed by the systematic acts of bullying and vandalism she was receiving from passers-by, Bennett eventually gave Miss Shepherd, and her van, sanctuary in his front garden:

Callers at the house had to squeeze past the back of the van and come down the side, and while they waited for my door to be opened they would be scrutinized from behind the murky windscreen by Miss Shepherd. If they were unlucky, they would find the rear door open with Miss S dangling her large white legs over the back. The interior of the van, a midden of old clothes, plastic bags and half-eaten food, was not easy to ignore, but should anyone Miss S did not know venture to speak to her she would promptly tuck her legs back and wordlessly shut the door. For the first few years of her sojourn in the garden I would try and explain to mystified callers how this situation had arisen, but after a while I ceased to care, and when I didn't mention it nor did anyone else.

The arrangement continued for 15 years, until her death.

*A*lan Bennett's story The Clothes They Stood Up In *is set in and around the nearby area of St John's Wood, with the protagonists, the Ransomes, living in 'an Edwardian block of flats the colour of ox-blood not far from Regent's Park'.*

HAMPSTEAD

*F*ew areas of London are fashionable for very long. Although most enjoy their turn at a place in the sun, London fashions are fickle, and an area that is all the rage at one point is unlikely still to be so 50 years later.

Hampstead is the exception. With its countrified air, huge tracts of untamed heath and position close to, but above and beyond, the metropolis, it has long been a beacon for writers who wish to enjoy the stimulation and raw material that London brings, together with the peace and seclusion they need to work and rest. (A rare sceptic was William Blake, who insisted that Hampstead air gave him 'a cold in my stomach' and complained that the long carriage journey gave him diarrhoea.) EM Forster called Hampstead 'the intellectual suburb', a distinction which it retained until as recently as the 1990s, when it began to be eclipsed by Islington.

One of the first groups to find Hampstead conducive to conviviality and debate was the Kit-Kat Club, a group of influential early eighteenth century Whigs which included the writers John Vanbrugh, Joseph Addison and Richard Steele. The club used to meet at the Flask Inn in Heath Street; Samuel Richardson's massive letter-novel *Clarissa*, published in 1748, includes scenes there.

Addison and Steele were close friends and colleagues: they had met at Charterhouse school and as adults co-edited the *Spectator*. Addison would take a coach from London and alight at a coaching inn which stood on the site of the Load of Hay pub at 94 Haverstock Hill. Steele lived opposite the inn, in a secluded cottage hidden behind a high bank (a useful location, as he was having trouble with creditors at the time). The present-day pub has a stained-glass window depicting Steele, who is also commemorated in nearby Steele's Road, Steele's Street and the Sir Richard Steele pub (97 Haverstock Hill).

One of the most influential literary figures ever to live in Hampstead was the editor and literary gadfly Leigh Hunt, who, with his brother John, founded and edited the *Examiner*. The *Examiner* was not only a forum for the new school of Romantic poetry , but it was also fiercely radical, fearlessly attacking targets such as the civil list, the Duke of York's mistress and, in March 1812, the august body of the Prince Regent, whom Leigh Hunt comprehensively described as 'a corpulent gentleman of fifty... a violator of his word, a libertine over head and ears in debt, a despiser

of domestic ties, the companion of gamblers and demi-reps, a man who has just closed half a century without one single claim on the gratitude of his country or the respect of posterity'.

This was a rash attack, even by the standards of the hot-blooded Hunt. But it was also a hypocritical one, for Hunt was himself seldom out of debt (and sponged shamelessly off his friends, including Byron) and a notorious womanizer (of his sister-in-law he once admitted that he liked to close his eyes and 'tickle the edge of her stockings, that my feelings may be kept tingling by imagining the rest'). The punishment for his comments was as harsh as it was predictable. Both Hunt brothers were sentenced to two years in jail and fined £1,000 each.

In the end, it was Leigh Hunt who had the last laugh. Setting himself up as a radical martyr, he continued to edit the *Examiner* from his prison cell in Horsemonger Lane, trebling its circulation almost overnight. It was on his release from jail

The Vale of Health overlooks the pond where Shelley once sailed paper boats.

151

John Keats (1795–1821), whose medical training at Guy's Hospital enabled him to nurse his brother Tom when he contracted tuberculosis.

that he moved to Hampstead, taking a house in the Vale of Health, in the south-western corner of the Heath, where he lived in a state of permanent chaos (physical and financial) with his wife, sister-in-law and – as more than one Romantic poet would complain – famously badly behaved children. One of them, Thornton, would recall Leigh Hunt as 'brilliant, reflecting, gay and kind, with a certain look of observant humour that suggested an idea of what is called shyness when it is applied to children or to a girl'.

Among the writers who came to visit the Hunts at their house, Vale Lodge, in the early part of the ninteenth century, were Shelley (who liked to sail paper boats on the pond near the house), Byron, Lamb, Hazlitt and Keats, whose first published poem 'O Solitude!' appeared in the *Examiner* in May 1816. Keats, like many of his contemporaries, was excited and flattered by Hunt's friendship (his cheerful sonnets 'On leaving some friends at an early hour' and 'Keen, fitful gusts are whispering here and there' were written while he was staying at Vale Lodge). Later, the friendship waned. Despite his charm, Hunt could behave like an interfering, gossipy old woman – a trait which Dickens later seized upon when he caricatured Hunt as the lazy, sponging dilettante Harold Skimpole in *Bleak House*.

Eventually Hunt's financial problems forced him to leave Hampstead and flee to the relative safety of Marlow. But the Vale of Health was destined to have other distinguished tenants. In 1915 DH

An early nineteenth-century illustration of Well Walk. Its residents have included John Masefield, DH Lawrence and JB Priestley.

Lawrence and his wife Frieda rented the ground-floor flat of 1 Byron Villas, where they made plans to form a commune which would include the writer and editor John Middleton Murry and his wife, the New Zealand born short-story writer Katherine Mansfield. The Murrys lived close by, at 17 East Heath Road, in a large house which they called the Elephant. (In a journal entry, Mansfield, who had left her first husband a few days after marrying him and, like her fellow Hampsteadites Lawrence and Orwell, was destined to die of tuberculosis, described number 17 as 'a tall, grave house with red geraniums and white daisies in the garden at the back'.) The commune scheme came to nothing, and meanwhile Lawrence's latest novel *The Rainbow* was declared obscene by

London magistrates. At this point, Lawrence announced he had had enough of England and was leaving for Florida. In the end he settled for Padstow in Cornwall.

John Keats obviously found Hampstead congenial. In April 1817 he and his younger brother Tom became lodgers at 1 Well Walk, sharing the house with the landlord, Mr Bentley, who was also the local postman, his wife and their lively ginger-haired children, whose 'horrid row' would later annoy Keats as he wrestled with his epic poem *Endymion*.

Keats's period at Well Walk was overshadowed by Tom's poor health. Within a few months of moving in, it became clear that Tom was seriously ill with 'consumption' (tuberculosis) and that he couldn't live much longer. Keats, who had trained as an apothecary, nursed his brother himself, knowing that by doing so he risked contracting the disease himself. When Tom died, aged 19, in December 1818, Keats had to move again – this time to a house called Wentworth Place, which stood on the edge of the heath. The house had been split in two, with one half occupied by the landlord and his family and the other by an old school friend of Keats, Charles Brown. Shortly after Keats moved in to share Charles's portion of the house, the landlords moved out and their place was taken by another family, the Brawnes, who had an 18-year-old daughter, Fanny.

The love affair between John Keats and Fanny Brawne is perhaps the most famous in English literature. Keats celebrated her beauty with an ardour that occasionally borders on the comic ('Her nostrils, small, fragrant, faery-delicate'), though he was under no illusions about her coquettishness. 'Ask yourself, my love, whether you are not very cruel to have so entrammelled me', he demands

in one of many passionate love letters. 'Will you confess this in the letter you must write immediately, and do all you can to console me in it – make it rich as a draught of poppies to intoxicate me – write the softest words and kiss them, that I may at least touch my lips where yours have been.'

Despite the pain she could cause him, this period of Keats's life was also one of immense happiness. Keats and his housemate Charles Brown got on well, playing cricket together on the heath (though on one occasion Keats received a black eye from being hit by the ball) and fighting duels with sticks of celery in the garden. And it was at this stage in

Keats's lodgings in Well Walk were next door to the Wells Tavern, then called the Green Man.

Keats faced his own death matter-of-factly. One February night he arrived home on a late coach from London, which had drawn up at the stop in Pond Street. As he climbed down from his usual position on the open roof, he began to feel feverish. When he arrived home, Brown immediately realized his friend was unwell, and told him to go straight to bed. When he followed him up a short while later to give him a glass of brandy, Keats was just getting into bed. As Brown recalled:

On entering the cold sheets, before his head was on the pillow, he slightly coughed, and I heard him say, 'That is blood from my mouth.' I went towards him; he was examining a single drop of blood upon the sheet. 'Bring me the candle, Brown, and let me see this blood.' After regarding it steadfastly, he looked up in my face, with a calmness of countenance that I can never forget, and said: 'I know the colour of that blood; – it is arterial blood; – I cannot be deceived in that colour; – that drop of blood is my death warrant; – I must die.'

Wentworth Place, where John Keats and Charles Brown fought celery duels in the garden.

his life that he wrote some of his finest poetry. As Brown later related, 'Ode to the Nightingale' was composed in the garden of Wentworth Place (now known as Keats House):

In the spring of 1819 a nightingale had built her nest near my house. Keats felt a tranquil and continued joy in her song; and one morning he took a chair from the breakfast table to the grass-plot under a plum tree, where he sat for two or three hours. When he came into the house, I perceived he had some scraps of paper in his hand, and these he was quietly thrusting behind the books. On enquiry, I found these scraps, four or five in number, contained his poetic feeling on the song of our nightingale.

Later that night, Keats suffered a massive lung haemorrhage – the first of several over the next few months. According to the medical wisdom of the time, the only hope for someone with advanced consumption was to live abroad, in a warm climate. Italy was suggested. This, of course, meant leaving Fanny behind.

On the morning of Wednesday 13 September 1820, Fanny walked with him to Pond Street and saw him on to the coach to London.

Leigh Hunt, who was carrying Keats's luggage, would recall that the couple could barely bring themselves to speak. When Keats died, in Rome, five months later, Fanny's last two letters to him were placed, according to his wishes, in his coffin, unopened. He couldn't bring himself to read them.

Some of the most vivid scenes in English fiction have been played out on and around Hampstead Heath. On the run after murdering Nancy, Bill Sikes makes an erratic journey here as *Oliver Twist* reaches its climax:

> *He went through Islington; strode up the hill at Highgate on which stands the stone in honour of Whittington; turned down to Highgate Hill, unsteady of purpose, and uncertain where to go; struck off to the right again, almost as soon as he began to descend it; and taking the foot-path across the fields, skirted Caen Wood, and so came out on Hampstead Heath. Traversing the hollow by the Vale of Health, he mounted the opposite bank, and crossing the road which joins the villages of Hampstead and Highgate, made along the remaining portion of the heath to the fields at North End, in one of which he laid himself down under a hedge, and slept.*

The 'road which joins the villages of Hampstead and Highgate' is Spaniards Road. Its famous inn, the Spaniards, features in both *The Pickwick Papers* and *Barnaby Rudge*. However, the most spell-binding

Hampstead scene in literature is arguably the opening of *The Woman in White*. Walter Hartright is walking home along the Finchley Road, through what was then open countryside, in the early hours of a sultry summer morning, when he is confronted by the electrifying figure of a woman, 'dressed from head to foot in white garments, her face bent in grave inquiry on mine, her hand pointing to the dark

cloud over London, as I faced her'.

Collins's description of the location is so precise that it is possible to locate the encounter almost exactly – at what is now the main crossroads where Fitzjohn's Avenue runs into Swiss Cottage. Oddly, two of the most entertaining novels of the 1990s begin in exactly the same place. Joseph Connolly's 1996 novel *This Is It*, opens with its accident-prone hero, Eric, lying in the middle of Fitzjohn's Avenue having just been run over by a bus and musing on how big the houses and trees look from this position. In the course of the novel, Eric's chaotic multiple life is revealed: his wife Bunty, whom he sees only at weekends,

Jack Straw's Castle on Hampstead Heath is a former coaching inn, named after one of the leaders of the Peasants' Revolt. Dickens, Wilkie Collins and Thackeray were all regulars.

155

The Spaniards Inn, still a little-changed and thriving establishment, was frequented by Keats, Shelley, Byron – and, legend would have it, Dick Turpin.

thinks he's a transvestite and keeps buying him women's underwear; his mistress Fiona, with whom he spends the rest of his time, thinks his weekends are spent writing a novel, of which he has completed just two lines. Time and again in the novel, Eric is obliged to visit the Royal Free Hospital to have various wounds attended to. At one point he muses on 'the great hulk of the Royal Free Hospital... its concrete stained by what? Life and death? No – rain: just the rain.'

Gilbert Adair's *Love and Death on Long Island* (1990) begins with its waspish, middle-aged narrator, an author of well-respected but unreadable novels, storming out of his house after being stood up by an interviewer and deciding on the spur of the moment to visit a cinema

(obviously based on the Odeon Swiss Cottage) to see *A Room with a View*. Unfamiliar with multiplexes, he wanders into the wrong auditorium and sits through the execrable *Hotpants College II* instead. To his own consternation and embarrassment, the elderly writer becomes hopelessly infatuated with the film's young star, one Ronnie Bostock, obsessively tracking down his back catalogue on video (*Tex-Mex; Skidmarks*), and ransacking teen magazines for details of Ronnie's personal life, before flying to America to try to meet him.

By the late twentieth century, only the richest, most successful writers could possibly aspire to a home in Hampstead. It was all very different in 1934, when George Orwell arrived to take up the job of part-time assistant in the cosily named Booklovers' Corner, at the corner of Pond Street and South

Church Row, described by WM Thackeray's daughter Anne as 'an avenue of Dutch red-faced houses, leading demurely to the old church tower that stands guarding its graves in the flowery churchyard'. Writers who have worshipped in St John's Church include Gerard Manley Hopkins, who lived at nearby Oak Hill Park, and the Du Mauriers.

End Road. (The building is now Perfect Pizza – the Orwell connection is marked by a plaque.) In *Keep the Aspidistra Flying*, Booklovers' Corner appeared virtually unchanged, with Orwell himself instantly recognizable as the permanently resentful Gordon Comstock. Gordon's lack of literary success (like Orwell a few years previously, Gordon is working on an epic poem about London), his resentment at those who have achieved it and his failure to persuade his conventional girlfriend Rosemary to sleep with him conspire to make him one of the most bad-tempered characters in fiction. The account of Gordon's incoherent fury when he turns up to a 'literary tea party' in 'Coleridge Grove' (obviously Keats Grove), only to find his hosts have gone out, is written with such venom that one suspects that it was prompted by a real-life incident. In later years, Orwell seems to have been embarrassed by the book, leaving (fruitless) instructions that it should not be reprinted after his death.

After living for six months in the flat above the shop, Orwell moved to a bedsit on the first floor of 77 Parliament Hill, the last house in a cul-de-sac on the very edge of the heath. It was at a party at the house that he met his first wife, Eileen O'Shaughnessy, then a psychology student at University College London. At about the same time, the writer Malcolm Lowry was a frequent visitor at number 68. Still in his early twenties, Lowry had already completed his first novel, *Ultramarine*, based on his experience as a merchant seaman. Like Orwell, Lowry had a taste for low life, which culminated in his building and living in a squatter's shack in British Columbia; like Orwell, too,

he died in his forties – from an overdose of sleeping tablets.

Another connoisseur of London's seamy side, Patrick Hamilton, also put in some useful time in Hampstead in the 1930s. For weeks at a time he would stay at the Wells Hotel, in Well Walk, soaking up the atmosphere at the bar and using it as raw material for his bar-life epic, *Twenty Thousand Streets under the Sky*. One of the most memorable scenes Hamilton ever wrote was the one in *Twenty Thousand Streets* where the waiter Bob and prostitute Jenny spend an afternoon on Hampstead Heath, looking down at the view of London 'out of sight and out of mind – far behind and far below'.

*W*ilkie Collins's distinctive physiognomy was a gift to caricaturists.

HIGHGATE

One day in April 1816, a Highgate physician named James Gillman, who had recently been elected as a member of the Royal College of Surgeons, received an unexpected letter from a fellow doctor, James Adams:

Samuel Taylor Coleridge in middle age, when he enjoyed a renaissance as 'the sage of Hampstead'.

Dear Sir,
A very learned but in one respect an unfortunate gentleman, has applied to me on a singular occasion. He has for several years been in the habit of taking large quantities of opium. For some time past, he has been in vain endeavouring to break himself off. It is apprehended [that] his friends are not firm enough, from a dread lest he should suffer by suddenly leaving it off, though he is conscious of the contrary; and has proposed to me to submit himself to any regime, however severe. With this view, he wishes to fix himself in the house of some medical gentleman, who will have courage to refuse him any laudanum, and under whose assistance, should he be the worse for it, he may be relieved. As he is desirous of retirement, and a garden, I could think of no one so readily as yourself.

The learned gentleman, Samuel Taylor Coleridge, duly turned up a week later, at Gillman's home close to St Michael's Church, Highgate,

overlooking what is now Waterlow Park. Coleridge was shown into the drawing room, where Gillman was already entertaining another visitor. As Gillman recalled many years later, 'Coleridge took his seat – his manner, his appearance, and above all his conversation were captivating. We listened with delight, and upon the first pause, when courtesy permitted, my [first] visitor withdrew, saying in a low voice, "I see by your manners an old friend has arrived."' Originally intending to stay for a few weeks while he was weaned off the drug, Coleridge remained with Dr Gillman, his wife Ann and their two young sons until his death 13 years later.

Coleridge was in his mid-forties when he arrived at Highgate, the intense, visionary years of his greatest creativity – the years that had produced 'The Rime of the Ancient Mariner', 'Christabel' and 'Kubla Khan' – far behind him. There was one great work to come – his philosophical prose work, *Biographia Literaria*, published in 1817. A late poem, 'Work without Hope', written, probably in the Gillmans' garden, in 1825, laments his lost powers:

All Nature seems at work.
Slugs leave their lair –
The bees are stirring – birds
are on the wing –
And Winter slumbering in
the open air,
Wears on his smiling face a
dream of Spring!
And I the while, the sole
unbusy thing,
Nor honey make, nor pair,
nor build, nor sing.

There were compensations, however. The publication of *Biographia* and, belatedly, of the 'Ancient Mariner' and 'Kubla

Khan' had finally made him famous, and distinguished visitors started making the pilgrimage up Highgate Hill to visit 'the sage of Highgate'. According to one of these visitors, Thomas Carlyle:

Coleridge sat on the brow of Highgate Hill, in those years, looking down on London and its smoke-tumult, like a sage escaped from the inanity of life's battle...The practical intellects of the world did not much heed him, or carelessly reckoned him a metaphysical dreamer: but to the rising spirits of the young generation he had this dusky sublime character; and sat there as a kind of Magus, girt in mystery and enigma; his Dodona oak-grove (Mr Gillman's house at Highgate) whispering strange things, uncertain whether oracles or jargon.

Carlyle's description of Coleridge's physical appearance, on his first visit to the 52-year-old 'sage' in 1824, was more prosaic:

Figure a fat, flabby, incurvated personage, at once short, rotund, and relaxed, with a watery mouth, a snuffy nose, a pair of strange, brown, timid yet earnest looking eyes, a high tapering brow, and a great bush of grey hair; and you have some faint idea of Coleridge. He is a kind good soul, full of religion and affection and poetry and animal magnetism. His cardinal sin is that he wants will. He has no resolution.

He was never 'cured' of his opium addiction, and there were frequent relapses. From the outset,

Gustave Doré's illustration of Dick Whittington on Highgate Hill. Today the Whittington Stone at the foot of Highgate Hill near Archway station marks the spot where according to folklore he heard Bow Bells ringing out 'Turn again, Whittington, Lord Mayor of London'.

Coleridge was scrupulously honest about his addiction, promising Gillman that he would never lie to him but that unless watched carefully he would probably smuggle opium into the house. A series of family traumas in the early 1820s drove him back into the arms of the drug. His son Hartley, the 'babe' to whom he had once addressed 'Frost at Midnight', was sent down from Oxford for persistent drunkenness, reminding Coleridge not only of his own past humiliations as an addict, but also of his failures as a father.

Gillman's ability to wean him from the drug was hampered by its easy availability (and legality): Coleridge had a secret account at a Highgate chemist's shop, Dunn's on the corner of Highgate Hill and Townshend Yard. He would enter through the side door, which gave on to the yard, and have his own half-pint bottle filled with 'tincture of opium' (heroin mixed with alcohol) at the back of the shop. On the day of Byron's funeral in

Dr Gillman's home at 3 The Grove, where Coleridge spent the last ten years of his life.

July 1824, Coleridge stood outside Dunn's, chatting to one of the assistants, Seymour Porter. As the cortege wound its way up Highgate Hill, Coleridge spoke with 'marvellous eloquence' of Byron's unhappy life and premature death.

On another occasion Coleridge was walking along Millfield Lane with a friend, the surgeon JH Green, when they met John Keats, who was living in Hampstead. The two poets had never met, but Green introduced them. After continuing on his way, Keats then hurried back and said, 'Let me carry away the memory, Coleridge, of having pressed your hand.'

In the autumn of 1823, the Gillman household moved to 3 The Grove, in Highgate village, a house which many years later was owned by JB Priestley. Coleridge's room was in the attic, looking out across the heath. He would sometimes invite the Gillman sons, Henry and James, to join him at the window

Coleridge in his attic room at the Grove which overlooked Hampstead Heath.

to admire the sunsets.

He died in the room, from heart failure, in July 1833 and was buried in the chapel of Highgate School. In 1961, his body was reinterred in St Michael's Church, in Highgate, where the Gillmans had put up a plaque commemorating him: 'Under the pressure of a long and most painful disease, his disposition was unalterably sweet and angelic. He was an ever-enduring and ever-loving friend, the gentlest and kindest teacher, the most engaging home companion.'

John Betjeman's *Summoned by Bells* begins with an account of his childhood at 31 West Hill, at the beginning of the twentieth century:

> *Safe in a world of trains*
> *and buttered toast*
> *Where things inanimate*
> *could feel and think,*
> *Deeply I loved thee, 31*
> *West Hill!*
> *At that hill's foot did London*
> *then begin,*
> *With yellow horse-trams*
> *clopping past the planes.*

Betjeman's father Ernest ran the

family firm, making everything from wooden cabinets to devices for hansom cabs, and hoped that his only son would eventually take over the business. But John knew even as a small boy that he had to be a poet:

... off to Hampstead Heath
I went with pencil and with
* writing-pad*
And stood tip-toe upon a little
* hill,*
Awaiting inspiration from
* the sky.*
'Look! there's a poet!', people
* might exclaim*
On footpaths near. The muse
* inspired my pen:*
The sunset tipped with gold St
* Michael's church,*
Shouts of boys bathing came
* from Highgate Ponds,*
The elms that hid the houses of
* the great*
Rustled with mystery, and
* dirt-grey sheep*
Grazed in the foreground...

During the First World War, Betjeman was a pupil at Highgate Junior School in Bishopswood Road, where other children bullied him because of his German-sounding name (in fact, it was Dutch). At the school, Betjeman had his poems bound into a book, precociously titled *The Best of Betjeman*, and showed it to one of his teachers, a Mr Eliot, who it was said 'liked poetry'. Writing in 1960, Betjeman mused over what the writer of 'The Love Song of J Alfred Prufrock' must have thought.

...He never says
When now we meet, across the
* port and cheese.*
He looks the same as then,
* long, lean and pale,*

Andrew Marvell's cottage near Waterlow Park. The house has gone, but is recorded by a plaque on the west side of Highgate High Street, opposite Number 112.

Still with the slow
* deliberating speech*
And enigmatic answers.

The Betjeman family grave is in Highgate Cemetery, which occupies both sides of Swain's Lane. John Betjeman's father died shortly after the poet had refused, for a second time, to take over the family business. In *Summoned by Bells* he confessed that

...now when I behold,
* fresh-published, new,*
A further volume of my verse,
* I see*
His kind grey eyes look
* woundedly at mine,*
I see his workmen seeking
* other jobs,*
And that red granite obelisk
* that marks*
The family grave in Highgate
* Cemetery*
Points an accusing finger to
* the sky.*

The cemetery was consecrated in 1839. Dickens buried his father, mother, brother, sister, and one of his own daughters here. George Eliot's obelisk is not far from Karl Marx's famous monument, on the east side of the cemetery. JamesThomson, Sir Leslie Stephen, Stella Gibbons and Radclyffe Hall are also buried at Highgate Cemetery.

*B*yron Cottage, AE Housman's rustic home in North Road.

*T*oday the village of Highgate retains much of the atmosphere of rural seclusion which attracted the poet and classical scholar AE Housman here in the 1890s. As an Oxford undergraduate he had fallen in love with a fellow student, Moses Jackson, and was deeply upset when Jackson emigrated to India and later married. At Byron Cottage, 17 North Road, he wrote *A Shropshire Lad*, a series of bucolic verses which made almost no impact on their publication in 1896, but became hugely popular during the First World War.

*'T*he massive forest skyline from Ken Wood, where the whole dangling necklace of ponds begins in a dark, ferny grotto.' Norman Collins: Bond Street Story, 1959.

ISLINGTON

*I*n Elizabethan times, Islington was known as 'merry Islington', renowned for its dairy farms and spring water. In the 1660s its hilltop position made it a place of refuge for Londoners fleeing the plague and, later, the Fire. Samuel Pepys came here often, to stroll in the fields, and eat and drink at the King's Head tavern.

In 1823, Charles Lamb moved to Colebrook Cottage at 64 Duncan Terrace. He was accompanied, as ever, by his sister Mary, whom he had cared for since 1795, when she had stabbed their mother to death in a bout of insanity. Writing to a friend, Bernard Barton, Charles described his new home as

a white house with six good rooms ... behind is a spacious garden with a vine (I assure you), pears, strawberries, parsnips, leek, carrots, cabbages, to delight the heart of old Alcinous [King of the Phaeacians in Homer's Odyssey]. You enter, without passage, into a cheerful dining-room, all studded over and rough, with old books; and above is a lightsome drawing-room ... I feel like a great lord, never having had a house before.

Among the friends who visited the Lambs here were Mary Shelley, Samuel Taylor Coleridge, and the short-sighted poet George Dyer, who on his departure walked straight out of the house and into the New River, which then flowed past the front door. Lamb hauled him out, and included the incident in one of his *Essays of Elia.*

In his book of alternative London walks, *Lights Out for the Territory* (1997), Iain Sinclair makes a pilgrimage to Duncan Terrace, hoping to run into the retired gangster 'Mad' Frankie Fraser, who is rumoured to exercise his small dog in a nearby park.

Noel Road, a couple of streets away, was the home of the playwright Joe Orton from 1959 until his death eight years later, at the hands of his lover Kenneth Halliwell. Flat 4, at number 25, was bought with Halliwell's money. Orton, then 26, had no real idea where his literary talents lay, and his output so far had consisted of a series of unpublished novels which the couple had written together (*The Boy Hairdresser* and *Between Us Girls* were eventually published in the 1990s). But Orton's latent, unfocused talent for satire was already beginning to emerge, initially in the long-running series of letters in the guise of 'Edna Welthorpe (Mrs)', which were written to entice credulous institutions into absurdist correspondence, such as an exchange with the manager of the Ritz Hotel over the loss of a handbag.

Other mischief-making was more destructive. Between 1959 and 1962, Orton and Halliwell systematically stole books from Islington Library in Holloway Road and pasted obscene drawings and fake blurbs inside them. The pair would then return the books to the library and blend in with other readers in the hope of witnessing a reaction. They were eventually arrested and charged with stealing and defacing 72 library books, including the removal of 1,653 plates from art

books, which Halliwell used to create several massive collages in the flat at Noel Road. Both men were sent to prison for six months – Halliwell to Ford Open Prison, near Arundel, and Orton to HM Prison East Church, in Sheerness, where he was given a job in the library.

Orton's fame came quite suddenly. His plays *Entertaining Mr Sloane* and *Loot* were a huge success – Terence Rattigan said *Sloane* was the best first play he had ever seen. Both were macabre, violent farces infused with corruption and sexual perversion in which Orton, as his biographer John Lahr put it, 'aspired to corrupt an audience with pleasure'. Orton's diary, begun in December

'A white house with six good rooms': the home of Charles and Mary Lamb in Duncan Terrace.

Joe Orton, photographed in the tiny studio flat he shared with his lover, Kenneth Halliwell.

1966, was written at the height of his success, when he was established as an international playwright, working on a new play *What the Butler Saw* (performed posthumously in 1969) and preparing a script for a new Beatles film, Up Against It.

Increasingly excluded from this new life was Halliwell. The pair had met in 1951, when they were both drama students, and it was Halliwell who had introduced Orton to literature and inititated their joint writing projects. But by the mid-sixties he was a morose, depressed figure, an uncomfortable presence at theatrical and literary gatherings where Orton was the witty, outrageous star turn and Halliwell the glum, tetchy 'wife'. The niggling, claustrophobic atmosphere in their tiny flat in Noel Road frequently comes across in the diary, with arguments 'breaking out like sudden flames on a dying fire'.

Much of Halliwell's simmering resentment came from the diary

itself, written and kept (almost literally) under his nose, and containing graphic descriptions of Orton's sexual expeditions to public lavatories in Holloway Road (see Holloway). As Lahr writes in his introduction, 'The diaries brought Orton's promiscuity off the streets and under their roof.' Even its title, 'The Diary of a Somebody' (a reference to Grossmith) could be seen as a form of provocation. Orton's decision to keep a diary in the first place was partly due to the influence of the actor Kenneth Williams, who had played in the first production of *Loot* and who kept a copious diary throughout his adult life.

In the early hours of 9 August 1967, Halliwell attacked and killed Orton with a hammer, then committed suicide by taking an overdose of sleeping tablets washed down with grapefruit juice. He left a note: 'If you read his diary all will be explained.'

Number 25 Noel Road, 9 August 1967. A policeman stands guard at the murder scene.

In 1820 the cabinet maker George Betjeman bought a group of workshops at 36–44 Pentonville Road, where he patented and produced a range of finely crafted domestic objects. In the early decades of the twentieth century, the family firm was being run by George's grandson, Ernest Betjemann (the extra 'n' was added during a craze for all things German, then removed again during the First World War). Ernest's son, the future Poet Laureate John Betjeman, recalled the premises in *Summoned by Bells* as a world 'of shining showrooms full of secret drawers / And Maharajahs' dressing-cases'.

Betjeman's father hoped that his only son would continue the family firm into its fourth generation, but Betjeman, knowing his talents lay elsewhere, refused to do so. The rift between them was never fully repaired – his father eventually retired through ill health and the workshops were closed down. Betjeman's decision was certainly correct – he had two left hands and would have made a hopeless businessman. But many years after his father's death, and with his own fame assured, Betjeman still felt a pang of guilt whenever he encountered the firm's ubiquitous range of products.

Canonbury Tower, in Canonbury Place, originally formed part of a medieval priory. Later additions turned it into a rather eccentric-looking manor house. The philosopher Francis Bacon lived there between 1616 and 1625. Later the building was divided into apartments. The poet and playwright Oliver Goldsmith moved into one of them in 1762 and wrote *The Traveller, or a Prospect of Society* there. The poem was greatly admired by Samuel Johnson, who contributed a few lines to it. The American humorist Washington Irving, mainly remembered now for his tales 'Rip Van Winkle' and 'The Legend of Sleepy Hollow' lived in the tower in the early nineteenth century.

In the 1930s and 1940s, Canonbury Square was an area of crumbling Georgian and Victorian terraces, inhabited mainly by working-class families and by a smattering of intellectuals of limited means. Evelyn Waugh was living at number 17a when his first novel, *Decline and Fall*, was published in 1928. The square had changed little when George Orwell moved into number 27b in late in 1944, after he was bombed out of his previous home at 10a Mortimer Crescent, in Maida Vale. The flat in Canonbury Square was on the third floor – an awkward location for Orwell and his wife Eileen, who had recently adopted a baby boy, Richard, and something of the atmosphere probably crept in to Winston Smith's flat at Victory Mansions in *Nineteen Eighty-Four*, with its broken-down lift and smell of cabbage in the corridors. However, Orwell seems to have been happy in the flat, taking particular pleasure in inviting friends to high tea, where he would indulge in his own favourite foods – huge oily kippers, scones, Cooper's Oxford marmalade, and very strong tea which he poured from a massive teapot. One guest, Paul Potts, would remember something

Canonbury Tower, the former home of Francis Bacon, is said to stand on 24 ley lines.

George Orwell, at work with his trademark roll-up cigarette, in his Canonbury Square flat in 1945.

*O*rwell's then
unfashionable
tenement in
Canonbury Square
may have inspired
Winston Smith's home,
Victory Mansions, in
Nineteen Eighty-Four.

'innocent and terribly simple' about Orwell: 'He loved being a host, as only civilised men can who have been very poor. There was nothing bohemian about him at all.' Orwell's financial position was still precarious – he had yet to enjoy the rewards of *Animal Farm* – and after tea he would disappear into his study, bashing out articles for *Tribune* on his typewriter while Eileen continued to entertain their guests.

Orwell was out of the country, reporting on the impending defeat of Germany when Eileen died during an exploratory operation for uterine cancer. For a time, Orwell remained in the flat with Richard, whose earliest memory of his father was of him making him a wooden cart on his workbench (Orwell was an enthusiastic, if unskilled, carpenter). In 1946, he moved, with Richard and his own sister Avril, to the island of Jura, where he wrote *Nineteen Eighty-Four*. By then, Orwell was seriously ill with tuberculosis. He died at University College Hospital on 21 January 1950.

HOLLOWAY

The name refers to the sunken highway which linked the hamlets of Upper and Lower Holloway. The countryside which lay between provided useful cover for the seventeenth-century highwayman Claude Duval, who was executed at Tyburn in 1670, but in the mid-nineteenth century the woods and fields rapidly disappeared under terraced houses and railway lines. By the last decade of the century the name Holloway was synonymous with drab suburbia. In George Gissing's *New Grub Street*, the just-about-respectable Alfred Yule is goaded almost beyond endurance by 'those Holloway people' – his impoverished, disreputable in-laws, who live in (fictional) Perker Street. However, Holloway's most famous literary son is Charles Pooter, narrator of George and Weedon Grossmith's *Diary of a Nobody* (1892). Pooter's diary, a minutely observed chronicle of middle-class pseudo-gentility, covers 15 months of his life at 'The Laurels', Brickfield Terrace: 'a nice six-roomed residence, not counting basement, with a front breakfast-parlour', and 'a nice little back garden which runs down to the railway'. Brickfield Terrace doesn't exist, but in his introduction to a recent edition, Ed Glinert tentatively suggests 1 Pemberton Gardens as the likely model.

Pooter is a fascinating character, partly because of his complete lack of self-awareness, and partly because he is so exactly a product of his time. In 1892, suburbs like Holloway were becoming increasingly popular with the rising, salaried middle class, but

social climbers like Pooter found to their disappointment that a regular income and a suburban villa did not necessarily entitle them to a role in polite society. Pooter's diary chronicles his almost daily humiliations at the hands of impudent tradesmen, obtuse servants and unpleasant neighbours, whose children throw rubbish into his garden. Meanwhile, Pooter's dreadful son Lupin, with his sudden fads and unintelligible slang, reminds us that middle-class family life has not changed so very much since the end of the last century but one. As for the diary format, the Grossmiths' influence can be seen in other novels told by similarly deluded diarists, among them Sue Townsend's *The Secret Diary of Adrian Mole Aged 13 3/4* (1984) and its sequels.

John Betjeman, who was born in 1906, recalled excursions into Pooter's territory in *Summoned by Bells*. He writes of childhood walks with his father,

> On sunny afternoons to
> great-great-aunts
> In tall Italianate houses:
> Aberdeen Park,
> Hillmarton Road and
> upper
> Pooter-land,
> Short gravel drives to
> steepish flights of steps
> And stained-glass
> windows in a
> purple hall,
> A drawing-room with
> stands of potted plants,
> Lace curtains screening
> other plants beyond.

Joe Orton's 'The Diary of a Somebody' (see Islington)

is a sort of anti-homage to Pooter, as redolent of the anxiously liberated 1960s as *Diary of a Nobody* is of the anxiously genteel 1890s. Orton's sojourns to the *pissoirs* of Holloway Road are recounted with impudent relish. An entry for 4 March 1967 recounts, in great detail, 'a frenzied homosexual saturnalia' with six other men, while 'no more than two feet away the citizens of Holloway moved about their ordinary business. I told Kenneth, who said, "It sounds as though eightpence and a bus down the Holloway Road was more interesting than £200 and a plane to Tripoli"' (a reference to a recent holiday the two had taken in Libya). Although homosexuality was decriminalized in 1967, cottaging was not, and Orton risked arrest, violence or worse on his night-time forays. In the event, retribution came not from an anonymous pick-up, but at home, in the form of a hammer attack from a no-longer-amused Kenneth Halliwell.

The bridge that spans the Holloway Road, scene of Orton's dangerous liaisons.

One of Weedon Grossmith's original illustrations for The Diary of a Nobody. *'We have a little front garden; and there is a flight of ten steps up to the front door, which, by-the-by, we keep locked with the chain up.'*

167

Graham Greene had a loathing for cremations in general and Golders Green Crematorium in particular. 'There was that slight stirring of excited expectation which is never experienced at a graveside. Will the oven doors open? Will the coffin stick on the way to the flames?' Travels with My Aunt, *1969.*

Nick Hornby's *High Fidelity* is set on and around the Holloway Road. Rob Fleming, who has just been dumped by his girlfriend, lives in a 'boxy first floor flat in a North London three-storey house' and works in a failing record shop. Championship Vinyl, in one of the quiet streets off the Holloway Road. Fed up with the greyness of his life, he wants some excitement bemoaning 'I'd like my life to be like a Bruce Springsteen song. Just once. I know I'm not born to run, I know that the Seven Sisters Road is nothing like Thunder Road, but feelings can't be so different, can they?'

Another of Nick Hornby's novels *Fever Pitch*, about one man's love-affair with Arsenal FC, marked the high-water point of an embarrassing few years in which middle-aged writers and broadcasters, who, one suspected,

were invariably the last to be picked for playground football teams and had spent Saturday afternoons doing biology homework, suddenly declared themselves to be lifelong fans of Chelsea, Man United, Charlton Athletic et al. Arsenal's home ground, where much of *Fever Pitch* takes place, can be found at Avenell Road, near Gillespie Park.

CROUCH END AND HORNSEY

Crouch End was originally 'Crux End' – a crossroads of ancient highways which developed into a medieval settlement. Today, the whole area is increasingly known as Crouch End. Although Hornsey is the setting for a brief scene in *David Copperfield* (the burial of Betsey Trotwood's villainous husband) the area remained relatively unsung until the 1970s, when the cheap but solidly built Victorian houses began to attract newcomers. For a time, Crouch End was known as a haunt of horror writers – Clive Barker, Peter Straub and Kim Newman are all former residents – and in the late 1980s the district (together with nearby Tottenham and Belsize Park) became the favoured setting for a younger group of horror writers known as 'miserablists'. Practised by, among others, M John Harrison, Michael Marshall Smith, Conrad Williams and Nicholas Royle, miserablism has been defined by Kim Newman as 'the literature of dole queues, bed-sits, relegated football teams, rainy British Sundays, loveless pick-ups and pub fights'. The anthologies *Darklands* and *Darklands Two* (both edited by Royle) and M John Harrison's collection *The Ice Monkey and Other Stories* are archetypal exercises in miserablism. Royle's work has gradually moved away from horror towards mainstream fiction, but in *The Director's Cut* (2000) he includes a scene deep inside miserablist territory. At the Jai Krishna restaurant in Stroud Green Road, a group of film-makers meet to plot, and film, the suicide of a cinema projectionist.

In Will Self's 1991 short story 'The North London Book of the Dead', the narrator meets his mother walking along Crouch Hill, some weeks after he has paid his last respects to her at Golders Green Crematorium. Later she explains the situation: when you die, you go and live in another part of London, and your new address is listed in *The North London Book of the Dead*, a sort of telephone directory of the afterlife. 'Why Crouch End?' demands her son.

'You hate Crouch End.'
'It could be worse,' his mother replies. 'Some dead people live in Wanstead.'

STOKE NEWINGTON

Once a Saxon village (the name means 'new town in the wood'), the centre of Stoke Newington (around Stoke Newington Church Street) has retained the atmosphere of a country town. In the seventeenth century, it was a sanctuary for religious dissenters, who were not permitted to live in the City. The ban was lifted, but Stoke Newington continued to be an important centre for nonconformism. Daniel Defoe, who was born into a dissenting family in 1660, was sent to school at the Nonconformist Academy at Newington Green. When, as an adult, Jonathan Swift dismissed him as an 'illiterate scribbler', Defoe angrily riposted that he 'understood' Latin, Spanish and Italian, 'could read' Greek and spoke French 'fluently'. Indeed, he left the Academy with all the qualifications he needed to become a minister, but instead he became first a liveryman, then a hosier in the City and, later, a pamphleteer, journalist and government agent. In 1709 Defoe was back in Stoke

Daniel Defoe was the son of a Stoke Newington butcher.

169

The spire of St Mary's Church dominates Stoke Newington.

Newington, living in a house on the north side of Stoke Newington Church Street. He built a second house on the site of number 95, where, in his late fifties and early sixties, he wrote his most famous works, *Robinson Crusoe, Moll Flanders* and *A Journal of the Plague Year.*

In 1783, Mary Wollstonecraft opened a school somewhere in the vicinity of Newington Green (the exact location is unknown). The school struggled on for two years without making a profit, but during this time Wollstonecraft gathered raw material for *Thoughts on the Education of*

Daughters (1787) and *Original Stories from Real Life, with Considerations Calculated to Regulate the Affections* (1788). She later fell passionately in love with a married man, the painter Henry Fuseli, lived in sin with a soldier, Gilbert Imlay, and finally married the philosopher William Godwin, dying from septicaemia shortly after giving birth to their daughter, Mary (see Somers Town).

In the *Dictionary of Biography*, the editor Leslie Stephen (father of Virginia Woolf) damned the mother of feminism with faint praise: 'Her faults were such as might be expected from a follower of Rousseau, and were consistent

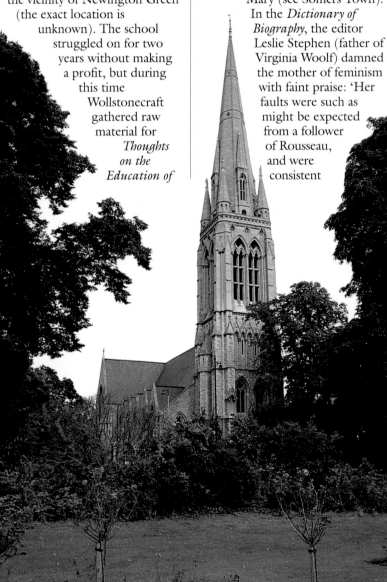

Stoke Newington stretches outwards like the rubber neck of a chicken. We drift past exotic minimarts, deleted cinemas, tributary name-plates with literary associations ... Stoke Newington is the perfect location in which to stay lost: limboland, London's Interzone. Large shabby properties that ask no questions. Internal exile with a phoney rent-book.

Daniel Defoe's former home, now a courier office.

Mary Wollstonecraft (1759–97) established a school in Newington Green. In November 1795, when her partner Gilbert Imlay deserted her, she tried to drown herself by jumping off Putney Bridge.

with much unselfishness and nobility of sentiment, though one could wish that her love-affairs had been more delicate.'

One of Stoke Newington's residents was Edgar Allan Poe who attended the Manor House School on the north side of Church Street. A plaque marks the former site. The school, which was run by the Reverend John Bransby, appears in his 1839 story 'William Wilson'.

Ernest Raymond's novel *We, The Accused* won the Book Guild gold medal in 1936 and was praised by John Betjeman for its 'sense of doom and impending murder and autumn mists in Clissold Park'. Alexander Baron's *The Lowlife* (1963) features Harryboy Boas, a literature-loving gambler on the run, and caught the atmosphere of Stoke Newington in the early sixties, as it began to be colonized by new arrivals from the West Indies. In *Lights Out for the Territory* (1997), Iain Sinclair explores Stoke Newington's seamy eastern borderland:

CHAPTER 3

EAST LONDON

◆

HACKNEY AND BETHNAL GREEN

Hackney occupies a large section of east London, stretching from Islington in the west to the river Lea in the east. Seventeenth-century Hackney was no more than a group of hamlets, set amid rolling countryside and highly popular as a day-trip destination for City dwellers of all classes.

Samuel Pepys's diary describes numerous excursions to Hackney, typically the one he made on a June evening in 1664, 'after dinner by coach with my wife, only to take the ayre, it being very warm and pleasant, to Bowe and old Ford and thence to Hackny; there light and played at shuffleboard, eat cream and good cherries; and so with good refreshment home'. Another east London outing, one Sunday in May 1667, moved Pepys to a mood of nostalgic reminisence seldom seen in the diary. After visiting a friend in Islington, Pepys and his wife 'walked over the fields to Kingsland and back again, a walk I think I have not taken these twenty years but puts me in mind of my boy's time, when I boarded at Kingsland and used to shoot with my bow and arrow in these fields. A very pretty place it is – and little did any of my friends think I should come to walk in these fields in this condition and state that I am.' Luck and hard work had made him a wealthy man, with the ear of the King.

Another visit the following August (on the day of his thwarted amours in St Dunstan's Church, Fleet Street) descended into farce. Motivated no doubt by guilt about his conduct earlier in the day (see Fleet Street), Pepys took his wife on an evening coach trip to Islington, via Kingsland,

but before we got to Islington, between that and Kingsland, there happened an odd adventure; one of our coach-horses fell sick of the staggers, so as he was ready to fall down. The coachman was fain to light and hold him up and cut his tongue to make him bleed, and his tail – the horse continued shakeing every part of him, as if he had been in an ague a good while, and his blood settled in his tongue, and the coachman thought and believed he would presently drop down dead. Then he blew some tobacco in his nose; upon which the horse sneezed, and by and by grows well and draws us the rest of the way as

*B*lossom Street (opposite) in Spitalfields, evocative of the dark atmosphere of the old East End described by Arthur Morrison and Jack London.

*T*he Boundary Street Estate (above) was built in 1900, after Arthur Morrison's slum novel A Child of the Jago caused a public outcry.

well as ever he did; which was one of the strangest things of a horse I ever observed – but he says it is usual.

In the early nineteenth century, rural Hackney, with its fields and market gardens, began to disappear under railway lines and factories. As the silk-weaving industry spread north from Spitalfields, Bethnal Green became progressively more urban in character, but when silk-weaving went into a decline in the first few decades of the nineteenth century, so too did Bethnal Green. By 1890 it was the scene of the most wretched poverty in London, with the highest infant mortality rate in the capital and almost 50 per cent of its population living below subsistence level.

One of the writers who worked

*I*ain Sinclair's *mesmerizing story* Hardball *(1993), which culminates in a macabre game of football, has its origin in one of Sinclair's former jobs, marking out scores of football pitches on Hackney Marshes.*

tirelessly to draw public attention to the plight of the East End poor was Sir Walter Besant. A distinguished historian (his biographies included one of Captain Cook, who lived in Mile End Road), as well as a scholar of French literature, Besant described the social make-up of Hackney and Bethnal Green in *All Sorts and Conditions of Men* (1882) and *Children of Gibeon* (1886). Besant was closely involved with the

People's Palace, a centre for education and recreation, opened in the Mile End Road by Queen Victoria in 1887, and destroyed in a fire in 1931. (The site is now occupied by Queen Mary and Westfield College.) The worst degradation of all was to be found in the 'Jago' area in the vicinity of Old Nichol Street. Arthur Morrison's novel *A Child of the Jago* (1896) is the story of Dick Perrott, a slum boy, who is drawn inexorably into violent crime, despite the efforts of a local priest to reform him. The novel, and Morrison's earlier *Tales of Mean Streets* (1894), about a factory girl's descent into street prostitution, influenced Somerset Maugham's first novel *Liza of Lambeth*, and its echoes can be heard in American working-class dramas of the 1930s such as Sidney Kingsley's play *Dead End* and Rowland Brown's story *Angels with Dirty Faces*, which was turned into a memorable film starring James Cagney.

Partly as a result of the publicity engendered by Morrison's novel, the Jago slums were demolished in 1900 and replaced by the acres of red-brick tenements which are still much in evidence around Old Nichol Street and Arnold Circus. Yet, according to Jack London, who visited the area shortly after the project was completed, the redevelopment had little real effect. In *The People of the Abyss* he describes how he 'visited the municipal dwellings erected by the London County Council on the site of the slums where lived Arthur Morrison's "Child of the Jago". While the buildings housed more people than before, it was much healthier. But the dwellings were inhabited by the better-class workmen and artisans. The slum people had

the thousands of Jews who came from Eastern Europe between approximately 1860 and 1914. One of the first writers to draw inspiration from the East End Jewish community was Israel Zangwill. The son of poor Russian immigrants, Zangwill's vivid, humorous novels of immigrant life *Children of the Ghetto* (1892) and *The King of Schnorrers* (1894)

'Only were to be seen the ubiquitous policemen, flashing their dark [sic] lanterns into doorways and alleys, and men and women and boys taking shelter in the lee of buildings from the wind and rain.' Jack London, The People of the Abyss, *1902.*

simply drifted on to crowd other slums or to form new slums.'

George Orwell, who had read and admired *The People of the Abyss* while he was still at school, undertook his own expedition into the East End shortly before Christmas 1931. Determined to get himself arrested, and thereby experience Christmas from a police cell, the 28-year-old Orwell dressed up in the tramp's clothing he had been using for undercover forays into London low life, and made for the Mile End Road, where he went to the nearest pub and proceeded to get very drunk. He was duly arrested as he tottered along the street and taken to Bethnal Green police station, on the corner of Bethnal Green Road and Ainsley Street (now the offices of the Providence Row Housing Association) before appearing at Old Street Magistrates' Court, charged with being drunk and disorderly. He used his brief experience of imprisonment for the scene in *Nineteen Eighty-Four* in which Winston Smith has to endure the stench of an unflushable cell lavatory while waiting to be interrogated.

Like neighbouring Whitechapel, Bethnal Green formed a refuge of sorts for

Emanuel Litvinoff was brought up in a tenement near Bethnal Green Road. A contemporary of George Orwell on the socialist journal Tribune, *Litvinoff described the local conditions in an article in 1946, as post-war slum clearance was getting under way:*

Side by side in a small street off Bethnal Green Road, twin tenements faced across six yards of cobbles and paving stones to a square factory building whose small windows were covered in wire mesh. These tall, forbidding buildings were the dominant features of a street of cramped artisan dwellings. There was little to distinguish the tenements from the factory except that the former was over-populous and their windows drably curtained and dimly gas-lit at night. Each consisted of ten apartments, erected like a structure of orange boxes placed one on top of the other, and each apartment of two rooms and a narrow scullery. Between them they gave shelter to a population of 100 to 120 men, women and children. A cobbler and his family of five lived and worked in one of the ground-floor flats, a furrier and his wife carried on a business next door to him, and two widows of the 1914–18 war supported large families by home dressmaking in upper apartments of the same tenement.

The lives of these inhabitants were exposed by day and night to the public ear in a pathetic, inescapable medley of sound. The rooms were soundboxes uninsulated against the neighbours and the street. A child cried with toothache monotonously, like the noise of water running down a drain, and people were kept awake until it fell asleep through exhaustion. The voices of men talking or quarrelling in bed penetrated the walls and ceilings of neighbouring flats. On the attic floor, six flights up the narrow stairs, there lived a woman who got drunk every Saturday night and wept maudlin tears until long after midnight. Down in the small stone passage the amorous scuffling of courting couples was audible to the top of the building.

Machines trundled: men and women laughed and quarrelled: people were born and died in this public atmosphere. Circumstances forced on them a kind of reluctant community. The sixty dwellers of each tenement shared the amenities provided by a tiny yard about 15 feet square filled with three w.c.s and a large wooden dustbin. Every morning a procession of people carried night-soil buckets down to the yard to be emptied into the w.c.s, of which no more than two seemed to be in working order at the same time.

'God's crucible ... where all the races of Europe are melting and re-forming.'

Among Zangwill's literary successors was the poet and novelist Emanuel Litvinoff. The mercurial Litvinoff made headlines in 1951, when he hijacked a poetry reading attended by TS Eliot to denounce Eliot's poem 'Burbank with a Baedeker: Bleistein with a Cigar' as anti-semitic. Eliot himself was heard to praise Litvinoff's poem.

In his autobiography, *Journey through a Small Planet* (1972), Litvinoff described how he returned to his birthplace, Bethnal Green, to find it much changed, its former Jewish inhabitants having moved to the suburbs and been replaced by a new generation of immigrants: 'Clumps of Muslim men stood aimlessly on corners and there was a curious absence of women ... The odour of spices mingled with the stench of drains.' The tenement in which Litvinoff had grown up had, however, survived unchanged – right down to the initials which he had carved on an outside window ledge when he was 12.

Iain Sinclair's Downriver describes a journey from Hackney Wick Station (above) to the strange landscape of North Woolwich (below) and the river beyond (far right).

earned him the sobriquet 'the Jewish Dickens'. Zangwill received his education at the Jews' Free School near Petticoat Lane Market, and later taught there. In *Children of the Ghetto*, he described the market as a place of 'bustle and confusion, in the cram and the crush, in the wedge and the jam, in the squeezing and shouting, in the hubbub and medley, such a jolly, rampant, screaming, fighting, maddening, jostling, polyglot, laughing broth.' Zangwill's 1907 play *The Melting Pot* coined a phrase and an enduring image of America as

Born in Wales in 1943, the writer Iain Sinclair has lived in Albion Drive, Hackney, since 1968. Like Dickens, Sinclair takes epic walks across London to find and record the city's secret nooks and crannies; unlike Dickens his work for the most part eschews plots and character development. Sinclair's most accessible book, the non-fiction *Lights Out for the Territory* contains a vignette of Hackney Marshes, or rather of the greyhounds that are exercised there, readied to perform at Walthamstow Stadium, on the far side of the marshes:

They're money on legs. You see them out on the Marshes in all weathers, being trained by fit young women: nerves on a string, shivering on the hottest day. They must have been hunters once – of a peculiarly dim kind. Who else would be stupid enough to chase a lump of old fur on a wire? Not just the first time, but every time; tongues lolling, or muzzled, up for it as soon as the trap opens. They don't have outsides, these dogs, no flesh cladding. They're all ribs and innards, X-rays of themselves. Febrile, bred to be elsewhere.

Sinclair's 1989 novel *Downriver* consists of 12 journeys, involving a certain amount of light fictionalization but a wealth of minute, accurate detail. Few other novelists, not even Dickens, would bother, or dare, to explore the rancid streets around Hackney Wick:

Once it was a shopping centre, somewhere to travel towards, a destination: the name alone survives. A hoop of gutted enterprises caught between the East Way and the rat-infested river. A station platform boasts of easy access to the Marshlands; where, in the twilight mists, razor-blade-chewing loners wait for their victims to stroll out of domestic banality into a definitive hothouse fantasy. The elevation of the tracks offers a momentary vision – of the hospital blocks; the Gormenghast on the hill, the Citadel of Transformation.

The ageing trains that call at Hackney Wick rattle across a landscape evoked in all its indifferent misery by George Gissing a century earlier in *The Nether World* – 'a city of the damned', with 'stations which it crushes the

Hoxton Square. The area has had various names, from Hocheston (in the Domesday book) to Hoggeston (in the time of Edward the III), Hogson and finally Hoxton.

heart to think should be the destination of any mortal'.

Sinclair's journey ends at North Woolwich, a stark, unfriendly Thameside landscape of abandoned railway engines and British Telecom saucer dishes. Here, Sinclair muses on an almost forgotten maritime tragedy which took place on this stretch of river in 1878: the collision of the pleasure steamer *The Princess Alice* and the collier *The Bywell Castle*, which resulted in some 600 deaths – the worst shipping disaster ever to take place on the Thames. Among the dead were the husband and children of Elizabeth Stride, who a decade later became one of the victims of Jack the Ripper – itself the subject of Sinclair's 1987 novel *White Chappell, Scarlet Tracings.*

SHOREDITCH AND HOXTON

Shoreditch and its northern neighbour Hoxton form an indeterminate area, not quite belonging to either the City or the East End. The region's literary credentials, however, are long-standing. In 1576 a travelling player named James Burbage, who was a

The nineteenth-century tightrope walker Charles Blondin was one of the star attractions at the Shoreditch Theatre. In 1860 he successfully crossed Niagara Falls on a high wire.

member of the Earl of Leicester's theatre troupe, leased some land near the present-day junction of Great Eastern Street and New Inn Yard, on which he erected London's first purpose-built playhouse. The Theatre, as it was named, opened in 1577, Burbage living in nearby Holywell Lane with his sons Richard and Cuthbert. The venture, which Burbage hoped would make his fortune, ended in tears: his business partner, John Brayne, discovered that Burbage had been using a duplicate key to open 'a commen box where the money gathered at the said playes was putt in' and secreting the contents 'in his bosome or other where about his bodye'. In due course, the partners came to blows. Burbage and Brayne 'went together by the eares', Burbage called Mrs Brayne a 'whore' and Burbage's son Richard attacked one of Brayne's men with a broom handle.

In the meantime, rival theatre managers were cashing in on the new craze for plays. The Curtain, in Holywell Lane, was opened by a man named Harry Lanman, or Laneman, in 1577. As a young actor, William Shakespeare performed at The Curtain and The Theatre, and lived in lodgings in Norton Folgate, south of Shoreditch High Street. According to a Privy Council inquiry, the area was then notorious for its wenches, soldiers and other 'dissolute, loose, and insolent persons' who frequented its teeming brothels and taverns. Shakespeare

drew on this local colour for the tavern scenes in *Henry IV*, where he depicts the debaucheries of Falstaff and Doll Tearsheet, but, according to some of Shakespeare's contemporaries, interviewed by the biographer James Aubrey, the Bard himself tended to avoid debaucheries with the excuse that he was 'in paine' – probably with toothache, but possibly a less respectable ailment.

James Burbage's son Richard also acted in The Theatre. Following his father's death in 1598, Burbage dismantled the building and used the timbers to build a new playhouse, the Globe, in Bankside. At the Globe he became the most respected actor of his day, playing the lead roles in Shakespeare's *Richard III*, *Hamlet*, *King Lear* and *Othello*. He also appeared in Ben Jonson's comedies *Every Man in his Humour* and *The Alchemist*. Both Burbages are buried at St Leonard's Church, in Shoreditch High Street. Also laid to rest there was an actor named Gabriel Spencer, murdered by Ben Jonson on 22 September 1598, in Hoxton Fields. They had met in the Marshalsea Prison the year before, when they and others had been jailed for their involvement in the satirical play *The Isle of Dogs*. In his defence, Jonson admitted killing Spencer, but claimed that they had been fighting a duel. He escaped the gallows because he was able to read the Bible in Latin

– sufficient to plead 'benefit of clergy', which exempted him from a normal criminal trial. Instead, he had his left thumb branded 'M' for 'murderer' with a hot iron and returned briefly to his old trade, bricklaying, before enjoying a huge success with his comedy *Every Man in His Humour*.

In the nineteenth century, Hoxton was still renowned for its theatres. The nearby Eagle, at 2 Shepherdess Walk was originally a tea-garden, immortalized in the nursery rhyme:

> Up and down the City
>   Road,
> In and out of the Eagle,
> That's the way the

Richard Burbage (1567-1619) acted in The Theatre, set up by his father, James, and later dismantled the building to build The Globe.

St Leonard's Church, Shoreditch, where Jonson's victim, Gabriel Spencer, is buried, together with Richard Burbage, and Henry VIII's jester Will Sommers.

Hoxton Square was called Hoxton Fields when Ben Johnson murdered Gabriel Spencer here in 1598.

money goes,
Pop goes the weasel!

A 'weasel' was a tailor's iron, pop was slang for pawn, but the meaning may be erotic. Dickens

In the early nineteenth century, the Eagle was one of the most fashionable night spots in East London. The atmosphere of the square is summed up by Dickens in 'Miss Evans and the Eagle' (1835) in Sketches by Boz.

described the scene in 'Miss Evans and the Eagle' (1835) in *Sketches by Boz*:

There were the walks, beautifully gravelled and planted – and the refreshment boxes, painted and ornamented like so many snuff boxes – and the variegated lamps

shedding their rich light upon the company's heads – and the place for dancing ready chalked for the company's feet – and a Moorish band playing at one end of the gardens – and an opposition military band playing away at the other.

The building was demolished and rebuilt in 1901, and the Eagle is now a large pub.

The Britannia Theatre at 188 Pitfield Street specialized in barnstorming melodramas and later became a music hall. When the actor-manager, Sam Lane, died in 1870, the Brit, as it was known locally, was taken over by his widow Sara Lane, who was still playing the principal boy in pantomime in her seventies. Near-by was Pollock's, a shop specializing in toy theatres, which Robert Louis Stevenson described in his essay 'A Penny Plain and Twopence Coloured': 'If you love art, folly or the bright eyes of children, speed to Pollock's.' The shop moved to Covent Garden in 1956, where it remains to this day.

In *David Copperfield* (1850), young David has just started working at Murdstone and Grinby, at Blackfriars, when he is introduced to Mr Micawber, in whose house he is to lodge.

'My address,' said Mr Micawber, 'is Windsor Terrace, City Road. I – in short,' said Mr Micawber, with the same genteel air and in another burst of confidence – 'I live there.'

I made him a bow.

'Under the impression,' said Mr Micawber, 'that your peregrinations in the metropolis have not as yet been extensive, and that you might have some difficulty in penetrating the arcana of the Modern Babylon in the direction of the City Road – in short,' said Mr Micawber, in another burst of confidence, 'that you might lose yourself – I shall be happy to call this evening, and install you in the knowledge of the nearest way.'

Mr Micawber's house turns out to be 'shabby like himself, but also, like himself, made all the show it could'. The only visitors are angry creditors, and eventually Mr Micawber is arrested in Windsor Terrace and carted off to

the King's Bench Prison in the Borough.

WAPPING, LIMEHOUSE AND THE ISLE OF DOGS

Wapping is the narrow strip of land which hugs the north shore of the Thames from the Tower of London to the Rotherhithe Tunnel. In his 1598 *Survey of London*, the historian John Stow described the area's main thoroughfare, Wapping High Street, as a 'filthy strait passage, with alleys of small tenements or cottages, built [and] inhabited by sailors' victuallers'. London's oldest surviving riverside pub, the Prospect of Whitby (57 Wapping Wall), first opened its doors in 1520 and has been frequented over the years by Pepys, Dickens and Thackeray.

By the nineteenth century, Wapping was overcrowded and squalid. Another historian, the American-born James Peller Malcolm, noted that the 'homes and workshops will not bear description' and left it at that. In *London Labour and the London Poor* (1851) Henry Mayhew

A scene from David Copperfield, illustrated by 'Phiz' (Hablot Knight Browne). Mr Micawber (standing) was partly based on Dickens's father.

The Prospect of Whitby pub which was originally called The Devil's Tavern. Pepys visited here regularly whilst working as Charles II's Secretary to the Admiralty and a coastal chart presented to him is displayed in the Pepys room upstairs where the Pepys society used to hold meetings.

detected a 'certain innate delicacy' about the sailors' women. The same could not be said about the taverns, which were among the most violent anywhere in London.

The writer WW Jacobs was born in Wapping in 1863, the son of a dock worker who later became a Civil Service clerk. Jacobs's stories of dockers and sailors first appeared in the *Strand* magazine in the 1890s, and later

River view from the Prospect of Whitby which was frequented by Dickens, Thackeray and Pepys.

in a series of collections such as *Many Cargoes* (1896), *Light Freights* (1901) and *Night Watches* (1914), though his best-known work is the much-anthologized horror story 'The Monkey's Paw'.

A merchant seaman for 20 years (1874–94), Joseph Conrad began and ended dozens of voyages along this stretch of the river. In Iain Sinclair's novel *Downriver* the book collector Todd Sileen is obsessively amassing Conrad's complete works. Sileen is first seen in the churchyard of St John's Church in Scandrett Street, which, Sinclair notes, was once colonized by marmosets, lemurs, genets, tamarins and sugar gliders – exotic

pets brought back to Wapping by sailors, and traded in the local taverns. According to Sinclair, some broke free and 'took cover behind the walls of this graveyard with its fox-mangy London planes, its chestnuts', where locals hunted them for their fur. (The passage is not quite as preposterous as it sounds: the first fuchsia to be seen in Britain was brought to Wapping by a seaman and sold to a market gardener in the Prospect of Whitby.) In the same novel, another Conrad collector, Dr Adam Tenbrücke, commits suicide in the manner reserved for eighteenth-century pirates – by manacling himself to a metal ring on the river wall at Wapping Old Stairs (at the end of the alley next to the Town of Ramsgate pub) and waiting to be drowned in the rising tide. In PD James's novel *Original Sin* (1994), an object is found floating in the Thames at roughly the same spot – 'something grotesque and unreal, like the domed head of a gigantic insect, its millions of hairy legs stirring gently in the tide' – in fact, the head of a drowned body.

Ratcliff Highway (now known simply as the Highway) forms Wapping's northern boundary. On 7 December 1811, Timothy Marr, a hosier who lived at number 29 (near the junction with present-day Betts Street), sent his maidservant to buy some oysters for supper. On her return, the front door was locked. A neighbour who gained entry found the bodies of Marr and his 13-year-old apprentice in the shop. Upstairs were Marr's wife and their child. All four had had their skulls smashed and their throats cut. The murder weapons, a chisel and

a maul (a heavy hammer) had been left on the shop floor.

Twelve days later, a publican, Mr Williamson, his wife Catherine and their maidservant, Bridget Harrington, were found hacked to death at the King's Arms inn, also in the Ratcliff Highway. A seaman's maul, marked with the initials JP, was found at the scene. The maul belonged to a Swedish sailor, John Petersen, who was at sea when the murders were committed but was a regular lodger at another Ratcliff Highway tavern, the Pear Tree. One of his fellow lodgers was John Williams, who had been seen walking towards the King's Arms on the night of the murders and had returned to the Pear Tree in the early hours with blood on his shirt. Williams was arrested but before he could be tried he hanged himself in his prison cell. As was the custom with suicides, he was buried with a stake through his heart; his grave is at the crossroads of Cannon Street Road and Cable Street.

The story of the Ratcliff Highway murders has fascinated a succession of writers. Much of Thomas De Quincey's provocative essay 'On Murder, Considered as One of the Fine Arts' was devoted to it; PD James co-wrote a book about it, *The Maul and the Pear Tree*; and the murder has featured in Peter Ackroyd's novels *Hawksmoor* (1985) and *Dan Leno and the Limehouse Golem* (1994). Both these novels also include scenes in and around the two local Nicholas Hawksmoor churches, St George in the East and St Anne's. In *Lights Out for the Territory* (1997), Iain Sinclair is dismissive of the view from Canary Wharf, but offers a paean to the prospect from Nicholas Hawksmoor's eighteenth-century masterpiece: 'Climb the true tower of St Anne's Church, and stand among

Wapping street children from Jack London's The People of the Abyss, *1902.*

The graveyard of St John's in Scandrett Street which Iain Sinclair describes in his novel Downriver.

The metal ring at Wapping Old Stairs features in Iain Sinclair's novel Downriver.

The significance of the stone pyramid in the grounds of St Anne's Church, Limehouse, has never been fully explained. St Anne's, and its architect Nicholas Hawksmoor, have long fascinated Iain Sinclair (Lud Heat) *and Peter Ackroyd* (Hawksmoor *and* Dan Leno and the Limehouse Golem).

Hawksmoor's crumbling Portland stone lanterns, pyramids set above catacomb arches, designed to be seen *through*, to keep vision alive; the river, all points of the compass – even the futile bluntness of Canary Wharf's phallic topping.'

Limehouse was named after the lime kilns which proliferated there in medieval times, but its heyday came in the eighteenth and early

nineteenth century, when it was one of the country's busiest shipbuilding centres.

Born in 1812, the year after the Ratcliff Highway murders, Charles Dickens knew Limehouse through childhood visits to his godfather, Christopher Huffam, a ship's chandler and sailmaker. Huffam's house was in Church Row (now called Newell Street), where the young Dickens would be lifted on to the dining room table to sing one of his favourite songs, 'The Cat's Meat Man' ('Down in the street cries the cat's meat man, / Fango, dango, with his barrow and can'). Limehouse, with its 'rows of houses, with little vane-surmounted masts uprearing themselves from among the scarlet beans', appears in *Dombey and Son*, where it is the home of the genial, reassuring Captain Cuttle. In *Our Mutual Friend*, The Grapes public house (76 Narrow Street) is renamed the Six Jolly Fellowship Porters. Today, The Grapes is still the most authentically Dickensian of the Thames riverside pubs, with its tiny, dimly lit bar and narrow upstairs dining room jutting out over the river. The twentieth-century novelist Angus Wilson also knew The Grapes. His father was born there, and Wilson was to write extensively on Dickens. At one point he and Benjamin Britten discussed a joint opera project, focusing on the Steerforth and Little Em'ly plot from *David Copperfield*, but the plan never came to fruition.

In the last year of his life, Dickens returned to Limehouse to gather material for his last novel,

The Mystery of Edwin Drood. Near the Ratcliff Highway he found the opium den which he describes in the opening scene of *Edwin Drood*. One of his companions, his American publisher James T Fields, recalled the scene 30 years later. 'In a miserable court, we found the haggard old woman blowing at a kind of pipe made of an old penny ink-bottle. The identical words which Dickens puts into the mouth of this wretched creature in *Edwin Drood* we heard her croon as we leaned over the tattered bed on which she was lying ... and the Chinamen and Lascars made never-to-be forgotten pictures in the scene.'

Oscar Wilde included a similar scene in *The Picture of Dorian Gray* (1890). Between then and the outbreak of the Second World War, the river fogs, gambling houses and opium dens of Limehouse would become a literary cliché, in much the same way that the mean streets and gasworks of Somers Town would become a cinematic cliché a century later. Sax Rohmer's arch-villain Dr Fu-Manchu ('the head of the great Yellow movement ... a menace to the civilized world'), who made his first appearance in 1913, is usually to be found somewhere in Limehouse, plotting to overthrow the British Empire and place it under Chinese rule.

The reality was less exotic. As the detective novelist Colin Watson wrote in his incisive study of crime fiction, *Snobbery with Violence*, the Chinese community in Limehouse was actually 'small, unobtrusive and industrious ... No pad-footed assassins. No Tong wars nor kidnapping nor torture chambers. Seldom in the history of racial intolerance had a minority shown itself so unco-operative in the matter of getting hated.'

Nevertheless, in the 1920s and 1930s groups of wealthy Londoners were still making forays into Limehouse in the hope of catching a glimpse of authentic Oriental villainy. As he recorded in his journal, Arnold Bennett

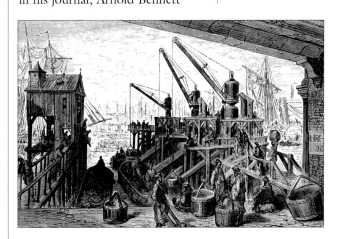

took a 'slumming party' to Limehouse one night in 1925, stopping off at two Chinese restaurants ('all very clean and tidy indeed') and a Chinese music club. He concluded the entry ruefully: 'On the whole a rather flat night ... We saw no vice whatsoever.'

A few years later, George Orwell witnessed an almost

The Angel Tavern, still a popular riverside inn at Bermondsey Wall, is mentioned in Pepys's diary. Judge Jeffreys regularly visited the Angel to watch pirates being hanged on the opposite bank of the river.

Limehouse Docks was at its peak in the early nineteenth century, when the young Dickens came here to visit his godfather, a local chandler.

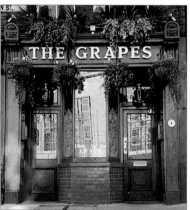

The Grapes, in Narrow Street, inspired the Six Jolly Fellowship Porters in Dickens's last completed novel, Our Mutual Friend *(1865).*

identical scene. In his guise as a working man, Orwell had secured a bed in a doss house in Limehouse Causeway, the kitchen of which was invaded one afternoon by 'a grave and reverend seignior in a frock coat, a lady sitting at a portable harmonium, and a chinless youth toying with a crucifix'. The trio embarked on an impromptu religious service, which, as Orwell recalled with some satisfaction in *Down and Out in Paris and London*, was roundly ignored by the lodgers.

'They did not offer the smallest rudeness to the slummers,' Orwell wrote. 'They just ignored them. By common consent everyone in the kitchen – a hundred men, perhaps – behaved as though the slummers had not existed. There they stood patiently singing and exhorting, and no more notice was taken of them than if they had been earwigs... Presently the slummers gave it up and cleared out, not insulted in any way, but merely disregarded. No doubt they consoled themselves by thinking how brave they had been, "freely venturing into the lowest dens", etc etc.'

The Isle of Dogs is not, in fact, an island but a peninsula, formed by a dramatic bend in the Thames at Limehouse Reach. Its curious name, of which the earliest known record is on a 1588 map, has never been satisfactorily explained: it may refer to the royal hunting dogs that were once kennelled there, to the dead dogs that were washed up there, or indeed to the people who lived there. Ben Jonson and Thomas Nashe's satirical play *The Isle of Dogs* may have drawn a parallel between the royal kennels and the slavering courtiers of Elizabeth I, but no one knows for sure, as the text has long since disappeared. Its contents, whatever they were, were strong enough for the play to be banned after one performance, and both writers – together with the cast – were sent to jail (see Borough).

The Isle of Dogs languished in relative obscurity until the 1980s, when it became the scene of frenzied building activity, culminating in the construction of Canary Wharf Tower, the tallest building in the country. The *Daily Telegraph* and *Reader's Digest* are among the high-profile publications which have recently set up shop in the vicinity.

In his novel *Downriver* (1989), Iain Sinclair imagines the Isle of Dogs (a 'peg of uncircumcised land') sold off by the developers to the Vatican and run by a papal Mafia, with its crowning glory, Canary Wharf Tower, 'a fortified nest, an angled chamber, the nearest point to the hand of God. He had only to uncurl His finger to touch it.' In *Lights Out for the Territory*, Sinclair turns his attention to the very tip of the Isle, where a pedestrian tunnel, excavated beneath the Thames between 1897 and 1902, links the Isle of Dogs with Greenwich. As Sinclair says, 'The lift chamber is sheer old-fashioned luxury, roomy and well-benched. The teak and polish of pre-war steamers. There are uniformed operatives, pitched by the mechanical repetition of duty into secret mindscapes. Passengers are no longer a reality. The cage has become a time-travelling module, connected to the outside world by a surveillance window: it's a Nautilus on

Gustave Doré's illustration of 'the room where The Mystery of Edwin Drood *opens', which Doré had visited to find a Lascar and a woman stirring opium over a small flame.*

Canary Wharf tower described as 'the nearest point to the hand of God' by Iain Sinclair.

wires, lowered into depths far stranger than Brother Thames can provide.'

'The little private doss houses, as a rule, are unmitigated horrors. I have slept in them, and I know.' Jack London, The People of the Abyss, *1902.*

WHITECHAPEL AND SPITALFIELDS

One morning in August 1902, the American writer Jack London hailed a taxi and ordered the driver to take him to the East End. 'Where, sir?' the driver asked. 'To the East End, anywhere,' London replied 'Go on.'

After some protests, when it became clear that the young American had no particular idea of where he wanted to go, the driver dropped him at an old-clothes shop in Stepney, where London kitted himself out in working man's clothes. After spending the night in a comfortable lodging house in Islington, he made his way to the East End in his new guise as a seaman down on his luck, and spent the next two months living among the poor and destitute in 'this human hell-hole called the East End'. In Frying Pan Alley, near Leman Street, London came across a woman in a doorway, nursing a baby 'at breasts grossly naked and libelling

all the sacredness of motherhood'; in the building behind her he climbed three flights of stairs, each landing 'heaped with filth and refuse' before coming across a sweat shop and, in an adjoining room, a 16-year-old boy dying of consumption. In Mile End Road he fell in with two unemployed men on their way to the workhouse. Puzzled as to why the men continually stooped down to the pavement without breaking stride, London eventually realized that they were picking up and eating tiny bits of orange peel, apple skin and crumbs of bread – 'and this, between six and seven o'clock in the evening of August 20, year of our Lord 1902, in the heart of the greatest, wealthiest, and most powerful empire the world has ever seen'.

The conditions which horrified Jack London had scarcely changed since the Jack the Ripper murders 14 years earlier. Between August and November 1888, five local women, four of them prostitutes, were stabbed and mutilated. Unsolved

188

to this day, the murders have featured in countless books, offering between them a plethora of suspects and solutions. (The idea of the Ripper murders as a jolly game – a sepia 'Cluedo' for armchair sleuths – received a jolt when the post-mortem photographs were first published, in their full ferocity, in 1972.) Among the more thoughtful literary works to have developed from the murders are Marie Belloc Lowndes's play *The Lodger* (1913), which was later filmed by Alfred Hitchcock, Colin Wilson's novel *Ritual in the Dark* (1960) and Iain Sinclair's *White Chappell, Scarlet Tracings* (1987), whose characters include a popular Ripper suspect, Queen Victoria's physician William Gull.

Sinclair's novel includes a present-day scene in which a group of antiquarian book-dealers discuss the Ripper victims at the Seven Stars pub in Brick Lane, in 'an oblique corner, bar still empty, sun puddle; the stripper not due on stage for another thirty minutes'. Paul West's novel *The Women of Whitechapel* (1991) also takes up the Ripper mythology, with a cast of characters which again includes Gull, together with the Ripper's last-known victim Mary Kelly. In *Downriver*, published the same year, Iain Sinclair seemed to be tiring of the whole subject, complaining that 'anyone who has ever written anything about Whitechapel, or the Whitechapel Murders, will soon discover that they have issued an open invitation to every conspiracy-freak who is not actually under lock and key... The events of nineteenth-century Whitechapel have been

overtold to the point of erasure; confirming nothing beyond their eternal melancholy. The puffers, sniffers, scribblers and scratchers are determined to keep that small flame dancing in the circle of their sour breath.'

Spitalfields, to the north of Whitechapel, takes its name from the medieval priory of St Mary Spital, which stood on the site of Spital Square. In the seventeenth century, the local population was swelled by Huguenot refugees, many of them silk-weavers. Their influence can still be seen in the rows of Georgian houses in Elder Street and Fournier Street, where the unusually large attic windows were designed to let in as much daylight as possible. Nicholas Hawksmoor's baroque masterpiece, Christ Church, was built in Commercial Street between 1714 and 1729 to serve the growing community.

The silk-weaving industry declined steadily from the early nineteenth century, and from then on much of Spitalfields consisted

A line of men waiting for the Whitechapel Workhouse to open in 1902. The workhouse was visited by Dickens on a winter night in 1855; finding a destitute woman outside he gave her a shilling to buy a night's lodging elsewhere.

Among those who have described the poverty of the East End is the Jewish poet Isaac Rosenberg (1890–1918), who went to school in Stepney until he was 14 and was then apprenticed as an engraver to an 'art publisher' and later trained at the Slade School. A Ballad Of Whitechapel, *describes the poverty and the chaos of the area.*

I watched the gleams
of jagged warm lights on shrunk faces pale.
I heard mad laughter as one hears in dreams,
Or Hell's harsh lurid tale.

The traffic rolled,
A gliding chaos populous of din.
A steaming wail at doom the Lord had scrawled
For perilous loads of sin.

of slum housing. However, the silk-weaving continued, in a much reduced form, until recent times. In ER Braithwaite's *To Sir, with Love*, published in 1959, Patrick Fernman comes from a family of Jewish silk-weavers who live 'in a neat walk-up flat in Jubilee Street'. In the course of the book, Patrick is stabbed with a knife used by his grandmother 'for cutting away tiny shreds of knotted silk during her weaving. It was always kept razor-sharp by a barber at Shadwell.'

Commercial Street runs crookedly between Whitechapel High Street and Shoreditch. Although much of Whitechapel and Spitalfields have been redeveloped, Commercial Street still retains some of the atmosphere of the Victorian East End. At night, the 'magnificent threat' (Iain Sinclair's phrase) of the illuminated Christ Church forms an exalted contrast to the darkened street below, with its sporadic late traffic, all-night mobile snack bar outside the church railings, and the street-walkers – among the last in London – who still ply their dangerous trade on this traditional stamping ground.

In *Hawksmoor* (1985) Peter Ackroyd creates an alternative East End, in which Christ Church is the work of Nicholas Dyer, an architect and secret devil-worshipper. Dyer escapes from his parents' plague-infected home off Brick Lane and goes on to design and build a series of churches, ostensibly Christian but in fact dedicated to Satan. The version of Christ Church in the novel is an amalgam of Christ Church at Spitalfields and St Anne's in Lime-house, but Ackroyd's description of 'the massive bulk which seemed to block off the ends of certain streets' is unmistakably Christ Church. (However, the mysterious pyramid, which in the novel marks the entrance to an underground labyrinth, can be seen in the churchyard of St Anne's.) In Iain Sinclair's *Downriver*, two film-makers visit a synagogue in Princelet Street, off Commercial Street, and climb on to the parapet to 'sit and watch the sun move behind the Portland dagger of Christ Church, and on to illuminate the Babylonian advance of the City's jagged towers'. As a child in the 1930s, the composer Lionel Bart, best remembered for his musical adaptation *Oliver!*, lived in a flat above what is now an off-licence on the corner of Princelet Street (west side) and Brick Lane. On summer evenings, Bart would climb on to the roof to get away from his quarrelling parents.

Some streets in Spitalfields seem to have been frozen in time for a century or more – none more than Brune Street, on the west side of Commercial Street. Ernest Stadler's 1913 poem 'Children in Front of a London Soup Kitchen' could have been written about the Brune Street Soup Kitchen for the Jewish Poor, which has miraculously been left almost untouched by developers.

They waited: soon the others
would be through, they'd be
admitted to the hall,
Served with bread and
vegetables, the soup in the
cups and all.
Oh, and then they'd grow
sleepy and their twisted
limbs would be untied.
And night and good sleep
would bring them to
rocking horses, to
Soldiers, the rooms of
marvellous dolls' houses
open wide.

The extreme poverty that Jack London witnessed in these streets almost exactly a century ago has never entirely gone away. The

Christ Church Spitalfields, as seen from Brushfield Street, which features in Peter Ackroyd's novel Hawksmoor.

The Soup Kitchen for the Jewish Poor. The atmosphere of the East End when there were a large number of Jewish residents is described by Israel Zangwill in Children of the Ghetto.

Tenter Ground, a few yards from the scene of the first Jack the Ripper murder in 1888.

Soup Kitchen was open as recently as the 1980s – as was Tower House, in Fieldgate Street. Known locally as the Monster Doss House, Tower House opened as a hostel for the homeless in Victorian times. Jack London mentions it in *The People of the Abyss*, and Stalin and Lenin stayed there in 1907 while attending the Fifth Congress of the Russian Social Democratic Labour Party in Fulbourne Street. In *Downriver* Tower House is described as 'a red-brick leviathan, studded with portholes. An Imperial fantasy: Wembley Stadium set in a grassless desert.'

ER Braithwaite's *To Sir, with Love*, set just after the Second World War, is the story of a West Indian teacher who goes to teach in an East End school. The book begins on the edge of the East End, on a bus 'inching its way through the snarl of traffic in Aldgate' (no change there), then swinging round Gardiner's Corner (now a

concrete round-about) just off Whitechapel High Street and into Commercial Road: a 'fleeting panorama of dingy shopfronts and cafés with brave large superscriptions telling of faraway places ... an international maypole with the name ribbons of Greece and Israel, Poland and China, Germany and Belgium, India and Russia, and many others; Semmelweiss and Smaile, Schultz and ChinYen, Smith, Seibt and Litobaraki'. Half a century on, the

character of Commercial Road is overwhelmingly Bangladeshi, though the occasional Jewish name survives above the myriad wholesale clothing businesses between Adler Street and Sidney Street. Some of the offshoots of Commercial Road remain recognizable – Watney Street is still a 'small dingy thoroughfare of small shops' – but the gaping bomb sites and Elizabethan-sounding goodies that Braithwaite found at the main crossroads have long since disappeared:

I crossed Commercial Road at the traffic lights into New Road... The few remaining buildings, raped and outraged, were still partly occupied, the missing glass panes replaced by clapboard or brightly coloured squares of tinplate, advertising Brylcreem, Nugget Shoe Polish and Palm Toffee. There was rubble everywhere, and dirt and flies. And there were smells.

The smells arose from everything, everywhere, flowing together and remaining as a sickening, tantalizing discomfort. They flowed from the delicatessen shop with its uncovered trays of pickled herrings, and the small open casks of pickled gherkins and onions, dried fish and salted meats, and sweaty damp walls and floor; from the fish shop which casually defied every law of health; from the Kosher butcher, and the poulterer next door where a fine confetti of new-plucked feathers hung nearly motionless in the fetid air; and from sidewalk gutters where multitudes of flies

buzzed and feasted on the heaped-up residue of fruit and vegetable barrows.

In December 1910 a group of anarchists shot and killed three policemen during a robbery at a Houndsditch jewellers. The following month the gang was traced to a tenement flat at 100 Sidney Street, off Commercial Road. The house was surrounded by armed police and a contingent of Scots Guards from the nearby Tower of London, and in the five-hour shootout which followed, the anarchists were killed and the house was burnt down. The Siege of Sidney Street, which was witnessed by the then Home Secretary Winston Churchill, was caricatured in Joe Orton's screenplay *Up Against It* (1967), but the film, intended for the Beatles, was shelved after Orton's sudden death. A more sober account of the siege is given in Emanuel Litvinoff's novel *A Death out of Season* (1973).

The 'Monster Doss House' in Fieldgate Street, described by Jack London (1902) and Iain Sinclair (1991).

CHAPTER 4

SOUTH LONDON

◆

RICHMOND AND BARNES

Originally a group of riverside fishermen's cottages, Richmond was called Sheen until Henry VII rebuilt a local manor house and named it after his estate in Yorkshire. As the manor house expanded to become Richmond Palace, the whole area prospered. Pageants and tournaments were held on Richmond Green, and courtiers built fine houses for themselves near the palace, particularly in Old Palace Terrace, Old Palace Place and Maids of Honour Row.

The Edinburgh-born poet James Thomson was enchanted by the view from Richmond Hill. 'Heavens! What a goodly prospect spreads around, of hills, and dales, and woods, and lawn, and spires, and glittering towns, and gilded streams,' he wrote in 1727. Thomson's civil service salary enabled him to buy a cottage near Kew Foot Road, where Fanny Burney, John Gay and Alexander Pope were among his visitors. Ironically, given his earlier encomium, he died from a chill after a boat trip on the river. The vista he described so enthusiastically has changed comparatively little, especially from Terrace Gardens, at the foot of Friars Stile Road.

In the 1720s, the poet and dramatist John Gay was a frequent guest of the Duke and Duchess of Queensberry at Douglas House, off Petersham Road, where he used the summer house as a study. Dickens and his wife Catherine spent the summer of 1839 at Elm Cottage (now Elm Lodge) in Petersham Road, where he wrote his monthly instalments of *Nicholas Nickleby* and posted them off to London to be printed. He also took early morning swims from the cottage to Richmond Bridge and went on an excursion to Eel Pie Island, the river islet, where he and his family enjoyed a 'cold collation, bottled beer, shrub, and shrimps' – an excursion which found its way into that month's number of *Nicholas Nickleby*.

An early morning view from Richmond Hill (opposite).

Late Victorian scullers near Richmond Bridge. Jerome K Jerome's comic classic Three Men in a Boat *(1889) features three lazy London clerks who set out from Kingston, a few miles upstream, to spend a fortnight on the Thames.*

The 'goodly prospect' from Richmond Hill is much as James Thomson knew it in the 1720s.

It was while he was in Richmond that Dickens had the idea for a weekly periodical, to be edited by himself, which became *Master Humphrey's Clock*. He also made frequent trips to London, to meet among others the actor William Charles Macready and the philanthropist Angela Burdett-Coutts, with whom he later set up a home for fallen women.

George Eliot's sojourn in Richmond was altogether less sociable. When, in October 1855, she and her partner George Henry Lewes set up house at 8 Parkshot, they deliberately avoided almost all contact with their neighbours – not because they were anti-social by nature, but because they knew that the neighbours would soon turn on them if they knew about their 'irregular' relationship. (Eliot and Lewes were not only *not* husband and wife, but Lewes was still married to his adulterous wife Agnes.) It was about this time that she adopted the Eliot pseudonym, to prevent further damage to her reputation if her novels turned out to be failures. She wrote *Adam Bede* and the early chapters of *The Mill on the Floss* in Richmond, before moving with Lewes to Wandsworth in 1859.

In his early twenties, Patrick Hamilton was a regular visitor to Richmond, especially its pubs. One evening, after he and a friend had refreshed themselves with the huge glasses of port served at the Greyhound, they rang repeatedly at the door of the Girls' Friendly Society. When someone eventually answered, Hamilton explained, 'You've got girls, and we want to be friendly.' When the door was slammed in his face, Hamilton tottered further down the road to a laundry, where he demanded to be washed.

The Hogarth Press, which Leonard and Virginia Woolf founded in 1915, was intended partly as a form of therapy for Virginia, who since childhood had suffered a series of mental breakdowns, culminating in a suicide attempt in 1913. The press was named after their new home, Hogarth House in Paradise Road. The printing press itself was bought in Farringdon Road, near Fleet Street, on the proceeds of some Thackeray manuscripts which the Woolfs sold to an American library. The first book to bear the Hogarth Press imprint was a modest pamphlet, containing two stories ('Three Jews' by Leonard, and 'The Mark on the Wall' by Virginia), price, including postage, 1s 2d. Writing the story was a welcome respite from the long, difficult novel Virginia was then engaged on, *Night and Day*. 'I shall never forget the day I wrote the "Mark on the Wall" – all in a flash, as if flying, after being kept stone-breaking for months', she remembered in 1930. The Hogarth Press went on to publish Katherine Mansfield's *Prelude*, John Middleton Murry's *The Critic in Judgement* and Sigmund Freud's *Collected Works*, as well as Virginia's own novels. However, the Woolfs felt obliged to turn down James Joyce's *Ulysses*, guessing correctly that whoever published it would be prosecuted for obscenity.

Wartime conditions in Hogarth House were difficult. During Zeppelin raids the Woolfs would sleep in the basement, Leonard on the kitchen table, Virginia underneath it. Her diary entry for Armistice Day 1918 was memorable:

Monday, November 11th. Twenty-five minutes ago the guns went off, announcing peace. A siren hooted on the river. They are hooting still. A few people ran to look out of windows. The rooks wheeled round and wore for a moment the symbolic look of creatures performing some ceremony, partly of thanksgiving, partly of valediction over the grave... So far neither bells nor flags, but the wailing of sirens and intermittent guns.

In the same month, TS Eliot visited the Woolfs at Hogarth House for the first time; 'that strange young man' was Virginia's verdict. In June 1922, however, he was invited back to Hogarth House, where he recited a poem he had been working on for the last eighteen months. As Virginia recalled,

He sang it and chanted it and rhythmed it. It has great beauty and force of phrase; symmetry; and tensity. What connects it together, I'm not so sure. But he read till he had to rush – letters to write about the London Magazine – and discussion thus was curtailed. One was left, however, with some strong emotion.

The Waste Land was published by the Hogarth Press the following year, shortly before the Woolfs left Richmond to move to 52 Tavistock Square.

George Eliot spent four reclusive years at 8 Parkshot, Richmond, in the 1850s.

Barnes, on the far side of the Kew peninsula, is the archetypal English village, its central pond surrounded by eighteenth-century houses and dark, welcoming pubs which seem to have been transplanted from deep within the English countryside. Henry Fielding bought Milbourne House, facing the pond, in 1748. The next year would be the most momentous of Fielding's life: he was appointed magistrate at Bow Street (see Covent Garden), where he managed to reverse the area's slide into total lawlessness, and he enjoyed an enormous popular

Henry Fielding wrote one of his most successful novels, Amelia, *at Milbourne House in 1752.*

success with his novel *Tom Jones*, which James Boswell claimed to have 'read through without stopping'. (Boswell's mentor, Samuel Johnson, was less charitable, calling the novel 'vicious' and its author 'a blockhead'.) Sadly, Fielding's health was already failing as a result of a variety of ailments, including chronic gout and asthma. He died in 1854, on a rest cure in Lisbon, and was buried in the English cemetery there.

CLAPHAM

Like so many districts of London, Clapham was a peaceful village well away from the metropolis, until its population was swelled by refugees from the plague and the Great Fire of London. Samuel Pepys, who remained in the City during both disasters, retired to Clapham in 1700, where he shared a house with William Hewer, his former servant, who is mentioned regularly in his diary (1660–69). John Evelyn wrote in his own diary: 'I went to visit Mr Pepys, at Clapham, where he has a very noble and wonderfully well-furnished house, especially with India and China curiosities. The offices and gardens [are] well accommodated for pleasure and retirement.' The house was on the site of The Elms, at 29 North Side, which was occupied by the nineteenth-century architect Sir Charles Barry, co-designer of the Palace of Westminster. Pepys died in 1703 and was buried in Seething Lane.

In the eighteenth century, a group of local evangelists and exponents of active Christianity became known as the Clapham Sect. The group worshipped at Holy Trinity Church, near The Pavement, and numbered, among others, Zachary Macaulay, father of the historian Thomas Macaulay, who lived at 5 The Pavement; William Wilberforce, whose house, Broomfield, was on the south-east

charm Clapham Common'. In *Psmith and the City* (1910), PG Wodehouse's eponymous Old Etonian manages to persuade his reluctant friend Mike to take an excursion there to listen to the political speeches on the common:

'The first thing to do,' said Psmith, 'is to ascertain that such a place as Clapham Common really exists. One has heard of it, of course, but has its existence ever been proved? I think not. Having accomplished that, we must then try to find out how to get to it. I should say at a venture that it would necessitate a sea-voyage. On the other hand, Comrade Waller, who is a native of the spot, seems to find no difficulty in rolling to the office every morning. Therefore – you follow me, Jackson? – it must be in England. In that case, we will take a taximeter cab, and go out into the unknown, hand in hand, trusting to luck.'

*H*oly Trinity Church was the headquarters of the Clapham Sect, whose members included Zachary Macaulay, William Wilberforce (the anti-slavery pioneer), and James Stephen.

*N*ovelist Pamela Hansford Johnson (1912–81) was born and educated in Clapham, and several of her novels make dramatic used of the area, particularly the common (below), including An Impossible Marriage and An Error of Judgement.

edge of Clapham Common, near present-day Broomwood Road (he had an opium addiction which rivalled Coleridge's but was considerably less publicised); and James Stephen, who was the great-grandfather of Virginia Woolf. In 1811, 16-year-old Harriet Westbrook was attending a school on the common. Among her fellow pupils were the sisters of Percy Bysshe Shelley. Harriet was introduced to the young poet, who had just been expelled from Oxford for writing an anti-religious pamphlet, and eloped with him to Scotland, but she later committed suicide (see Kensington).

Clapham's village atmosphere, with its common and its dignified Queen Anne houses is little changed today. In *The Newcomes* (1855), Thackeray declared that 'of all the pretty suburbs that still adorn our metropolis, there are few that exceed in

Graham Greene, whose career as a novelist spanned almost 60 years, from The Man Within *(1929) to* The Captain and the Enemy *(1988), published when he was 84.*

'I expect you could get there by tram,' said Mike.

Psmith suppressed a slight shudder.

'I fear, Comrade Jackson,' he said, 'that the old noblesse oblige traditions of the Psmiths would not allow me to do that. No. We will stroll gently, after a light lunch, to Trafalgar Square, and hail a taxi.'

Later, after the meeting has descended into a free-for-all, Psmith and Mike are invited to Mr Waller's home, 'one of a row of semi-detached villas on the north side of the Common', where they endure one of the most excruciating dinner parties in comic literature.

In 1935, Graham Greene and his wife Vivien moved into 14 North Side, one of the eighteenth-century houses overlooking Clapham Common. Greene wrote enthusiastically to his mother:

The whole appearance of Clapham Common is lovely, like a wide green plateau on a hilltop above Battersea, with the common stretching out of sight in one direction, and on three sides surrounded by little country-like shops and Queen Anne houses, a pond and in the middle of the Common, the eighteenth-century church to which the Clapham set belonged.

Number 14 North Side would be the last home in which Greene and his wife lived together. The house was destroyed by an incendiary bomb in 1940, by which time Vivien and the couple's young son and daughter were living in Oxford, and Greene was doing nightly duty as an ARP warden in Gower Street (see Fitzrovia). But 14 North Side was destined to make two appearances, barely disguised, in Greene's fiction. In *The End of the Affair* (1951) Sarah lives with her husband at 17 North Side, while the narrator, Bendrix, lives at 14 South Side. After assignations with Sarah, Bendrix watches 'her torch trail across to the opposite side of the Common like the tail-light of a slow car driving away'. In the novel, Bendrix's house, like Greene's, receives a direct hit during an air raid. One night Bendrix follows Sarah around Clapham, waiting for the opportunity to tell her to leave her husband. He eventually tracks her down at 'the church at the corner of Park Road' – clearly St Mary's – where she is 'sitting in one of the side aisles close to a pillar and a hideous statue of the Virgin'.

Greene's disturbing short story 'The Destructors' (1954) seemed to revel in the destruction of his former marital home. In the story an elderly man lives in a Queen Anne house which has been damaged in the Blitz. The house is invaded by a gang of youths, who systematically dismantle it from within. When Vivien Greene read the story, she wept.

BATTERSEA

The original name was Batrices Ege (Batric's Island), coined when the original Anglo-Saxon settlement was surrounded by marshland. The fertile soil made Battersea famous for its market gardens, and its agricultural past is recalled in some of the local street names – Lavender Hill, Plough Road, Sheepcote Lane. Catherine Boucher, the wife of William Blake, was the daughter of Battersea market gardeners who had fallen on hard times. Blake was visiting her parents, who were distant relatives on his father's

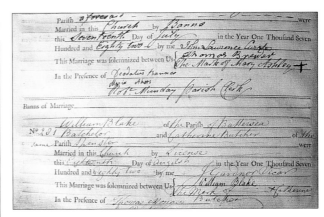

side, and as soon as he came in the room Catherine, as she told a friend, 'instantly recognized her future partner' and 'was so near fainting that she left his presence until she had recovered'. They were married at St Mary's Church, by the river, Catherine signing the register with a '+', suggesting that she was illiterate or perhaps merely embarrassed by her poor handwriting. It was an enduring and loving marriage, though on one occasion Catherine told an acquaintance, 'I have very little of Mr Blake's company. He is always in Paradise.'

From the mid-nineteenth century, Battersea's fields and market gardens began to disappear under small factories, terraced houses and the miles of railway lines threading their way into central London. By the turn of the

The signature of William Blake, and the '+' of his bride Catherine, can be seen in the marriage register of St Mary's Church, Battersea.

Catherine Blake, sketched by her husband William Blake. She was described by Edith Sitwell as 'the most wonderful wife who has ever comforted and supported a man of genius'.

century, Clapham Junction station was the busiest in the world, with more than 2,000 trains passing through daily.

On 21 November 1895, Clapham Junction was the scene of the most degrading moment of Oscar Wilde's downfall. Convicted of indecency and sodomy, he was initially

'I can see now the gloomy Battersea Park Road, newly set with electric arc-lamps, tall, futurist standards, that began to hiss and splutter at dusk, and needed no kindling by a man with a pole, as did the homely gas-lamps in our side-streets.' Richard Church, Over the Bridge (1955).

imprisoned at Wandsworth prison, then brought to the station to be transferred to Reading. Standing on the platform in his prison uniform, he was recognized by bystanders, and for half an hour, as he waited for the train to arrive, he was jeered and spat at by the crowd. He wrote in *De Profundis*: 'For a year after that was done to me, I wept every day at the same hour and for the same space of time.'

Richard Church's lyrical autobiography *Over the Bridge* opens on 1 January 1900, with Church, then aged seven, and his brother Jack slowly and painstakingly carrying a fish tank (with goldfish) over Battersea Bridge – the gift of a family acquaintance in Chelsea – and growing increasingly nervous as they near home: 'I knew that, once across the bridge, we were likely to encounter school-fellows, bands of marauding freebooters of the Battersea gutters, ripe for any action, so long as it was destructive. I knew that the sight of a large glass aquarium in the arms of a boy somewhat more warmly dressed than themselves would rouse their hunting gusto.' In the event, the brothers managed to escape a crowd of curious and hostile boys, but only because their would-be attackers were distracted by a more dramatic sight: a navvy and his wife engaged in a drunken pavement brawl.

Church, whose father was a Post Office worker and his mother an elementary school teacher, lived near Surrey Street, between Battersea Park and St Mary's Church. He gives a vivid eye-witness account of working-class Battersea at the very beginning of the twentieth century:

The little streets had a character that made me think of sailors rather than industrial workers. This may have been caused by the tidal waters of the Thames that ebbed and flowed round the parish, giving it a strand of mud enlivened with washed pebbles, and salt-breasted gulls that screamed as though a herring-fleet were coming in.

The streets, too, aided the illusion, for most of the householders maintained the practice of lime-washing their yards, front and back, and even the lower courses of the house-walls, to preserve the health of their copious livestock: rabbits, poultry, pigeons, and even goats. The effect of this was to give the impression of sailors ashore; of holystone and white-scrubbed decks, of painted masts, of furled sails and gleaming port-holes.

Church's description of Battersea nights, when the soft London gaslight so evocative of Dickens and Conan Doyle, was beginning to be replaced with a harsher form of illumination is also memorable:

The lamp-lighter was a half-fairy figure, always followed by a number of children who danced about him and shouted with glee when he stopped at a lamp, flipped open a little glass trap-door at the bottom of the lantern, pushed his brass-topped pole into it, and kindled a fish-tail flame that flashed into life with a pop like a bursting balsam-seed. Then the magician, with his chorus of urchins, went on to the next lamp-post, the flame inside the brass head of his caduceus flickering, but never quite expiring.

Intriguingly, two classic ghost stories, Edward Bulwer-Lytton's 'The Haunted and the Haunters' (1859) and Henry James's 'The Jolly Corner' (1906) both include scenes in which narrators, terrified almost beyond endurance by

supernatural events in houses, derive momentary comfort by looking out of the window at the reassuring gas lamps flickering in the street.

Graham Greene first got to know Battersea in 1926, when he was living at his aunt's house in the area and working at night as a special constable during the General Strike. 'The river's lovely at that time,' he wrote to his future wife Vivien. 'Chelsea Bridge, with the light of the police boat creeping fearfully quietly along the edge. You can't see the boat at all, only the light, until it's right up

'The stranded barges and the paper mill...the blackened chimneys of Lots Road.' Graham Greene, The Ministry of Fear *(1943).*

underneath you, and then you just get one glimpse of two mysterious muffled figures sitting very stiff like Egyptian Kings in the stern and then it's gone again. Absolutely no noise but the stir in the water.'

He wrote vividly of Battersea in *It's a Battlefield*, his panoramic thirties novel of London life: 'The trams came screeching like a finger drawn on glass up the curve of Battersea Bridge and down into the ill-lighted network of streets beyond; on the water the gulls floated asleep.'

Set in wartime London, *The Ministry of Fear* (1943) was written in Sierra Leone, where Greene was working for military intelligence. In the novel his amnesiac hero Rowe finds his way to a friend's home, in a block of

flats overlooking Battersea Park, from which 'the war came back into sight. Most of the church spires seemed to have been snapped off two-thirds up like sugar sticks, and there was an appearance of slum clearance where there hadn't really been any slums.' Afterwards Rowe walks along the riverside edge of Battersea Park towards Chelsea Bridge, where he meets a vaguely sinister man who 'took a piece of bread and threw it towards the mud. Before it had reached the river the gulls had risen: one out-distanced the others, caught it and sailed on, past the stranded barges and the paper mill, a white scrap blown towards the blackened chimneys of Lots Road.' More than half a century on, the view is unchanged, except that the paper mill is now a recycling plant.

Battersea Park also appears in Iris Murdoch's *Under the Net* (1954), in which Jake Donaghue and Hugo Belfounder meet regularly on Chelsea Bridge before going drinking in the King's Road. Jake arranges to meet Hugo in the usual place but, guilty about appropriating some of his philosophical theories for a book of his own, is unable to face his friend.

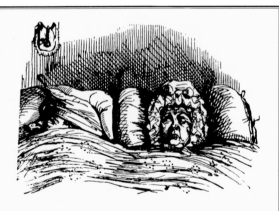

A Charles Keene illustration from Douglas Jerrold's Mrs Caudle's Curtain Lectures *(1845). The lectures are doled out by the nagging Mrs Caudle every night to her long-suffering husband Job. The lectures provide a wealth of information about the mores and attitudes of everyday Victorian London. They also tell us about the geography of nineteenth-century London, which was very different, with places like Battersea and Hornsey being regarded as villages outside of the city. On this occasion, Mrs Caudle is discussing where they should have an out of town cottage:*

'What do you say to Hornsey or Muswell Hill? Eh? Too high? What a man you are! Well then—Battersea? Too low? You're an aggravating creature, Caudle, you must own that! Hampstead, then? Too cold? Nonsense...'

Our appointment was at five-thirty. I spent the afternoon drinking brandy – and about five o'clock I went out into Battersea Park. A sort of calm had descended on me, as I knew now that I should not meet Hugo that day, or any other day ever again. A tragic fascination drew me to the riverside, from which I could see the bridge. I sat on a seat and smoked two cigarettes. Hugo walked up and down. After a while longer I saw him

*cross the bridge to the south
bank and I knew he was going
to my lodgings. I lighted
another cigarette. Half an
hour later I saw him walk
slowly back across the bridge
and disappear.*

PECKHAM

Nowadays one of the less glamorous districts of south London, Peckham has an unexpectedly rich literary history. As a child in the 1760s, the poet William Blake had the first of his many 'visions', or hallucinations, on Peckham Rye Common – then open farmland, used for grazing cattle. During one of the long walks he took in and around London when he was about ten, he looked up to see an oak tree full of angels, their 'bright angelic wings bespangling every bough like stars'. Back home in Soho he recounted the experience to his parents, and it was only through his mother's intervention that he escaped a thrashing from his father for telling a lie. Blake's vision is now depicted in a mural on the east side of Goose Green, near Hinckley Road.

In the summer of 1867, Charles Dickens rented 16 Linden Grove, under the name Charles Tringham. The house was intended not for him but for his long-standing companion, the actress Ellen Ternan, though he did write some of *The Mystery of Edwin Drood* here.

The location was highly convenient for Dickens. Peckham was sufficiently far from central London to constitute a discreet bolt-hole, but the railway stations which opened the following year at both Peckham Rye and Nunhead

meant that Ellen's house was within easy reach of his office in Wellington Street (see Strand). In addition, Dickens had been using another set of lodgings, opposite the Five Bells pub on the corner of New Cross Road and Hatcham Park Road, for some years as a place where he could work in peace. Part of *Great Expectations* had been written there.

The local geography has changed little, although the fields which once surrounded Linden Grove have since been engulfed by the massive Nunhead Cemetery. It's tempting to think of Dickens, an inveterate London walker, strolling from Hatcham Park Road to Linden Grove via Pepys Road –

During the last decade of his life, Dickens rented lodgings near the Five Bells pub in New Cross Road.

the most direct route, though with a punishingly steep hill which Dickens, no longer in good health, may have avoided. What is actually known, through Peter Ackroyd's assiduous research, is that on 22 June 1867 he waited for Ellen for some time outside 16 Linden Grove to show her the property.

Peckham makes one of its few appearances in fiction in Muriel Spark's *The Ballad of Peckham Rye* (1960). The novel tells the story of one Dougal Douglas – actually the devil incarnate – who spreads mayhem among the local citizens. On the first page of the novel, one of Dougal's victims, Humphrey Place, whom Dougal has goaded into deserting his fiancée at the altar, embarks on an epic pub crawl which can still be followed today. Starting at the Rye Hotel (31 Peckham Rye), Humphrey crosses the road to the White Horse (29 Peckham Rye), then goes to the Morning Star (231 Rye Lane), the Heaton Arms (249 Rye Lane) and the Harbinger, which is probably based on the Hope (corner of Elm Grove, in Rye Lane). It's here that

Humphrey runs into his best man, Trevor Lomas, and the pair begin a fight which continues outside the Rye Hotel (the open-air swimming baths closed in 1999).

Two courting couples returning from the dusky scope of the Rye's broad lyrical acres stepped to the opposite pavement, leant on the railings by the swimming baths, and watched. Eventually the fighters, each having suffered equal damage to different features of the face, were parted by onlookers to save the intervention of the police.

DULWICH

In 1605, Edward Alleyn, who had made his fortune as an actor and bear-baiting impresario on Bankside, bought the manor house of Dulwich for £5,000. In 1613, he founded a local school, which since 1870 has been called Dulwich College. Much expanded over the years, the school's spectacular terracotta buildings, all pinnacles and towers, stand in extensive grounds in College Road. Among the distinguished Old Alleynians, as past pupils are called, was Raymond Chandler, who was born in Chicago in 1888 but educated in England. Chandler returned to America in 1912, and worked successfully in the oil industry before learning his craft as a crime writer in the 1930s.

As the creator of Jeeves, Bertie

'The dusky scope of the Rye's broad lyrical acres.' Muriel Spark, The Ballad of Peckham Rye, *1960.*

Wooster, Psmith, Ukridge et al. PG Wodehouse prided himself on writing books which had no message whatsoever. He is probably the greatest writer of humorous prose in the language, though the Irish playwright Sean O'Casey famously dismissed him as 'English literature's performing flea'. Wodehouse took the phrase as a compliment and used it as the title of his autobiography.

Wodehouse, who attended Dulwich College from 1894 to 1900, is practically unique among writers in that he enjoyed every moment of his schooldays. This was partly because he was athletic – as has often been said, no schoolboy who is good at games is ever unpopular. Wodehouse was offered additional incentives to shine on the cricket field. His father established a highly organized tipping system on a sliding scale: five shillings for six wickets, ten shillings for 50, a pound for a century. Wodehouse's 1899 school report predicted the shape of things to come: 'He has the most distorted ideas about wit

and humour; he draws over his books and examination papers in the most distressing way and writes foolish rhymes in other people's books. Notwithstanding, he has a genuine interest in literature and can often talk with much enthusiasm and good sense about it. He does some things at times astonishingly well, and writes good Latin verses.' The language of Bertie Wooster is a hotch-potch of half-remembered Latin tags and classical allusions, the detritus of a public school education. Bertie's governing ethic – a chap must never let down his pals, whatever the cost to himself – also has its roots firmly in the public school system to which Bertie and his idiotic chums ('Bingo' Little, 'Stilton' Cheesewright, the newt-fancier Gussie Fink-Nottle and the rest) owe their allegiance and homage.

In his early novel *Psmith in the City* (1910), the intensity of Wodehouse's feelings about school

Unlike most, PG Wodehouse (left) really did believe his schooldays at Dulwich College (above) were the happiest days of his life. He once commented 'to me the years between 1894 and 1900 were like heaven'.

in general, and Dulwich College in particular, are explicit. Wodehouse's hero Mike has left his own public school, Wrykyn, but because of a downturn in his father's fortunes he must abandon his plans to go to university and instead earn a living in the City. On his first evening in London, Mike decides to take lodgings in Dulwich, 'principally because there was a school at Dulwich, and it would be a comfort being near a school'. After taking lodgings in Acacia Road (actually Acacia Grove), then, as now, a street of respectable nineteenth-century houses, Mike wanders towards Dulwich College. There he finds the gate by the railway bridge unlocked (just as he would today) and sits on a bench, contemplating the cricket and football fields. 'Up till now the excitement of a strange venture had borne him up; but the cricket-field and the pavilion reminded him so sharply of Wrykyn. They brought home to him, with a cutting distinctness, the absolute finality of his break with the old order of things. Summers would come and go, matches would be played on this ground with all the glory of big

scores and keen finishes; but he was done.' For Mike, as for Wodehouse, leaving one's school is like an expulsion from Eden.

Dulwich village, about a quarter of a mile from the college, was little more than a hamlet until the eighteenth century, when Dulwich Wells (near the corner of Dulwich Common and Lordship Lane) became a popular spa and the settlement began to expand. Mr Pickwick retires to Dulwich at the end of *The Pickwick Papers* (1836), where, Dickens tells us, he 'may still be frequently seen, contemplating the pictures in the Dulwich Gallery, or enjoying a walk about the pleasant neighbourhood on a fine day'. Dulwich picture gallery, like the college, was founded by Edward Alleyn and its first exhibits came from his personal collection. In *Over the Bridge* the poet and novelist Richard Church describes the village in the 1900s, when he was a pupil at Dulwich Hamlet School: 'Towering over both the tall villas and the low cottages stood the ancient trees, so close and abundant that the whole village had the character of being abandoned at the bottom of a canyon green in summer, and brown in winter.'

SYDENHAM AND CRYSTAL PALACE

Isolated, thickly forested Sydenham was barely known until the mid-seventeenth century, when healthful springs were found in what is now Sydenham Wells Park. In the nineteenth century, much of the former common land was covered by tracts of suburban housing. The writer and naturalist Richard Jefferies lived at 20 Sydenham Park Road in the 1880s. His best-known book *Bevis, The Story of a Boy* (1882) was an idyllic evocation of his Wiltshire boyhood, but *After London* (1885) was less comforting. In it, the city has reverted to swampland, the Thames is a vast lake and the surrounding forests are inhabited by vicious dwarfs.

In 1854 the Crystal Palace was removed from its original site in Hyde Park, where it had been used to house the Great Exhibition, and rebuilt at Anerley Hill. As the focal point of Crystal Palace Park, the vast glass building was variously used as a theatre, concert hall and exhibition centre. Charles Dickens came to Crystal Palace with the music critic and novelist Henry Chorley to hear Arthur Sullivan's music for *The Tempest*, then walked back to Chorley's home in Knightsbridge – a distance of some ten miles.

The Canary Wharf Tower of its day, the glinting form of the Crystal Palace could be glimpsed from all over London. John Ruskin, in Herne Hill, was unimpressed, complaining that the building had 'no more sublimity than a cucumber frame' and mourning 'the ghastly squalor of the once lovely fields of Dulwich', which had been churned to mire by the daily influx of visitors. In the 1900s, VS Pritchett could see it from Dulwich village, 'like a sad and empty conservatory', while DH Lawrence, who taught in a school in Croydon, four miles away, described it as a fairy-like blue bubble. The building burnt down in 1936, but the huge replica dinosaurs dotted around the lake in Crystal Place Park, have survived. Designed by the sculptor Waterhouse Hawkins, from designs supplied by the Victorian palaeontologist Sir Richard Owen, the dinosaurs were constructed from brick and iron and covered in stucco. Shortly before they were completed in 1854, a party for 20

The erection of Crystal Palace was celebrated in comic fashion by Thackeray:

With ganial foire,
Thransfuse me loyre,
Ye sacred nymphs of Pindus;
The while I sing
That wondrous thing,
The Palace made o' windows.

Say, Paxton, truth,
Thou wondrous youth,
What stroke of art celestial,
What power was lint
You to invint
This combination cristial?

guests was held inside the model iguanadon. The Poet Laureate Sir John Betjeman also had a fondness for the dinosaurs, which now enjoy the status of listed buildings.

HERNE HILL

In 1823, when he was four, John Ruskin and his parents moved from their home at 54 Hunter Street, Holborn, to a villa at 28 Herne Hill, with a large garden and country views. The Ruskin household was one of stern asceticism: Margaret Ruskin was a strict Puritan who thought toys sinful and, it was said, insisted that the pictures in the house be turned to face the wall on Sundays. Mother and son studied the Bible together, reading alternate verses aloud, she 'watching every intonation, allowing not so much as a syllable to be missed or mis-placed'. When they finally reached the last page, Mrs Ruskin began again at Genesis the next day.

John was encouraged to keep a diary and write his own verses, for which his parents paid him a shilling a page. When he was in his teens, the whole family began to travel together in Europe, by carriage – 'the golden days of travelling', as Ruskin called them

in *The Stones of Venice*, 'now to return no more'. The family tours would continue until his parents' deaths some 30 years later.

The house on Herne Hill remained the family home until 1842, when the Ruskins moved to 163 Denmark Hill, which stood in seven acres of land, including a stable and farmyard. By then, Ruskin was beginning to make his name as a writer on natural history, architecture and painting, par-ticularly the work of Turner and the Pre-Raphaelites. Ruskin's five-volume study *Modern Painters*, published between 1843 and 1860, sealed his reputation as the most influential art writer of his day, though his outspokenness made him many enemies in the art world. Whistler sued him for libel after Ruskin said of one of the *Nocturnes* that he 'never expected to hear a coxcomb ask for two hundred guineas for flinging a pot of paint in the public's face'. *Punch* once lambasted him using the persona of an exasperated artist:

I paints and paints,
Hears no complaints,
And sells before I'm dry;
Till savage Ruskin
Sticks his tusk in
And nobody will buy.

Ruskin's own comments on his working methods offer an insight into his character: 'I knew exactly what I had got to say, put the words firmly in their places like so many stitches, hemmed the edges of the chapters round with what seemed to me the graceful flourishes, touched them finally with my cunningest points of colour, and read the work to Papa and Mamma at breakfast next morning, as a girl shows her sampler,' he trilled. In 1848 he married Euphemia Chalmers Gray ('Effie') but the marriage was never consummated – apparently Ruskin, whose previous experience of naked women was confined to marble statuary, rejected her on their wedding night because he was dismayed by the sight of her pubic hair. After living for a while in Mayfair, Ruskin moved with his wife back to Herne Hill, where his father had bought them a house, 30 Herne Hill, next door to the former family home. Ruskin would work in the study at Denmark Hill every day, where his wife would join them for dinner. By 1854 Effie had begun an affair with the painter Millais, one of the Pre-Raphaelites whose work Ruskin had championed, and the marriage was annulled. Ruskin now moved permanently to 163 Denmark Hill, where he remained until his parents' deaths. In 1872 he moved to Brantwood, in Cumbria, where he was kept busy writing, lecturing and drawing. However, he led an isolated and unhappy existence. He became infatuated with a series of young girls, particularly Rose La Touche, who had come to him for drawing lessons. For the last decade of his life, he wrote nothing. 'Poor finger!' he said to a friend. 'It will never hold a pen again. Well, it has got me into so much trouble, perhaps it is better

so.' All three houses where Ruskin lived have been demolished, though he is commemorated by Ruskin Park, opposite the site of 163 Denmark Hill.

In 1905 Richard Church moved with his family from Battersea to a detached house in Herne Hill. Ruskin Walk was lined with aspen trees, with meadow land and derelict farm buildings beyond. As he recalled in *Over the Bridge* (1955), it was 'a little piece of country, stone-dead, waiting to be buried by the jerry builders. Similar patches of rural survival littered the district, gradually disappearing, with their hedges of hawthorn, their uncut grass, their nettle-beds, as the builders nibbled with teeth of brick and slaver of mortar.' His mother's death five years later, when Church was 17, marked an end of innocence both for him and for the land around him. *Over the Bridge* ends with the extraordinary image: 'I can hear still the crunching and stamping of wheels and horses' hooves, as the hearse bearing my mother's body turned from our front door, to be the first vehicle to cross the loose-metalled, newly-made road beside the house, watched reverently, cap in one hand, an axe in the other, by the workmen who were felling the aspen trees and silencing their music, the very music of the past.'

The poet and teacher Eric Mottram lived at 40 Guernsey Grove, Herne Hill, from 1972 until his death in 1995, where he wrote his best-known volume of poetry, *A Book of Herne* (1981).

John Ruskin (1819–1900) lived most of his life at 26 Herne Hill. A near neighbour at Number 51 was Arthur Henry Ward, alias Sax Rohmer, creator of the inscrutable underworld mastermind Fu Manchu.

THE BOROUGH

From Chaucer to Shakespeare, from Gower to Jonson and Keats, from Charles Dickens to Peter Ackroyd ... the Borough has seen them all. Its rich literary heritage has much to do with its position. For centuries, the Borough was, quite literally, a last staging post for travellers heading north across London Bridge to the City or, alternatively, a starting point for those journeying south, to Surrey, Kent and beyond.

Not surprisingly, Borough High Street was lined with inns – 'a continued ale house with not a shop to be seen between' was how the seventeenth-century playwright Thomas Dekker saw it. One of the most famous was the Tabard, which occupied what is now Talbot Yard, just off the High Street. Chaucer's pilgrims gather here at the beginning of the *Canterbury Tales*:

> *Bifil that in that*
> *seson on a day,*
> *In Southwerk at the*
> *Tabard as I lay*
> *Redy to wenden on*
> *my pilgrymage*
> *To Caunterbury with ful*
> *devout corage,*
> *At nyght was come into that*
> *hostelrye*
> *Wel nyne and twenty in a*
> *compaignye,*
> *Of sondry folk, by aventure*
> *yfalle*
> *In felaweship, and pilgrimes*
> *were they alle,*
> *That toward Caunterbury*
> *wolden ryde.*

It is the innkeeper at the Tabard who suggests that each pilgrim tells a story in order to while away the journey. The Tabard (the name refers to a

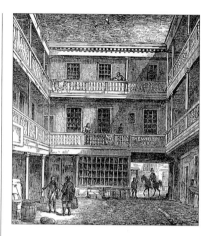

knight's sleeveless jacket) was destroyed in a fire in 1676, rebuilt, and finally demolished in 1873. A similar fate eventually befell one of its neighbours. The White Hart Inn, two streets away in White Hart Yard, was partially burnt down in 1669 and pulled down for good in 1889 – 56 years after Dickens, in *The Pickwick Papers*, had included it among 'some half-dozen old inns, which have preserved their external features unchanged, and which have escaped alike the rage for public improvement, and the encroachments of private speculation'. (Dickens was writing in 1833, when stagecoaches and coaching inns were already disappearing because of the railways.) It's at the White Hart that we first meet the resourceful Sam Weller, who becomes Mr Pickwick's faithful servant, polishing boots in the inn yard. Dickens's description of the yard, and the Phiz illustration that accompanied it, are now a valuable documentary record:

> *Three or four lumbering*
> *waggons, each with a pile of*
> *goods beneath its ample*
> *canopy, about the height of the*
> *second-floor window of an*
> *ordinary house, were stowed*

away beneath a lofty roof which extended over one end of the yard; and another, which was probably to commence its journey that morning, was drawn out into the open space. A double tier of bedroom galleries, with old clumsy balustrades, ran round two sides of the straggling area, and a double row of bells to correspond, sheltered from the weather by a little sloping roof, hung over the door leading to the bar and coffee-room. Two or three gigs and chaise-carts were wheeled up under different little sheds and pent-houses; and the occasional heavy tread of a cart-horse or rattling of a chain at the further end of the yard announced to anybody who cared about the matter, that the stable lay in that direction. When we add that a few boys in smock frocks were lying asleep on heavy packages, wool packs, and other articles that were scattered about on heaps of straw, we have described as fully as need be the general appearance of the yard of the White Hart Inn, High Street, Borough, on the particular morning in question.

Happily, a similar inn has survived. The George, in George Inn Yard, is London's only surviving galleried coaching inn. Before the Globe Theatre opened in 1599, plays were performed in the courtyard; as a young actor, Shakespeare himself is said to have performed from the back of a cart in the courtyard. The White Hart gets a mention in *Henry VI Part II:* the rebel leader Jack Cade sets up his headquarters there.

Southwark Fair, which occupied much of Borough High Street, as well as the side streets and various inn yards, was held every September from 1462 onwards. Like Bartholomew Fair in the City, it was famous for its performers and puppet shows, and was visited by the diarists John Evelyn and Samuel Pepys. Evelyn, who came in 1660, described the trained monkeys, who danced on ropes: 'They saluted one another with as good grace as if instructed by a dancing master; they turned heels over head with a basket having eggs in it without breaking any; also with lighted candles in their hands and on their heads without extinguishing them, and with vessels of water without spilling a drop.' Complaints from local shopkeepers, whose business

The George in Borough High Street, London's last galleried coaching inn. Shakespeare is said to have acted in plays staged in the courtyard here before The Globe was built.

was sorely affected, and high levels of petty crime finally led to the closure of the fair in 1763.

In October 1814, John Keats moved to the Borough to complete the medical training which would enable him to practise as an apothecary. This would, in essence, make him a GP to the poor, who could not afford the services of a fully qualified surgeon or physician. Keats's apprenticeship had begun in Edmonton when he was only 15, where his tasks included cleaning the surgery, making up prescriptions, attending post-mortems, bleeding, dressing wounds, extracting teeth and delivering babies. At Guy's Hospital, he was now required to attend lectures (his fellow students would later recall him sitting in the same window seat, staring into space 'in a deep poetic dream')

John Keats was a medical student at Guy's Hospital, but abandoned medicine in favour of poetry.

and observe operations. These were conducted in an amphitheatre, in a highly charged atmosphere. During major operations, the room would be crowded with students, pushing and shoving to get a good view; sometimes the surgeon had to clear a space around the patient. There was no anaesthetic other than alcohol, and as a surgeon's assistant, as he became later in his course, Keats's duties included holding down the patients and stifling their cries.

Conditions at Keats's lodgings, at 28 St Thomas Street, near the hospital gates, had a similarly medieval flavour. During the hot summer of 1816, a former resident, George Cooper, arranged for a corpse to be delivered there, so he could continue his anatomy studies. Not surprisingly, Keats swiftly found alternative accommodation, at 8 Dean Street – now Stainer Street, which is now almost completely concealed under one of the railway viaducts leading to London Bridge Station.

Keats's posthumous reputation as the swooning nancy-boy of English literature is not borne out by his activities in the Borough. He enjoyed snuff and cigars, played billiards, attended boxing matches, cockfights and bear-baitings and slept with local prostitutes, from whom he contracted at least one dose of venereal disease. Stocky and occasionally pugnacious, he never lost the cockney accent he acquired in his native Moorgate.

He was, however, beginning to write poetry. In May 1816, Leigh Hunt published one of his early efforts, 'To Solitude', in the *Examiner*, and from then on Keats began to spend more time on his verses and proportionately less studying for his medical examinations. 'To Solitude', written shortly after he arrived in the Borough, suggests he was lonely, at least at first, and the opening lines almost certainly refer to his surroundings:

> *O Solitude! if I must with*
> *thee dwell,*
> *Let it not be among the*
> *jumbled heap*
> *Of murky buildings...*

Keats's celebrated poem 'On First Looking into Chapman's Homer' was written in Dean Street in the summer of 1816. He had visited an old schoolfriend, Charles Cowden Clarke, at Clarke's lodgings in Clerkenwell, where the two young men had sat up all night reading George Chapman's translation of *The Iliad* and *The Odyssey*, first published in 1616. On his way home, Keats began to plan a sonnet, which he wrote up as soon as he returned to Dean Street at six o'clock in the morning. When he finished it, he gave it to a messenger to take to Clarke. The poem, with its famous opening line 'Much have I travelled in the realms of gold', duly arrived on Clarke's breakfast table at ten o'clock that morning.

A few weeks later, Keats had his first meeting with Leigh Hunt, at his home in the Vale of Health (see Hampstead). They had been near-neighbours in the Borough, though it was never likely that their paths would cross: Hunt had spent two years in Horsemonger Lane Prison (now the site of Newington Recreation Ground, off Harper Road) for insulting the Prince Regent ('a corpulent gentleman of fifty') in the pages of the *Examiner*. Hunt made the best of his captivity. He had his cell decorated with flowered wallpaper and the ceiling painted with the sky and fluffy clouds; there was a piano, and fresh flowers were delivered every few days. He also continued to edit the *Examiner* from his cell, but the experience of imprisonment had been more traumatic than he let on – for months after his release he refused to leave his house. Hunt and Keats hit it off from the outset, and it was largely because of Hunt's influence that Keats decided to abandon his medical career and make his living as a writer.

Horsemonger Lane was one of several local prisons which existed from medieval times until the mid-nineteenth century. The King's Bench Prison, near the present site of Little Dorrit Court, was used mainly for debtors and was renowned for its relaxed regime: inmates who could obtain money from friends and relatives could eat in style, and there were 30 gin shops within the prison grounds. The novelist Tobias Smollett spent three months at the King's Bench in 1759 – in his case for libel rather than debt (he had written an article in the *Critical Review*, which he edited, accusing Admiral Sir Charles Knowles of cowardice). While he was incarcerated, he wrote part of *The Life and Adventures of Sir Launcelot Greaves*. The tale, inspired by *Don Quixote*, which Smollett had translated, contains the memorable line, 'I think for my part one half of the nation is mad – and the

Keats's home in Stainer Street was obliterated during the expansion of London Bridge Station in the 1840s.

'Thirty years ago there stood, a few doors short of the church of Saint George, in the borough of Southwark, on the left-hand side of the way going southward, the Marshalsea Prison. It had stood there many years before, and it remained there some years afterwards; but it is gone now, and the world is none the worse without it.' Dickens, Little Dorrit, 1855.

Lant Street, where Dickens's lodgings were a few minutes' walk from his father's cell in the Marshalsea.

other half not very sound.'

Mermaid Court, off Borough High Street, is on the site of the Old Marshalsea Prison, opened in the fourteenth century. In 1381 the prison was attacked during the Peasants' Revolt and the prisoners were freed. Ben Jonson served two sentences at the Marshalsea. In 1597 he and various members of the cast of *The Isle of Dogs* were incarcerated there when the play was deemed to contain 'very seditious and slandrous matter'. One of the actors who was locked up with him was Gabriel Spencer, whom Jonson murdered the following year (see Shoreditch). Jonson managed to escape punishment for the murder, but in 1605 he was back in the Marshalsea after some anti-Scottish dialogue in *Eastward Hoe* was brought to the attention of the recently crowned James I. In 1609, the poet Christopher Brooke also found himself a guest of the Marshalsea, after acting as a witness at the wedding of John Donne and Anne More. The pair had married in secret, without troubling to ask the permission of the bride's father.

Although *The Pickwick Papers* is the most cheerful of his novels, Dickens's experience of the Borough was traumatic. When he was 12, his improvident father, John Dickens, was imprisoned for debt in the Marshalsea. By then, the prison had moved up the road to Angel Place (the site is now filled by the suitably penitential-looking headquarters of the Health and Safety Executive). Mr Micawber's strictures on financial improvidence to the young David Copperfield – 'Annual income twenty pounds, annual expenditure nineteen nineteen six, result happiness. Annual income twenty pounds, annual expenditure twenty pounds ought and six, result misery' – is now one of the most famous passages in English literature; but at the time, few readers suspected that the remarks had been made, almost word for word, to Dickens himself by his father, in his cell in the Marshalsea. Both Mr Micawber and, later, Mr Dorrit reflect John Dickens's mixture of verbosity, essential goodness and a congenital inability to live within his means. Sent to work in a blacking factory off the Strand, Charles himself was installed in

cheap lodgings in nearby Lant Street, where he had a back attic overlooking a timber yard. He described the local ambience in *The Pickwick Papers*, in which Bob Sawyer too has lodgings in Lant Street.

> *There is a repose about Lant Street, in the Borough, which sheds a gentle melancholy upon the soul... The chief features in the still life of the street are green shutters, lodging-bills, brass door-plates, and bell-handles; the principal specimens of animated nature, the pot-boy, the muffin youth, and the baked-potato man. The population is migratory, usually disappearing on the verge of quarter-day, and generally by night. His Majesty's revenues are seldom collected in this happy valley; the rents are dubious; and the water communication is very frequently cut off.*

The Marshalsea Prison dominates Dickens's later novel *Little Dorrit*, whose heroine, a debtor's daughter, is born in the prison and grows to adulthood there. Writing more than 30 years after his own father's incarceration, the middle-aged Dickens described – or rather, recalled – the building as 'an oblong pile of barrack building, partitioned into squalid houses standing back to back, so that there were no back rooms; environed by a narrow paved yard, hemmed in by high walls duly spiked at top'. After the Marshalsea closed in 1842, the exercise yard became part of the churchyard of St George the Martyr. Sitting there one day, Dickens's greatest biographer,

Peter Ackroyd, had the idea for his own first novel, *The Great Fire of London* (1982), in which a group of loosely related characters – among them a film director, a

murderer and a university academic – are all in various ways influenced by *Little Dorrit*. The church itself features in Dickens's novel. Locked out of the prison one night, Little Dorrit sleeps in the vestry, using the burial register as a pillow, and she is married there at the end of the novel. She is now depicted, kneeling, in one of the stained-glass windows.

The church of St George the Martyr is known locally as 'the Little Dorrit Church'.

Southwark Cathedral, or the Cathedral Church of St Saviour and St Mary Overie to give its full name, stands at the northern end of Borough High Street, just below London Bridge.

John Gower's tomb in Southwark Cathedral.

cathedral. He was buried in the nave. Gower's most important work was *Vox Clamantis* (1380), a 10,000 line poem on statesmanship, written in Latin. Gower was a friend of Chaucer (*Troilus and Criseyde* is dedicated to him) and he speaks the Prologue to Shakespeare's late play *Pericles*, the plot of which is based partly on Gower's 'Apollonius of Tyre'.

BANKSIDE

The stretch of riverfront immediately west of the present Southwark Bridge was London's ultimate den of iniquity. From medieval times until the late seventeenth century, Bankside was a seething mass of brothels (licensed and regulated by the Bishops of Winchester, who owned the land), cockpits, gardens for bear- and bull-baiting, and theatres – considered by the Church to be the most sinful places of all. 'The cause of plagues is sin, if you look to it well,' reasoned one preacher, Thomas White, at St Paul's in 1577. 'The cause of sin are plays: therefore the cause of plagues are plays.'

Admittedly, Elizabethan theatre people were hardly the gushing luvvies of modern caricature. When James Burbage fell out with his business partner John Brayne at The Theatre they settled their differences with a fist-fight (see Shoreditch); the playwright Christopher Marlowe was involved in a street fight in which a man was killed, and was himself murdered in a tavern brawl (see Deptford); and Gabriel Spencer, the actor killed during a duel with Ben Jonson, had himself murdered a man some years earlier. Public suspicion of actors was fuelled by rumours of paedophilia (probably

In 1616, when most of London's theatres were in the vicinity, the then chaplain, the Reverend Sutton, preached a sermon in which he denounced those 'who dishonour God... by penning and acting of plays'. Ironically, numerous dramatists and actors have memorials in the cathedral. John Fletcher (who co-wrote *Henry VIII* with Shakespeare) and Philip Massinger are both buried here, as was Shakespeare's brother Edmund, an actor, in 1607. Shakespeare himself is remembered in the form of a stained-glass window and an alabaster statue, carved in 1912. Next to the statue is a tablet dedicated to Sam Wanamaker, founder of the present-day Globe Theatre.

From about 1377 until his death in 1408, the writer John Gower lived in the monastery which was then attached to the

suspicion of actors was fuelled by rumours of paedophilia (probably due to the presence of boy actors in theatre companies), and travelling theatre companies could find themselves barred from rural towns and villages because they were thought to be carrying the plague. The actor's life was a precarious one: theatres were routinely closed by the authorities during outbreaks of plague and rioting – both regular occurrences, the latter often being instigated by the notoriously rowdy City apprentices. The actors were not the only ones taking risks. One Bankside theatre-goer was stabbed to death by an usher after questioning the price of admission.

The first of the Bankside theatres was the Rose, a thatched, polygon-shaped building opened by Philip Henslowe in 1587, in what is now Rose Alley. Henslowe employed the best dramatists of his time to write for his theatre, and even lent some of them money, though as he noted in his *Diary* (written between 1592 and 1609 and giving a vivid insight into the world of the Elizabethan theatre), 'when I lent I wasse a frend & when I asked I wasse unkind'. Shakespeare probably acted at the Rose when he first arrived in London, and his early play *Henry VI Part I* had its first performance there – as did Thomas Kyd's *The Spanish Tragedy* and Christopher Marlowe's *Tamburlaine the Great*, *The Jew of Malta* and *Dr Faustus*. The leading actor was Edward Alleyn, the founder of Dulwich College. The Rose's lease ran out in 1605 and the theatre was abandoned, but in

1989 the remains of the building were discovered by workmen clearing the site for a new office block.

The legendary Globe Theatre was built during the winter of 1598–9, using timber from The Theatre in Shoreditch. The wood was piled on to wagons and driven across London Bridge to what is now the junction of Park Street and Southwark Bridge Road. Owned jointly by, among others, Richard Burbage and William Shakespeare, the Globe was polygon-shaped like the Rose, about 100 feet across and only partly thatched. The centre of the building was open to the elements, restricting performances to the summer months.

The first play to be performed there was probably Shakespeare's *Julius Caesar*, followed by *Henry V*, in which the Chorus begins by alluding to the physical limitations of the Globe – 'this cockpit... this wooden O' – before appealing to the audience to 'piece out our imperfections with your thoughts'. In 1613, a performance of Shakespeare's new play, *Henry VIII*, included

William Shakespeare (1564–1616). Oscar Wilde once observed that 'Shakespeare never wrote anything but doggerel lampoon before he came to London, and never penned a line after he left.'

The original Globe Theatre, owned by Richard Burbage and William Shakespeare among others, existed for just 14 years.

the firing of real cannon to mark the entry of the King. The thatch caught fire, and the Globe burnt to the ground within half an hour. The poet and diplomat Sir Henry Wotton, who was at the scene, recorded that 'nothing did perish but wood and straw, and a few forsaken cloaks; only one man had his breeches set on fire, that would perhaps have broiled him, if he had not by the benefit of a provident wit put it out with bottle ale'. The Globe was rebuilt the following year, but by then its star playwright had retired to Stratford. In the 1640s it was closed down and demolished by the Puritans.

In 1934, a 15-year-old American youth named Sam Wanamaker visited the World Fair in Chicago, where he saw a group of actors performing Shakespeare in a small plywood replica of the Globe. After becoming an actor himself, Wanamaker visited the site of the Globe in 1949, where it occurred to him to build a replica of the original theatre. Investing much of his own money in the project, Wanamaker was finally

able to start building work in 1987; the 1989 discovery of the Rose Theatre revealed new details about the probable construction of the Globe which were incorporated in the plans. Wanamaker died in 1993, before the new Globe could be completed. It opened in the summer of 1997, with a performance of *Henry V*.

Shakespeare's former boss Philip Henslowe took advantage of the destruction of the original Globe by converting a bear-baiting arena into a theatre, called the Hope, which had a removable stage so that animal baiting could continue between plays. The Hope's first production was Ben Jonson's *Bartholomew Fair* in 1614, but two years later it had reverted to a bear pit, its site now marked by a small street called Bear Gardens.

Animal baiting continued to be a source of guilty pleasure to Londoners for another three centuries. In 1670 John Evelyn came with some friends to see a display of miscellaneous animal-fighting: 'One of the bulls tossed a dog full into a lady's lap as she sate in one of the boxes at a considerable height from the arena. Two poor dogs were killed, and so all ended with the ape on horseback, and I most heartily weary of the rude and dirty pastime.' Samuel Pepys once witnessed a fencing match in one of the local taverns between a butcher and a waterman,

The third Globe Theatre. Like the original Globe, it opened with a Shakespeare play, this time Henry V.

frequent guest at the home of Henry Thrale, a brewer, and his wife Hester in Deadman's Place (now Park Street). Johnson wrote Thrale's election speeches when he stood for Parliament, and worked on *Lives of the English Poets* in the room which was set aside for him in their brewery gatehouse. The friendship ended abruptly when, three years after Henry Thrale's death, Hester married an Italian musician named Gabriel Piozzi, of whom Johnson disapproved.

Bankside's dog fights and bear-baiting were banned by the Puritans – not because they brought suffering to the animals, but because they gave pleasure to the spectators.

which ended in a free-for-all when the butcher deliberately cut his opponent's hand. At the height of the Great Fire of London, Pepys came with his wife and some friends to Bankside, where they watched the progress of the flames on the other side of the river, 'as far as we could see up the hill of the City, in a most horrid malicious bloody flame, not like the flame of an ordinary fire... we saw the fire as only one entire arch of fire from this to the other side of the bridge, and in a bow up the hill, for an arch of above a mile long. It made me weep to see it. The churches, houses, and all on fire and flaming at once, and a horrid noise the flames made, and the cracking of the houses at their ruine.'

'I took my wife & son to Bankside in Southwark where we behold the whole city in dreadful flames near the Waterside' *John Evelyn, Sept. 1666*

During the 1750s Oliver Goldsmith practised, not very successfully, as a physician in Bankside. From the early 1760s, Samuel Johnson was a frequent guest at the home of

Hester Thrale's diaries and other writings were belatedly published as *Thraliana* in 1942.

Bankside's long period of relative obscurity ended in the 1990s, with the opening of the new Globe Theatre, and later of the Tate Gallery's modern art collection in the former Bankside Power Station. The building's vast brick façade and single, malevolent-looking chimney were used to good advantage in Ian McKellen's 1993 film version of Shakespeare's *Richard III*, in which it appears as an alternative version of the Tower of London.

The Anchor Inn in Southwark, where John Evelyn and his family watched the progress of the Great Fire of London, and where Samuel Johnson met his friends Henry and Hester Thrale. The Thrales owned the nearby (now demolished) Anchor brewery, where Johnson had a room in which to write.

221

LAMBETH

The name Lambeth now describes a huge south London borough stretching from Waterloo Station to the suburbs of Streatham and West Norwood. Until the nineteenth century, however, Lambeth was merely the area of marshland across the river from Westminster.

Samuel Pepys found Lambeth a convenient location for the occasional daytime dalliance. On 23 July 1664 he plotted, in Westminster Hall, with Mrs Lane 'to go over the water; so met at Whites stairs in Channel row, and over to the old house at Lambeth marsh and there eat and drank and had my pleasure of her twice'. At the beginning of Peter Ackroyd's novel *Dan Leno and the Limehouse Golem* (1994), set in the 1880s, Lizzie Cree lives in Lambeth Marsh with her mother, earning a living sewing sails for Thames fishermen.

In 1790, William Blake and his wife Catherine moved from their home in Soho to 13 Hercules Buildings, a terraced house with a small garden and a view of the Thames from the upstairs windows. (The house is on the present site of 23 Hercules Road.) In his 1995 biography, *Blake*, Peter Ackroyd points out that a large flour mill, Albion Mill, lay just north of Hercules Buildings in Blackfriars Road. In 1791 the mill was burnt down – possibly by disaffected

A street flood in Lambeth in Victorian time captured by John Thomson in Victorian London Street Life, *(1887), one of the first photogaphic records of how the poor lived.*

workers – and remained a burnt-out shell until it was pulled down in 1809. Ackroyd speculates whether these events may have influenced Blake's lyric 'Jerusalem', with its lines

And was Jerusalem builded here,
Among these dark Satanic Mills?

Blake's ten years in Lambeth were not without incident. On at least one occasion he was 'mob'd and robbed' by one of the local gangs who used to attack passers-by in the lanes around the marsh; he once saw a ghost of 'scaly, speckled, very awful' figure coming down the stairs, causing him to flee the house; and he twice had visions of the Angel Gabriel: one in his study, the other in one of the local taverns. He also accepted some bizarre commissions to help make ends meet, including a series of engravings of urinary tract stones for a medical book, *Practical Observations on the Operation for the Stone.*

He also revealed himself as an early naturist. One day a friend, Thomas Butts, found Blake and his wife sitting in their summer house, stark naked, reciting passages from *Paradise Lost*. Blake was unperturbed, cheerfully calling out, 'Come in! It's only Adam and Eve, you know!'

In 1815, the Bethlehem Royal Hospital, popularly known as 'Bedlam', moved from its previous site in Moorfields to a new building in the Lambeth Road. As they had done in the City, crowds flocked to the hospital to watch the mentally ill patients, who were kept in cages. In his verse autobiography *The Prelude*, Wordsworth lists Bedlam among the 'sights' he most looked forward to seeing in London, along with St Paul's Cathedral and the Tower of London.

The painter and poet Richard Dadd, who illustrated scenes from *A Midsummer Night's Dream* and *The Tempest*, was sent to Bedlam in 1843 after murdering his father. He eventually spent 43 years in the hospital, dying there in 1886. The architect and writer Augustus Pugin, who co-designed the Houses of Parliament, was treated in the hospital in the mid-nineteenth century, and the novelist Antonia White also spent some time there in 1922 after trying to drown herself in the Thames. In 1930, the hospital moved to Kent and the building in Lambeth Road became the Imperial War Museum. The main hall of the museum, with its fighter aircraft and V2 rocket suspended from the ceiling, has been likened by the writer Tim Newark to a boy's bedroom on a massive scale.

In the nineteenth century, despite its proximity to the seat of government, Lambeth acquired an unenviable reputation as one of the worst slum areas in London. George Gissing, once described as 'an epicure of London's uglier aspects', set much of his 1887 novel *Thyrza* in the area round Lambeth Walk. The heroine of Somerset Maugham's *Liza of Lambeth* lives in fictional Vere Street, near Westminster Bridge Road. Maugham had got to know the area as a medical student at St Thomas's Hospital, near

Westminster Bridge, which he portrayed as St Luke's in *Of Human Bondage* and *Cakes and Ale*. Required to attend at least 20 childbirths in order to qualify, Maugham would be called out to slum houses all over Lambeth, 'up stinking alleys and into sinister courts where the police hesitated to penetrate, but where your black bag protected you from harm'. In three weeks, Maugham helped deliver babies to 63 women, many of whom would have been women like Liza – a flirtatious, vivacious, factory girl, who has an affair with a married man which culminates in a shocking street fight between Liza and the wronged wife. The world described in the novel – in which whole streets go on wagon outings to Chingford, where girls dance with girls and men with men to the accompaniment of a barrel

Somerset Maugham (above) would barely recognize most of modern Lambeth, but this stretch of Lambeth Walk is the exception.

organ, and where house-holders sit on doorsteps shelling peas – seems so distant that it's hard to believe that Maugham was still alive in the era of the Beatles, Harold Wilson and the Ford Cortina.

Christopher Marlowe was stabbed through the forehead in a local tavern, apparently in an argument over the bill. The circumstances surrounding Marlowe's death are still shrouded in mystery. It was only in the 1920s that Marlowe's killer was identified as one Ingram Frizer (or possibly Frezer), one of a trio of shadowy figures, all of them almost certainly government agents, who had spent the day eating and carousing together.

It was always on the cards that Marlowe would die violently and young (he was 29): in 1589 he had been present at a street fight in which a man was killed, and in 1592 he was deported from Holland for forgery. His plays *The Jew of Malta* and *Edward II* were physically and verbally violent, even by the standards of their own time, and Marlowe loved to shock, especially with his much-quoted observation that 'All they that love not tobacco and boys are fools.' At the time of his death he was due to appear before the Privy Council, charged with blasphemy.

Frizer's claim that he had killed in self-defence was accepted and he was granted a royal pardon by Elizabeth I. Marlowe is buried in the churchyard of St Nicholas church in Deptford Green, where he is remembered in a tablet quoting his most famous work: 'Near this spot lie the mortal remains of Christopher Marlowe, who met his untimely death in Deptford on May 30 1593. *Cut is the branch that might have grown full strength* – Dr Faustus.' Anthony Burgess's novel *A Dead Man in Deptford* is an imaginative re-creation of Marlowe's life and violent times.

As a senior Navy official, Samuel Pepys visited the Royal Naval Dockyard once a week or

DEPTFORD

Deptford ('deep ford') was a fishing village until Henry VIII built the Royal Naval Dockyard there in 1513 to construct and maintain his fleet ('the wood wall of England'). Like much of the commercial river-front, Deptford was (and occasionally still is) a dangerous area. In 1593 the playwright

GREENWICH

The name comes from Anglo-Saxon, meaning 'green port', but Greenwich's prosperity came from its royal patronage. This began in 1426, when Humphrey, Duke of Gloucester, the brother of Henry V, enclosed the land between the river and Greenwich Hill to create Greenwich Park, and built a manor house by the river. Greenwich Palace, as the house became, was the favourite home of Henry VIII and Elizabeth I, but it fell into disrepair under Oliver Cromwell and was subsequently demolished. Sir Christopher Wren's Royal Naval Hospital (subsequently the Royal Naval College) now stands on the site, though its vast, split façade – designed to give an unimpeded view from the river of the Queen's House on the hill behind – prompted Samuel Johnson's observation that the

more, usually travelling by barge from Westminster or the Tower of London. After one visit, in April 1662, he noted in his diary that he was 'much troubled today to see a dead man lie floating upon the waters; and had done (they say) these four days and nobody takes him up to bury him, which is very barbarous'. Pepys's friend and fellow-diarist John Evelyn moved into a house in Sayes Court (now Sayes Court Street, off Evelyn Street), after many years travelling on the continent with the poet Edmund Waller. Evelyn then spent over 40 years in Deptford before inheriting the family seat in Surrey.

After one visit to the Royal Naval Dockyard at Deptford, Pepys wrote in his diary, 'Never till now did I see the great authority of my place, all the captains of the fleet coming cap in hand to us.'

A botched attempt to blow up Greenwich Observatory inspired Joseph Conrad's novel The Secret Agent.

building was 'too magnificent for a place of charity, and too much detached to make one great whole'. Wren's assistant was the architect Nicholas Hawksmoor, who later designed the church of St Alfege in Greenwich High Road. The church features in Peter Ackroyd's novel *Hawksmoor* (1985). Hawksmoor also worked on various architectural projects with the playwright and architect Sir John Vanbrugh, author of Restoration comedies such as *The Relapse* and *The Provok'd Wife* (both 1697). Vanbrugh Castle, the fortress-like home which he designed for himself on Maze Hill, has been called Britain's first folly.

Sir John Vanbrugh occupied this unusual house on Maze Hill from 1719 until his death in 1726.

During the summer of 1838, a rather priggish 19-year-old girl from Warwickshire named Mary Ann Evans visited London with her brother Isaac. A devoted member of the then fashionable evangelical movement, Mary Ann took an instant dislike to St Paul's (too frivolous) and the theatre (too sinful), though she did claim to enjoy a visit to the Royal Naval Hospital. In middle age, as the novelist George Eliot, she somewhat revised her position on organized religion and conventional morality (see Marylebone, Chelsea and Richmond). She returned to Greenwich in 1861, for a whitebait dinner in her honour to celebrate the publication of *Silas Marner*. Eliot was the only woman present at the gathering, Victorian convention dictating that it was acceptable for men, but not other women, to be in the same room as a fallen woman.

The tradition of holding a whitebait dinner in Greenwich to celebrate the completion of a novel had begun in 1851, when Harrison Ainsworth invited some friends to the Trafalgar Tavern, in Park Row, when he finished *Mervyn Clitheroe*. Dickens, Thackeray and Wilkie Collins (not to mention Dick Turpin and Dr Crippen) became frequent visitors to the Trafalgar, and to the nearby Ship Tavern in King William Walk (since demolished) for their own completion dinners. Dickens's son Charley wrote in his *Dictionary of the Thames*, 'There is no next morning headache like that which accompanies a Greenwich dinner.'

Henry James, too, enjoyed his fish suppers at the Trafalgar: 'I would try to express how pleasant it may be to sit in the company of clever and distinguished men

before the large windows that look out upon the broad brown Thames,' he wrote in *English Hours*. 'The ships swim by confidently, as if they were part of the entertainment and put down in the bill; the light of the afternoon fades ever so slowly.' The large windows and deep-blue river dusks are still much in evidence in the Trafalgar, though today the view is dominated by the Millennium Dome, a mile or so downstream.

James made his first visit to Greenwich full of childhood memories of 'large maps which had a glazed, sallow surface... hung so high that my eyes could only reach to the lower corners, and these corners usually contained a print of a strange-looking house perched among trees upon a grassy bank that swept down before it with the most engaging steepness'. This was Greenwich Observatory. Finally seeing the building itself, James felt 'terribly old' on discovering that he had lost his boyhood urge to roll down the hill. Some years later, in 1894, an anarchist named Martial Bourdin travelled to Greenwich intending to plant a bomb in the observatory, but tripped on one of the tree roots on the hill and blew himself up instead. Joseph Conrad, who was then living in Victoria, read about the incident and used it in his 1907 novel *The Secret Agent*, in which Stevie, the unwitting bomb carrier, is killed in precisely the same place, and in the same way (see Victoria).

The thriller writer Edgar Wallace had a fleeting relationship with Greenwich: he was found abandoned in a street there when he was a few days old, and was subsequently brought up by a Billingsgate fish porter and his wife. In May 1939 George Orwell and his wife Eileen O'Shaughnessy stayed at her brother's home, at 24 Crooms Hill. Laurence O'Shaughnessy was a doctor, and arranged for Orwell to have some tests for TB, of which he was beginning to show symptoms. The tests found nothing wrong, and for the time being Orwell received no further treatment. Laurence was killed in the Second World War, and one wonders whether Orwell might have survived longer if swifter treatment had been more forthcoming.

On a later visit to Crooms Hill, in August 1940, Orwell stood at the front door watching an air raid on East India Docks. The novelist and Poet Laureate C Day-Lewis lived at 6 Crooms Hill from 1957 until his death in 1972.

In his demanding novel *Downriver* (1989), Iain Sinclair offers the image of a cricketer, Arthur Singleton, going in to bat at a charity cricket match for victims of the *Princess Alice* disaster (see Hackney and Bethnal Green). Singleton is 'leaning breathless against the brass line of zero longitude' while 'a pale stripe of virtue ran away from his navel and down Maze Hill, between the twin domes of Greenwich Hospital, across the river, and far around the red-splashed globe: to pierce, on its return, his psychic body'.

BLACKHEATH AND SHOOTERS HILL

Like many visitors today, Henry James came across this open, windswept area by accident – through one of the gates at the southern end of Greenwich Park which open unexpectedly onto the common of Blackheath. James found it 'a great, green, breezy place where lads in corduroys were playing cricket' and got into a conversation with a soldier, who suggested he might enjoy the walk to neighbouring Woolwich.

Shooters Hill Road, which bisects Blackheath, took its name from the highwaymen who used to haunt it. To discourage them, a gibbet was kept at the bottom of Shooters Hill itself: in 1661 Samuel Pepys 'rode under a man that hangs at Shooters Hill and a filthy sight it was to see how the

flesh is shrunk from his bones'. Dickens's *A Tale of Two Cities*, set during the French Revolution, opens with a mail coach lumbering along Shooters Hill Road on the long journey to Dover.

During the nineteenth century, Blackheath was dotted with schools, some good, some notorious for the cruelty of their regimes and the illiteracy of their teachers. Benjamin Disraeli attended the Reverend John Potticary's school on Blackheath. The hero of *David Copperfield* is sent to Salem House School on the heath, after being banished from home for biting his stepfather. (Salem House was partly based on Dickens's old school, Wellington House Academy in Hampstead Road.) Later in the novel, David sleeps in a haystack by the school wall during his long journey on foot to the South Downs. As the American consul in Liverpool (1853–7), the American writer Nathaniel Hawthorne, who had recently published one of the first great American novels, *The Scarlet Letter*, spent a few months in Blackheath in 1856. Hawthorne describes 4 Pond Road, a New England-style clapboard house, in *Our Old Home*.

In 1928, 19-year-old Malcolm

Lowry was living in a room at 5 Woodville Road, where he began his first novel. *Ultramarine* was based on Lowry's recent voyage to Yokohama, as a deckhand on the SS *Pyrrhus*, but it also owed a good deal to *Blue Voyage* by his friend Conrad Aiken (Lowry appears as 'Hambro' in Aiken's autobiography *Ushant*). Lowry had been influenced by the work of Melville, Conrad and Jack London and after leaving school wanted to experience life at sea before going to university. He went up to Cambridge in 1929, and subsequently travelled widely in Canada and Mexico, the latter, the setting for his 1947 masterpiece *Under the Volcano*.

WOOLWICH

Like Deptford, the Thames waterfront at Woolwich was first developed by Henry VIII, who built a dockyard here to construct his 1,500 ton flagship, the *Great Harry*. Woolwich Dockyard continued to expand during the seventeenth and eighteenth centuries. As newly appointed Clerk of the King's Ships, Samuel Pepys made one of his first visits to the dockyard in December 1660, to see the ship *Assurance*, 'which lies there under water; only the upper deck may be seen, and the masts'. One night in 1665, during the plague, Pepys walked through the centre, and 'in the street did overtake and almost run upon two women, crying and carrying a man's Coffin between them: I suppose the husband of one of them'.

In a travel essay 'London at Midsummer' (1877) Henry James describes walking from Blackheath to Woolwich at the suggestion of a

soldier (see Blackheath) and finding Woolwich Common dotted with strolling soldiers and townspeople, the whole vista dominated by the Royal Artillery Barracks. The scene aroused in James an odd, vicarious patriotism – 'an admiration for the greatness of England' – which came to fruition nearly 40 years on when he finally threw in his lot with his adopted country and became a British citizen.

With the closure of the Royal Dockyard in the 1860s, and the slow decline of the Woolwich Arsenal, which during the First World War employed some 40,000 workers, Woolwich's prosperity began to ebb away. However, the free river ferries, introduced in 1889, continue to shuttle like waterboatmen across the river to North Woolwich (see Hackney and Bethnal Green).

Henry James described the 'interminable façade' of the Royal Artillery Barracks in 1877.

Iain Sinclair visited Woolwich in 1994, during one of the epic walks recounted in Lights Out for the Territory. *'We're so far off the map that nobody has found it worthwhile to close down the free ferry... First-time voyagers sprint around the decks looking for the bar, the duty-frees. Old hands take up the position that will let them off first when the moving platform swings into place on the north shore.'*

CHAPTER 5

WEST LONDON

◆

TWICKENHAM

In 1719, Alexander Pope marked his growing status as the pre-eminent writer and literary socialite of his day by moving into a new house in the increasingly fashionable village of Twickenham, at the side of the Thames and some ten miles from central London.

Born in 1688, the son of a City linen draper, Pope was a precocious child, studying French, Italian, Latin and Greek literature 'like a boy gathering flowers'. At 12 he was acting out scenes in Homer. But at some point in his childhood, he was afflicted by a medical condition which curved his spine and permanently restricted his growth. As an adult he measured no more than four foot six. He also suffered from constant headaches and, it would appear, insomnia – according to Dr Johnson, Pope once got his servant up four times in a night so that he could write down thoughts which had just occurred to him. His stringent criticism of other writers and their work earned him the sobriquet 'the Wasp of Twickenham'.

Pope's home was in a road called Cross Deep, named after this stretch of the Thames, and included gardens which ran right down to the water. Pope, who was

Alexander Pope (1688–1744) devoted much of his spare time to creating a perfect home, well away from 'the pomps of the town'.

an early enthusiast of landscape gardening, took great pleasure in laying out the grounds himself, planting them with imported trees and shrubs (the first weeping willows seen in Britain are said to have been planted by him), and employing an architect, James Gibbs, to turn the house into a Palladian-style villa. As the conversion took place, Pope revelled in its increasingly eccentric appearance. He boasted that 'My building rises high enough to attract the eye and curiosity of the

passenger from the river, when, upon beholding a mixture of beauty and ruin, he inquires what house is falling, or what church is rising.' To a friend, Edward Blount, he wrote, 'From the river Thames you see through my arch up a walk of the wilderness, to a kind of open temple, wholly composed of shells in the rustic manner.' This was his famous grotto, made of shells, rock crystals and pieces of looking-glass. When Henrietta Howard drew up plans for her new house at Marble Hill, from funds donated by her lover, the Prince of Wales, she asked Pope to help with the design. It was Pope's idea to borrow some sheep from his friend Lord Bathurst to keep the lawns short.

Pope remained in Twickenham for the rest of his life. His translation of Homer's *Iliad*, completed in 1720, was described by Coleridge as 'an astonishing product of matchless talent and ingenuity', though Pope's friend Richard Bentley pointed out that it was 'a pretty poem, but not

Pope's 'little kingdom' at Cross Deep.

Homer.' Pope's fast and loose approach to great literature was again in evidence when he edited *The Dramatic Works of Shakespear* in 1725. The Shakespearian scholar Lewis Theobald published a pamphlet, 'Shakespeare Restored', in which he listed 'many of Mr Pope's errors'. Pope was furious, and made Theobald the target of his satire *The Dunciad*, while quietly adding many of Theobald's corrections to the second printing of his *Shakespear*.

When Pope died in 1744, at the age of 56, he was buried at the church of St Mary the Virgin, in Church Street, where his parents were buried, and where he had erected a graceful tribute to his

Pope's memorial to his nurse, Mary Beach, at the church of St Mary the Virgin, Twickenham. A brass plate in the floor of the nave is dedicated to Pope, but he is actually buried under the adjoining slab, which is marked with a letter P.

TO THE MEMORY OF
MARY BEACH
WHO DIED NOV. 5. 1725 AGED 78
ALEX. POPE, WHOM SHE NURSED IN
HIS INFANCY AND CONSTANTLY AT-
TENDED FOR THIRTY EIGHT YEARS
IN
GRATITVDE TO A FAITHFVL OLD SERVANT
ERECTED THIS STONE.

Twickenham resident Horace Walpole (1717–97) pioneered the 'Gothic novel'.

nurse, Mary Beach (see left).

Pope's house quickly fell into a state of neglect. After passing through the hands of several owners, it was bought by Sophia Howe. In 1807, tired of the steady stream of visitors to her property, she demolished the house and garden, and wrecked the grotto, a remnant of which remains in the grounds of the girls' school in Cross Deep. Sophia Howe's actions earned her the title 'Queen of the Goths' among Pope's followers.

Horace Walpole, who had admired Pope's creation and lamented its sad decline, moved to Twickenham three years after Pope's death and started work on his own, unconventional dwelling. 'Strawberry Hill' (off Waldegrave Road) had been the home of a retired coachman employed by the Duke of Bedford. Under Walpole, who enjoyed a substantial private income, the unpretentious villa was turned into a Gothic extravaganza. Over the next 40 years he added battlements, arches, stained-glass windows, Tudor chimneys and two towers – all modelled on buildings which Walpole had either visited or seen in illustrations. The rooms were stocked with furniture, paintings, statues and other *objets d'art*, which Walpole carefully catalogued in a 'Description of the Villa of Horace Walpole... at Strawberry Hill, near Twickenham, with an Inventory of the Furniture, Pictures, Curiosities, &c'. The catalogue was printed on Walpole's own press, in a cottage near the house, which he used to publish works by himself and by friends, such as Thomas Gray. His Gothic novel *The Castle of Otranto*, however, purported to be the work of 'William Marshal, Gent, from the original Italian of Onuphrio Muralto, Canon of the church of St Nicholas of Otranto'. Fearful that this extravagant tale of castles, graveyards, vaults, ghosts and bleeding statues might provoke ridicule, Walpole only revealed himself as the author when the novel became a runaway success. Generally regarded as the first of the 'Gothic novels', it was imitated by writers such as Ann Radcliffe and 'Monk' Lewis, though the form was later parodied by Jane Austen in *Northanger Abbey* and Thomas Love Peacock in *Nightmare Abbey* and *Gryll Grange*. In his seventies, Walpole became friendly with two sisters, Agnes and Mary Berry, and he arranged for them and their father to move in to a house in the grounds, 'Little Strawberry', which has since been demolished.

Walpole died in 1797, leaving Strawberry Hill to a friend, Mrs Damer. Unlike Pope, he took the precaution of adding an additional bequest of £2,000 to ensure that

the home which had given him so much pleasure was kept in good condition. In the nineteenth century, Strawberry Hill was owned by Countess Waldegrave, who like Walpole was an inveterate builder, increasing the height of the towers, and having a railway line built to the front door. It is now the home of St Mary's University College.

Strawberry Hill, Walpole's mad Gothic pile which grew and grew.

Originally known as the Dove Coffee House, the Dove in Upper Mall was known from 1860–1948 as the Doves, after a signboard painter erroneously depicted two birds rather than one. The pub appears as The Pigeons in AP Herbert's novel The Water Gypsies.

HAMMERSMITH, CHISWICK AND SHEPHERD'S BUSH

William Morris (1834–96) twice rowed all the way from Kelmscott House (below right) to his rural Thameside home in Lechlade, a distance of some 130 miles.

Since its earliest days, Hammersmith has been less a destination in itself than a glorified crossroads – a function which was accentuated by the opening of a massive flyover in the early 1960s. Its proximity to the river has occasionally attracted writers. Leigh Hunt spent his last few years in straitened circumstances at 7 (now 16) Rowan Road. He was living there when Dickens published his unflattering portrait of him as Harold Skimpole in *Bleak House*.

Upper Mall was more salubrious. A narrow riverside street, it boasted a popular pub, the Dove, which continues to flourish at number 19. James Thomson wrote 'Rule, Britannia!' here around 1740, and the pub appears, as the Pigeons, in

AP Herbert's most popular novel, *The Water Gypsies* (1930). George MacDonald lived at 26 Upper Mall from 1868 to 1878, and wrote his strange, beautiful children's novels *At the Back of the North Wind* and *The Princess and the Goblin* here. He leased the house to the designer, novelist and poet William Morris, who wrote his utopian fantasy *News from Nowhere* here in 1890. It was Morris who renamed the house Kelmscott House, after his country home in the Cotswolds. He used his London home to set up the Kelmscott Press, designing the fonts and borders himself, and publishing his own works and those of other writers. Morris died in Hammersmith in 1896, shortly after completing the Kelmscott edition of Chaucer; the edition was hailed as the finest printed book ever produced. His Hammersmith house is now occupied by the William Morris Society.

Chiswick Mall, which continues west along the Thames beyond Black Lion Lane, was immortalized in the opening scene of Thackeray's *Vanity Fair*, where

his impudent heroine Becky Sharp emerges from Miss Pinkerton's academy for young ladies on her very last day of school and hurls her leaving present – a copy of Johnson's *Dictionary* – out of the carriage. As a boy, Thackeray had himself gone to school in Chiswick Mall – at Dr Turner's Preparatory School for Young Gentlemen at Walpole House.

In 1876, the portrait painter John Butler Yeats moved to 8 Woodstock Road, near Turnham Green Station, with his family; his son, the 11-year-old William Butler Yeats would remember the original William Morris wallpaper.

He was a day boy at the Godolphin Boys' School in Iffley Road, Hammersmith, which was (and is) 'a Gothic building of yellow brick'.

Marie Louise de la Ramée was living at Bessborough House, at 11 Ravenscourt Square, in 1859 when her neighbour introduced her to his cousin, the novelist Harrison Ainsworth, who was then the editor of *Bentley's Miscellany*. Ainsworth was impressed by her short stories and published 17 of them over the next 18 months. Under the pseudonym 'Ouida' (a childhood mispronunciation of Louise), she

Chiswick Mall, scene of the memorable opening of Thackeray's Vanity Fair *(1848), where Rebecca Sharp throws her prize out of the carriage as she leaves the school with Amelia Sedley.*

235

dogs which she rescued from the street. When she died, from pneumonia, in 1908, an anonymous fan paid for a monument to be erected over her grave, depicting a recumbent Ouida with a dog at her feet.

The busy, unglamorous byways of Hammersmith and Shepherd's Bush have, on occasion, been put to good use by imaginative novelists. Richard Marsh's vigorous exercise in Victorian science fiction, *The Beetle* (1898), begins with the discovery of a giant insect in an abandoned house in Hammersmith. The middle section of Patrick Hamilton's London trilogy *Twenty Thousand Streets Under the Sky* (1935) recounts Jenny Maple's inexorable fall from respectable servant girl to street prostitute. Jenny meets her friend

The Godolphin School in Hammersmith, where William Butler Yeats was teased for being Irish and bad at games.

subsequently became the Barbara Cartland of her day, producing 45 novels of which the best known was *Under Two Flags* (1867). Ouida's literary talents were summed up shortly after her death by the *Dictionary of National Biography*: 'She described love like a precocious schoolgirl, and with an exuberance which, if it arrested the attention of young readers, moved the amusement of their elders.' She was an ardent humanitarian, anti-vivisectionist and an opponent of women's suffrage. The enormous popularity of her novels enabled her to live in style in Florence, but she went out of fashion after about 1890 and spent the rest of her life in poverty, sharing a tenement flat in Viareggio with abandoned

The Mawson Arms in Chiswick, then a private house, became home to Alexander Pope from 1716–1719, after he fled the anti-catholic mood in London following the Jacobite rebellion. Pope translated the greater part of the Iliad *while living here.*

Violet at the Arcade entrance to Hammersmith Underground Station and, while wandering aimlessly in the direction of Baron's Court, the pair allow themselves to be picked up by two men. The ill-fated drinking session which follows takes place in the King's Head, 'a large and respectable house in the most crowded section of King Street with chocolate-coloured wood panelling, and copper-covered tables all round'. In Nicholas Royle's novel *The Director's Cut* (2000), would-be film auteur Fraser Munro murders his namesake, an established film-maker, on the Isle of Mull, then drives to London, where he moves into a 'one-storey abandoned building on the opposite side of Wood Lane from the BBC'. Standing nearby are the derelict Exhibition Halls, built to house the 1908 Franco-British Exhibition and the Olympic Games, where the novel's atmospheric dénouement takes place.

KENSAL GREEN

'For there is good news yet to hear and fine things to be seen Before we go to Paradise by way of Kensal Green.'

So wrote GK Chesterton of one of London's great Victorian cemeteries. The novelist Arthur Machen, who was living near the cemetery in the early 1880s, described it as 'the goblin city'. George Orwell, who visited it in 1931, was predictably sniffy, dismissing the elaborate, Gothic monuments and tombs as 'a last attempt on the part of the corpse to get himself noticed'.

The narrator of Alan David Price's story 'The Rolling Road to Kensal Green' (1991) goes to the cemetery to spend the last few hours before nuclear armageddon. When the bomb falls, Kensal Green is consigned, like the rest of London, to a giant underwater crater – 'a Victorian Atlantis'. Iain Sinclair came to the cemetery in 1994 to attend the funeral of the crime writer Robin Cook (also known as Derek Raymond). Sinclair describes the scene in *Lights Out for the Territory*: 'pyramids and stone mansions whose original pomposity has been weathered by long indifference into something more democratic: a sanctuary for wild nature, a trysting-place for work-experience vampires'.

When the cemetery was consecrated in 1833, it was intended that funeral barges should deliver their charges from the adjacent Grand Union Canal. This never actually happened, but in Nicholas Royle's *The Director's Cut* the funeral of cinema projectionist Iain Burns is interrupted by the arrival by blazing funeral barge,

Kensal Green Cemetery – 'Whenever I feel in the least tempted to be business-like or methodical or even decently industrious I go to Kensal Green and look at the graves of those who died in business.' Saki (1870–1916)

laden with flammable ciné film and bearing the body of a second man.

It was the bucolic atmosphere of Kensal Green that attracted the novelist Harrison Ainsworth here in 1835. His house, Kensal Lodge, at the Willesden end of the Harrow Road had 'a superb panorama' of woods and fields, and his 1839 novel *Jack Sheppard*, about the eighteenth-century high-wayman, was set in the area. Ainsworth is seldom read now, but in the late 1830s and early 1840s novels such as *Guy Fawkes* and *Old St Paul's* enjoyed a popularity that rivalled that of Dickens. Dickens and Ainsworth got on well – both relished hard work, long walks and hearty social gatherings – and it was at Ainsworth's home that Dickens made some of his most enduring friendships, including those with the painter Daniel Maclise

Originally a horse market, Portobello Road market now specializes in antiques and bric-a-brac. George Orwell lived at 22 Portobello Road in the late 1920s.

and with the editor and biographer John Forster, who was Dickens's closest literary associate and his first biographer. Both Ainsworth and Forster are buried at Kensal Green Cemetery, as are Thackeray, Leigh Hunt, Trollope and Wilkie Collins.

NOTTING HILL AND LADBROKE GROVE

Ever since it ceased to be farmland in the nineteenth century, Notting Hill has been characterized by an unhappy combination of opulent housing and out-and-out slums. George Orwell observed this uneasy social mixture in 1927–8, when he was living at 22 Portobello Road, as the lodger of Mrs Craig and her family. One day, she, her husband and Orwell were locked out of the house, and Orwell was dispatched to fetch a ladder from a relative, a mile away. Borrowing one from

the working-class family who lived next door was out of the question: Mrs Craig, who was a former lady's maid and a rampant snob, had not spoken to them once in the 14 years she had been living in the house, and she had no intention of starting now. Orwell, who had recently resigned from the colonial police in Burma, spent his time in Portobello Road learning to be a writer, composing poetry and beginning the under-cover visits to the East End which would make him, in the words of VS Pritchett, the first British writer to 'go native' in his own country.

The local atmosphere, particularly that of the lengthy, meandering antiques market, is fully realized in Muriel Spark's 1956 short story, 'The Portobello Road', which is told by a ghost. During this period, Notting Hill enjoyed a reputation as an outpost of Soho – a reputation enhanced by the presence of the self-consciously bohemian writer Colin Wilson, who lived at 24 Chepstow Villas. The milieu was probably best described by Colin MacInnes in his novel *Absolute Beginners* (1957).

The novelist Will Self has a particular affection for the raised arterial road known as the Westway. In an essay he has described his first 'grown-up' ride on it, on a summer night, on a moped pillion: 'A road sweeping across the city's Cubist scape; clean, shiny, slicing by block after block in elegantly plotted curve after curve. Then tantalising with a final roller-coaster plunge over the Marylebone flyover, before depositing you, dazed by the hubbub after the cool heights, in the bebop beat of central London.'

Despite its confusing title, which is also the name of a green space in Hackney, Martin Amis's *London Fields* (1989) is set in and around Notting Hill. Keith Talent is an unsuccessful armed robber turned con-artist who lives in 'the lone tower block at the end of Golborne Road' – actually, Trellick Tower, whose architect, Erno Goldfinger, gave his name to a James Bond villain. (Keith's long-standing challenge to the staff at his local Indian restaurant, the Indian Mutiny, is to make a curry so hot that he can't eat it.) Keith Talent's alter ego is Guy Clinch, who lives with his humourless wife and revolting baby, Marmaduke, in middle-class misery in Lansdowne Crescent.

Golborne Road is overshadowed by Trellick Tower, one of the unglamorous Ladbroke Grove locations in Martin Amis's London Fields.

PADDINGTON AND BAYSWATER

Paddington and Bayswater form a triangle-shaped area north of Hyde Park. During its history, the district has been dominated by two focal points. The gallows at Tyburn, near what is now Marble Arch, attracted huge, unruly crowds between 1388 and 1783, and Paddington Station, which opened in 1838, is probably the most written-about of all the London railway termini.

Completed in the mid-nineteenth century, the stately avenues Westbourne Terrace and Bayswater Road were among the

Talbot Road, takes its name from the setting of many of his novels.

In 1870, Dickens rented a house at 5 Hyde Park Place, overlooking Bayswater Road and Hyde Park. At work on his last, unfinished novel *The Mystery of Edwin Drood*, Dickens spent the last few months of his life alternating between this house, Ellen Ternan's home in Peckham and his own country home at Gad's Hill.

William Hogarth's 1747 engraving of a mass execution at Tyburn shows the triangular gallows, which was used to hang up to 20 criminals at a time. Dr Johnson commented 'Scarce can our fields, – such crowds at Tyburn die –, / With hemp the gallows and the fleet supply.' The site of the gallows is now a traffic island at the bottom of Edgware Road.

most desirable in London. In George Gissing's *New Grub Street* (1891), Amy Reardon deserts her impoverished writer husband and goes home to her mother, who lives in opulent surroundings in Westbourne Park

When the novelist Laurence Sterne died in 1768, he was buried in a graveyard near Bayswater Road, on the site of Hyde Park Place. Two days later his body was dug up by grave robbers and sold to Charles Collignon, a professor of anatomy at Cambridge University. The body was lying on a slab awaiting dissection when it was recognized by one of Sterne's friends and subsequently returned to its grave in Bayswater. In 1969 the body was dug up again, this time by the Sterne Trust, and reinterred in the churchyard at Coxwold, in north Yorkshire, where Sterne had been vicar. Thomas Hardy, whose body was also subjected to one or two posthumous indignities (see Westminster) lived at 16 Westbourne Park Villas from 1863–7, when he was studying to be an architect (see Strand). The Wessex Gardens Estate, near

Oscar Wilde was married, on 29 May 1884, at St James's Church, Sussex Gardens. Wilde designed his bride's wedding dress. According to the *New York Times*, the dress was made of 'rich creamy satin … with a delicate cowslip tint; the bodice, cut square and somewhat low in front, was finished with a high Medici collar; the ample sleeves were puffed; the skirt, made plain, was gathered by a silver girdle of beautiful workmanship, the gift of Mr Oscar Wilde; the veil of saffron-coloured Indian gauze was embroidered with pearls and worn in Marie Stuart fashion; a thick wreath of myrtle leaves, through which gleamed a few white blossoms, crowned her fair frizzed hair; the dress was ornamented with clusters of myrtle leaves; the large bouquet had as much green in it as white'. Somehow, Wilde had found time to design the bridesmaids' dresses as well.

Aldous Huxley was living at 155 Westbourne Terrace in 1921, when he published his exuberant first novel *Crome Yellow*, in which he tried out some of the themes which he developed fully a decade later in *Brave New World*. AJ Cronin, who later enjoyed enormous popular success with novels such as *The Stars Look Down* (1935) and *The Citadel* (1937) had a medical practice at 152 Westbourne Grove between 1925 and 1930. His collection of stories, *The Adventures of a Black Bag*, formed the basis of the long-running television series *Dr Finlay's Casebook*.

In 1921, when he was 17, Graham Greene was sent to stay with a psychoanalyst, Kenneth Richmond, and his wife Zoë, at their home at 15 Devonshire Terrace. Greene had suffered a nervous breakdown, triggered mainly by systematic bullying at his school, Berkhamsted, where his father was headmaster. As part of his treatment, Greene was required, at 11 o'clock every morning, to recount the previous night's dreams. One night he had an erotic dream about Zoë Richmond's breasts, which he dutifully recounted. It was the sort of reckless honesty which would get him into trouble later.

Whether he was conscious of the link or not, there was a long-standing connection in Greene's life between illicit sexuality and Paddington, with its increasingly seedy terraces and anonymous hotels. In the 1940s, Greene and his then mistress Dorothy Glover went to a cheap lodging house near Paddington Station. To Greene's embarrassment, the door was opened by a woman who had worked as a stage technician on the dramatized version of his novel *Brighton Rock*. In *The End of the Affair* (1951), based on Greene's affair with Catherine Walston, the narrator and his mistress leave Rule's restaurant in Maiden Lane

'with the same intention in both our minds' and take a taxi to 'Arbuckle Avenue' – the nickname which was then given to Leinster Terrace, 'the row of hotels that used to stand along the side of Paddington Station with luxury names, Ritz, the Carlton and the like' where rooms were paid for by the hour. Greene betrays some confusion here – Leinster Terrace is some distance from Paddington Station, though Eastbourne Terrace does run alongside it.

Beginning in 1945, the American novelist August Derleth wrote a long series of Sherlock Holmes pastiches featuring the detective Solar Pons, who has rooms at 7b Praed Street. After Derleth's death in 1971, the series was continued by the British horror writer Basil Copper.

In a poem, 'On the Demolition of the Odeon Cinema, Westbourne Grove' (1988), John Heath-Stubbs notes sadly that

Thomas Hardy (1840–1928) lived in Paddington before returning to his native Dorset to become a novelist.

Its soft innards, I guess, are
gone already:
The screen, the lighting, the
plush seats; the ghosts
likewise –
Shadows of shadows, phantoms
of phantoms,
The love goddesses, the butcher
boy heroes,
The squawking cartoon-
animals.

Nicholas Royle's novel *The Director's Cut* (2000) takes up the same theme – again with a Paddington setting. Angelo lives in a sixth-floor flat at 208 Gloucester Terrace, overlooking the main railway line into Paddington Station, and has a collection of video boxes – containing not the films themselves but the air from the cinemas where they were shown. He explains to a friend, Naomi:

'You can tear down the screen
and bulldoze the walls, but
you can never destroy the space
itself. This is a small part of
that space.'
'Space?'
'The space between the walls
and the floor and the screen
and the people watching the
films night after night. You
think that space can remain
unaffected by all of that
emotion, all of that drama?'

'At Paddington Station,' moaned the sensitive John Ruskin, 'I felt as if in hell.' As a rule, however, writers have found the station a stimulating place. At Hyde Park Place, Dickens enjoyed waking at dawn to hear the sound of wagons bringing produce from Paddington Station, and Anthony Trollope used the station for a pivotal scene in *The Small House at Allington*, where Johnny Eames attacks Adolphus Crosbie after hearing of his ungentlemanly conduct towards Lily Dale.

Oliver Goldsmith (1728–74) lived in various houses in London, including this farmhouse off the Edgware Road. He started out in London as a physician in Southwark and undertook various jobs until he attracted notice with his Enquiry into the Present State of Polite Learning in Europe *and subsequently achieved fame as a poet, novelist and dramatist.*

In a passage in *English Hours* that appears to have been written after an exceptionally good dinner at the Athenaeum, Henry James even argued the case for the aesthetic charms of 'Mr WH Smith's bookstalls – a feature not to be omitted in any enumeration of the charms of Paddington and Euston'.

It is a focus of warmth and light in the vast smoky cavern; it gives the idea that literature is a thing of splendour, of a dazzling essence, of infinite gas-lit red and gold. A glamour hangs over the glittering booth, and a tantalising air of clever new things. How brilliant must the books all be, how veracious and courteous the fresh, pure journals!

Graham Greene's wartime novel *The Ministry of Fear* (1943) ends at a blacked-out Paddington Station, where 'the season-ticket holders were making a quick get-away from the nightly death'. The novel ends with a piece of delicious black comedy in the men's toilets, with the hero's tormentor, Hilfe, obliged to cadge a penny in order to shoot himself in one of the cubicles.

In Agatha Christie's *The 4.50 from Paddington* (1957), Mrs McGillicuddy catches a train from platform three and subsequently witnesses a murder taking place on another train as the two carriages draw parallel.

The following year, Michael Bond, a former BBC cameraman, published *A Bear Called Paddington*, which fast became popular with children, in which the Brown family find an abandoned bear on Paddington Station, with a label marked 'Please look after this bear'.

KENSINGTON AND HYDE PARK

Previously an area of scattered farms, market gardens and occasional manor houses and private schools, Kensington's present-day character was shaped by Victorian munificence. By the turn of the century its character was clearly defined. As HG Wells summed it up in *Tono-Bungay*, Kensington was – and remains – a place of 'hugely handsome buildings and vistas and distances, a London of gardens and labyrinthine tall museums, of old trees and remote palaces and artificial waters'.

Thackeray lived at various addresses in Kensington. From 1846 to 1853 he was at 16 Young Street, a bulging brick house, now part of an American university, Richmond College. Thackeray wrote *Vanity Fair*, *Pendennis* and *The History of Henry Esmond* here. In May 1850, he invited Charlotte Brontë to a

Isambard Kingdom Brunel's design for the roof of Paddington Station, which has been mentioned by writers from Ruskin and Dickens to Greene and Agatha Christie, was inspired by the Crystal Palace. The station forecourt now has a statue of the famous bear 'from darkest Peru' to which it gave its name.

*K*enneth Grahame
lived in this solid
Kensington villa while
he was Secretary of the
Bank of England.

*A*n illustration
by William
Makepeace Thackeray
for Vanity Fair, the
first novel to give a
view of London society
with its combination of
the traditional upper
classes and the new
social climbers.

party at the house, after she had
expressed her admiration for his
work by dedicating her novel *Jane
Eyre* to him (see Bloomsbury).
Also present were Thomas and
Jane Carlyle, but conversation
failed to ignite and Thackeray
eventually made his excuses and
escaped to his club. The
Greyhound pub, on the other side
of the road, replaced an earlier
hostelry of the same name which
Thackeray mentions in *Henry
Esmond*: Lady Castlewood's home
is 'over against the Greyhounds'.
Passing 16 Young Street with a
friend some years after he had
moved out, Thackeray bellowed:
'Down on your knees, you rogue,
for here *Vanity Fair* was penned,
and I will go down with you, for I
have a high opinion of that little

production myself.'

After a reading tour of America
in 1853, Thackeray moved to 36
Onslow Square, described by his
daughter Anne as 'a pleasant,
bowery sort of home, with green
curtains and carpets, looking out
upon the elm trees'. Thackeray
wrote *The Virginians* and his last
completed novel *The Adventures of
Philip* here, before moving to his
final home, 2 Palace Green, next
to Kensington Palace. He died
suddenly there on Christmas Eve
1863. For a few months in 1862,
his greatest rival, Dickens, rented a
house at 16 Hyde Park Great
South, but the arrangement was
not a success: he called it 'this
odious little house' and 'this
London box'.

The first of Oscar Wilde's
several flirtations with the
Roman Catholic Church
occurred at the Brompton
Oratory, in Brompton Road.
In April 1878, Wilde, who was
then a student at Oxford, was due
to be formally received into the
Church. On the appointed day,
Wilde failed to materialize,
sending instead a large bunch of
lilies by way of apology. It was
one of several rather half-hearted
attempts to become a Catholic,
though later Wilde was to remark
that 'The Catholic Church is for

saints and sinners alone. For the respectable people, the Anglican Church would do.' Graham Greene would no doubt have agreed.

Kenneth Grahame, then the Secretary of the Bank of England lived at 16 Phillimore Place from 1901 to 1908, the year in which he resigned from the Bank and completed *The Wind in the Willows*. The book developed out of a series of stories which Grahame told his son Alastair, who was partially blind, and whom he affectionately called 'Mouse'.

In a letter to Theodore Roosevelt, who was an enthusiast of his work, Grahame was at pains to dismiss any notion of a 'message' in *The Wind in the Willows*. 'Its qualities, if any, are mostly negative – i.e. – no problems, no sex, no second meaning – it is only an expression of the very simplest joys of life as lived by the simplest beings of a class that you are specifically familiar with and will understand' – in other words, the class of bluff, unintellectual, upper middle-class countryfolk. Like so many books with 'no second meaning', *The Wind in the Willows* was nothing of the sort. The good-hearted Rat, Mole and Badger can be seen as symbols of the old order of rural England, under threat from the forces of suburbia (the 'Wide World' beyond the Wild Wood) and socialism (the weasels who take over Toad Hall and have to be repelled by force). Several of the characters were drawn from life: Rat was an amalgam of Grahame's friends WE Henley (who also inspired Long John Silver), Frederick Furnivall, who ran a rowing club on the river, and Edward Atkinson, another water enthusiast who at one time owned some 30 boats. As for the mercurial Toad, he has been described by one of Grahame's biographers as 'irresistibly suggestive of an adult manic-depressive'. Toad's misadventures were partly intended as a dire warning to 'Mouse', whose childhood tantrums were of epic proportions.

After some delay (*The Times* lamented that 'as a contribution to natural history, the book is negligible') *The Wind in the Willows* became a phenomenal success, going through numerous reprints in Grahame's lifetime. In 1929 the book enjoyed another surge of popularity through AA Milne's play *Toad of Toad Hall*, which became a Christmas institution in the West End. For Grahame, however, there was little more to do or say: he had put everything into one brilliant book and the rest of his life was spent in what his biographer, Peter Green, described as 'paralysing indolence'. There was also great unhappiness. Mouse was miserable and isolated at school, and had to be removed first from Rugby, then from Eton, completing his education with a private tutor. During his third year as an undergraduate at Christ Church, Oxford, his body was found on a railway line: apparently he had lain down on the rails and waited to be

William Makepeace Thackeray (1811–63) first attracted attention writing and drawing for Punch *and went on to write novels and edit the* Cornhill *magazine.*

decapitated. An inquest recorded a verdict of accidental death.

Grahame was initially resistant to having illustrations in *The Wind in the Willows*. The early editions had none – when Grahame was asked whether the railway scene should have Toad life-size or train-size, Grahame unhelpfully replied that Toad was train-sized and the train was Toad-sized, so there could be no pictures. However, when EH Shepard, who had earlier illustrated the *Winnie the Pooh* stories, visited Grahame at his home in Pangbourne in 1930, he 'listened patiently while I told him what I hoped to do. Then he said, "I love these little people, be kind to them." Just that; but sitting forward in his chair, resting upon the arms, his fine handsome head turned aside, looking like some ancient Viking, warming, he told me of the river nearby, of the meadows where Mole broke ground that spring morning, of the banks where Rat had his house, of the pools where Otter hid, and of the Wild Wood way up on the hill above the river.'

Kenneth Grahame (1859–1932) had a great love for rivers and boating which can be seen in Rat's love of the river.

Early in 1886, Henry James finally left the rooms off Curzon Street which he had been occupying ever since he took up residence in London nine years earlier (see Mayfair). His new home, 34 De Vere Gardens, was in a huge and, from the outside, rather anonymous mansion block. De Vere Gardens was a wide, quiet, avenue with a view of Hyde Park at the end of the road which probably reminded James of the similar view of Green Park from Bolton Street. Three days after moving in to his set of apartments on the fourth floor, James was writing enthusiastically to his brother William: 'The place is excellent in every respect, improves on acquaintance every hour and is, in particular, flooded with light like a photographer's studio. I commune with the unobstructed sky and have an immense bird's-eye view of housetops and streets … I shall do far better work than I have ever done before.' His output during the dozen years he would spend at De Vere Gardens would include the novels *The Princess Casamassima*, *The Aspern Papers* and *What Maisie Knew*, his ambitious 1897 novel, written from the point of view of a small girl who is used as a pawn by her warring parents. James's elaborate prose style, which he adopted in his later novels, was unsuited to this novel, but his attempt to tell the story entirely from the child's perspective was a significant development in fiction. The following year, he developed the theme of innocence corrupted by experience with his seminal ghost story, 'The Turn of the Screw', about two children haunted by the malign ghosts of former household servants.

Much commented on by visitors to 34 De Vere Gardens were James's own servants, Mr and Mrs Smith. Mr Smith, who served James as butler and valet, was inclined to be obtuse. 'When I gave him an order,' James complained to his friend Edith Wharton, 'he had to go through three successive mental processes before he could understand what I was saying. First he had to register the fact that he was being spoken to, then to assimilate the meaning of the order given to him, and lastly to think out the practical consequences which might be expected to follow if he obeyed it.' Eventually both Smiths took to heavy drinking and had to be fired.

It was while James was living at De Vere Gardens that he experienced his worst professional humiliation when he attempted, disastrously, to become a playwright. His first attempt was a dramatization of his novel *The American*. When the producer, Edward Compton, came to De Vere Gardens to discuss the project, he brought his seven-year-old son Monty, later known as Sir Compton Mackenzie. The future author of *Whisky Galore* was to remember the tools of James's trade. 'On the right of the window was a desk at which he could write, standing; along the wall on the left was a day bed with a swivel-desk attached on which he could write, lying; in front of the window was a large knee-hole desk at which he could write, sitting. Observing my eyes wandering round these engines of his craft, Henry James explained to me with elaborate courtesy their purposes.'

James endeared himself to the cast of *The American*. Every day while they were rehearsing, he would take a carriage to the theatre from De Vere Gardens, with a hamper full of food for the actors. No one in the company could remember a writer doing such a thing before.

Although *The American* was only a modest success, James felt confident enough to write a completely new play. Set in the eighteenth century, *Guy Domville* was the story of a man torn between becoming a priest and continuing his family name by marrying and having children. On its first night, at the St James's Theatre in King Street, off Pall Mall, James was too nervous to watch his own play and spent the evening at the nearby Haymarket Theatre watching Oscar Wilde's latest hit, *An Ideal Husband*.

James arrived back at the St James's just after the

The memorial to Prince Albert in Kensington Gardens, completed in 1876. Osbert Sitwell later described Albert's statue as a 'gilded and pensive giant on his dais under the Gothic canopy, strewn with white mosaic daisies of a blameless life'.

curtain came down. The production had been a disaster. Patrons started tittering at the eighteenth-century costumes, and as one actress came on stage wearing an enormous plumed headdress a section of the audience started chorusing the popular song 'Where Did You Get That Hat?' When the leading actor, George Alexander, launched into his climactic speech, beginning, 'I'm the last, my lord, of the Domvilles,' a voice yelled down from the gallery 'It's a bloody good thing you are!' The play ended to a chorus of jeers and boos and ironic shouts of 'Author! Author!' Unaccountably, Alexander decided to take these calls at face value. Seizing James's hand, he led him onto the stage, where they took the full force of the audience's wrath. HG Wells, who was beginning his career as a drama critic, described James facing the storm, 'his round face white, his mouth opening and shutting' before he and Alexander finally escaped to the sanctuary of the wings.

James walked home, in the January drizzle, to De Vere Gardens. A few days later, after

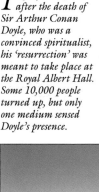

In July 1930, a week after the death of Sir Arthur Conan Doyle, who was a convinced spiritualist, his 'resurrection' was meant to take place at the Royal Albert Hall. Some 10,000 people turned up, but only one medium sensed Doyle's presence.

Edward Compton's wife had suggested that he write another play, he told her how 'as I walked home, alone, after that first night, I swore to myself an oath never again to have anything to do with a business which lets one into such traps, abysses and heart-break'.

Among James's Kensington friends was Leslie Stephen, who, as editor of the *Cornhill* magazine had published James's hugely successful novella 'Daisy Miller' in 1879. His daughter Virginia Stephen, later Virginia Woolf, was born at 22 Hyde Park Gate on 25 January 1882. Viriginia established her storytelling credentials early on: when the lights were extinguished in the top-floor nursery, she would entertain her sister Vanessa and her brothers Thoby and Adrian with fantastic nightly serials. At the age of nine, she produced her own newspaper, the *Hyde Park Gate News*, which appeared every week for four years, and in which she published her first story, 'A Midnight Ride' and a comedy, 'A Cockney's Farming Experiences'.

Woolf's childhood was wrecked by two events when she was 13. First, her mother died suddenly from influenza at the age of 39. Shortly afterwards, her 27-year-old half-brother George Duckworth, her mother's son by a previous marriage, began visiting her in the night nursery in order to abuse her sexually. Within a few months of her mother's death Virginia had a nervous breakdown, characterized by the 'horrible voices'

which would accompany many future bouts of mental illness and which eventually drove her to suicide. (See Bloomsbury.)

G K Chesterton (the initials stood for Gilbert Keith) was born in an unassuming three-storey house at 32 Sheffield Terrace, between Campden Hill Road and Kensington Church Street, in 1874. When he was five, the family moved to 11 Warwick Gardens, near Kensington High Street. Chesterton made his name as a journalist in turn-of-the-century Fleet Street and subsequently as an author. His most popular novels were his detective stories featuring the clerical sleuth Father Brown. Chesterton's 1904 novel *The Napoleon of Notting Hill* anticipates Orwell, being set in the London of 1984; here, London is divided into separate, feudal areas, each governed by its own monarch.

Henry James admired and envied Chesterton's ability to write on the hoof, apparently undistracted by the world around him whether it was a drawing room or a corner of Fleet Street, where he could occasionally be seen scribbling furiously. James, did, however, find Chesterton's vast girth disconcerting, describing him to his secretary Theodora Bosanquet as 'the unspeakable Chesterton ... a sort of elephant with a crimson face and oily curls'. During his many lecture tours, Chesterton became widely known both for his bulk and his ability to disarm audiences. While he was addressing a crowd during the First World War, a woman shouted, 'Why aren't you out at the Front?' 'If you would care to step to the side, madam,'

Chesterton replied, 'you will see that I am.'

In 1909, the prolific novelist, poet and journalist Ford Madox Hueffer scandalized Edwardian society by separating from his wife Elsie and living with his long-term lover Violet Hunt at her home, South Lodge, at 80 Campden Hill Road. Violet was a novelist, a committed member of the women's suffrage movement and a famous literary hostess of her day. Her salon at South Lodge was attended by, among others, Hardy, James, Hugh Walpole and the journalist Douglas Goldring, who in his book *South Lodge* recalled Ford as 'a flabby lemon and pink giant who hung his mouth open as though he were an animal at the zoo inviting buns – especially when ladies were present'. After serving in the Army during the First World War, Ford changed his name to the less Germanic Ford

G K Chesterton (1874–1936), who was educated at St Paul's school and studied art at Slade School, was an occasional illustrator as well as a prolific writer.

249

Ezra Pound (1885–1972), was a regular at Violet Hunt's Kensington soirées before the First World War.

Church Walk, he was visited by another American poet, TS Eliot, who had recently arrived in London. It took Eliot two months to pluck up the courage to approach the older, more established Pound.

On 10 January 1957, when Eliot married his secretary Valerie Fletcher at St Barnabas's Church in Addison Road, he and his new wife were invited for breakfast at the priest's house – which, Eliot was startled to discover, was at 10 Kensington Church Walk. In the 1920s Pound had moved to Paris, then to Italy, where he made a series of pro-Nazi radio broadcasts during the Second World War. In 1945 he was arrested by the US forces in Italy, and charged with treason. In Washington he was found to be unfit to plead and confined to a mental hospital. The decision to release him in 1958 was due in large part to the efforts of Eliot.

Madox Ford and wrote a wartime quartet, *Parade's End*. His 1915 novel *The Good Soldier*, is a story of interlocking relationships notable for its unreliable narrator and cunningly planted revelations.

Another figure who was frequently to be seen at Violent Hunt's literary soirées was the Idaho-born poet Ezra Pound, who came to Europe in 1908. In 1909 he moved in to a first-floor front-room flat at 10 Kensington Church Walk, a tiny, narrow street leading to the church of St Mary Abbot. Pound's bath, which was kept under his bed and was filled with water from the kitchen boiler, became the subject of a poem, 'The Bathtub'. Pound remained in the flat, with his 'unique and treasured landlady' Mrs Langley, until 1914, when he married Dorothy Shakespear. In his last year at 10 Kensington

Eliot himself had first lived in Kensington in the early 1930s, after he ended his marriage to his first wife, Vivien. Soon after the break-up he moved into a boarding house at 33 Courtfield Road, near Gloucester Road tube station. Eliot attended mass at St Stephen's Church in Gloucester Road, and when the priest, Father Eric Cheetham, offered him rooms in his presbytery, Eliot accepted. When Virginia Woolf came to visit him at his new home, 9 Grenville Place, she was disconcerted by how dingy the place was (his bedroom overlooked the railway line), but Eliot remained at Grenville Place until 1940, becoming church warden at St Stephen's and, during the Second World War, serving as a local air raid warden.

Graham Greene's life contained

some curious parallels to Eliot's. Both embraced Christianity as young men; both married, then abandoned, wives called Vivien; both were wartime ARP wardens.

In *Journey Without Maps* Greene describes an unnerving

encounter in Kensington Gardens when he was 17, and staying at the home of his psychoanlyst in Paddington. An elderly, well-spoken man engaged him in a prurient conversation about corporal punishment at girls' schools before, 'suddenly taking a grip of the poor sliding brain, he rose and moved away with stiff military back, the old Etonian tie, the iron-grey hair, a bachelor belonging to the right clubs, over the green plain among the nursemaids and the babies wetting their napkins'.

Other writers have also focused on the sadder, seedier side of Kensington. In *The Death of the Heart* (1938), Elizabeth Bowen describes two unhappy Kensington houses, built for 'a class doomed from the start, without natural privilege, without grace', which are joined together to form an equally unhappy hotel. The Karachi Hotel could be any one of a hundred similar establishments in west London: 'the nude-looking windows exist in deserts of wall: after dark the high-up electric lights die high in the air above unsmiling armchairs.' Angus Wilson's short story 'Saturnalia' (1947) is set in the drab-genteel Mendel Court

Hotel during an awkward New Year's Eve party for servants and staff in which 'a class barrier of ice' prevents all but the most stilted conversation. Lynne Reid Banks's *The L-Shaped Room* and Muriel

*M*ervyn Peake *(left), whose last London home was this pleasant house off Old Brompton Road (below).*

251

Speakers' Corner has been a Hyde Park insitution since 1872. Writers who have attended meetings and spoken here include Karl Marx, Friedrich Engels, William Morris and George Orwell.

Spark's *The Bachelors* and *A Far Cry from Kensington* are all set in lonely, communal flats and bedsits in Kensington, Chelsea and Fulham.

Mervyn Peake was born in 1911 in China, where his parents were working as missionaries. During the Second World War he worked as a war artist, visiting Belsen in 1945. After the war he lived for three years on the Channel island of Sark. Peake's experience of closed, alien communities probably fuelled his vision of Gormenghast, the fantastical castle which provides the setting for his trilogy *Titus Groan* (1946), *Gormenghast* (1950) and *Titus Alone* (1959), novels which defy simple classification but have been variously been described as 'Gothic', 'grotesque' and 'fantastic realist'. Peake was also a gifted artist, illustrating classic works such as 'The Hunting of the Snark', 'The Rime of the Ancient Mariner' and *Treasure Island.* As a portrait artist, Peake was fearless, scouring London for subjects and stopping them in the street to make an on-the-spot sketch. In the late 1950s, however, Peake began to develop Parkinson's disease, which left him progressively unable to draw or to write. He spent the last eight years of his life (from 1960 until shortly before his death in 1968) in Kensington, living at 1 Drayton Gardens, just off Old Brompton Road.

'It takes London to put you in the way of a purely rustic walk from Notting Hill to Whitehall,' ruminated Henry James in 1888. 'You may traverse this immense distance – a most comprehensive diagonal – altogether on soft, fine turf, amid the song of birds, the bleat of lambs, the ripple of ponds, the rustle of admirable trees.' He meant, of course, the route from Kensington Gardens and Hyde Park, followed by Green Park and St James's Park, which can still just about be done without stepping on asphalt.

Hyde Park was used by Henry VIII and Elizabeth I for hunting deer and wild boar, but in the early seventeenth century it was opened to the public. Samuel Pepys recorded a visit in 1663, when he dressed up in his finest clothes hoping to be noticed by the King (he wasn't). A few years later, after an affair with his maidservant had all but wrecked his marriage, he came looking for the girl in Hyde Park, but she affected not to see him.

In the eighteenth century, Hyde Park was a notorious haunt of highwaymen. In 1749 a pair of them held up Horace Walpole at blunderbuss-point and relieved him of eight guineas and his watch. Following Britain's victory at the Battle of Trafalgar, a huge fair was held in the park, with the battle itself re-enacted on the Serpentine while an orchestra played the national anthem. Charles Lamb deplored the debris that was left behind. 'The whole surface of Hyde Park is dry crumbling sand, not a vestige or hint of grass ever grows there,' he wrote to Wordsworth. 'Booths and drinking places go all round it for a mile and a half, I am confident – the stench of liquors, bad tobacco, dirty people and provisions conquers the air, and we are stifled and suffocated.'

Henry James was particularly impressed by the view from bridge which crosses the Serpentine: 'The towers of Notre Dame, as they rise in Paris from the island that divides the Seine, present themselves no more impressively than those of Westminster as you see them looking doubly far beyond the shining stretch of Hyde Park water,' he wrote in *English Hours*. 'Equally delectable is the large river-like manner in which the Serpentine opens away between its wooded shores.' In 1816, Shelley's pregnant wife Harriet drowned herself here, after he abandoned her for Mary Godwin.

In John Galsworthy's famous *Forsyte Saga* published between 1906 and 1928, the upper-middle-class Forsytes all live at intervals around Hyde Park, 'the fair heart of London'. Old Jolyon stayed at Stanhope Gate, the Jameses in Park Lane, the

'The shining stretch of Hyde Park water' was one of Henry James's favourite views.

The Peter Pan statue was the subject of questions in the House of Commons when it appeared without warning in Kensington Gardens.

Soameses 'in their nest off Knightsbridge', and the Rogers in Princes Gardens.

In 1895, the playwright JM Barrie moved in to 133 Gloucester Road. Since arriving in London from his home town of Kirriemuir, near Forfar, Barrie had collaborated with Sir Arthur Conan Doyle on *Jane Annie; or, the Good Conduct Prize*, a libretto which was performed without much success by the D'Oyly Carte opera company. He had also been commissioned to write *The Professor's Love Story* for Sir Henry Irving, but the actor-manager was not happy with the work and refused to perform it. Recently, however, Barrie's career had begun to take off. His play *The Little Minister* was a West End hit.

Barrie frequently walked in Kensington Gardens, accompanied by his Newfoundland dog Luath, the inspiration for Nana in *Peter Pan*. It was next to the Round Pond that he encountered five-year-old George Llewelyn Davies and his younger brothers Jack, aged three, and baby Peter. Barrie first met their mother, Sylvia Llewelyn Davies, after sitting next to her at a dinner party. She was married to a barrister, Arthur Llewelyn Davies, and Barrie became a regular visitor to their home at 31 Kensington Park Gardens, where he kept the boys entertained with his stories. Barrie's novel *The Little White Bird* (1902) was a rudimentary version of the

included an unsympathetic portrait of him, as the irritable Mr Darling, in *Peter Pan*. When Llewelyn Davies died from cancer in 1907, followed by his wife in 1910, Barrie adopted their five boys (Michael was born in 1900, and Nicholas in 1904), giving rise to rumours, which persist to this day, that his actions were motivated by paedophilia. Two of the boys died prematurely: George was killed in Flanders in 1915 and Michael drowned in the Thames near Oxford in 1921, a possible suicide. A third son, Peter, committed suicide in 1960.

In his biography of Rudyard Kipling, Angus Wilson describes a bizarre scene: the 16-year-old Kipling and the classical scholar and future chairman of the League of Nations Gilbert Murray stoning a cat in Kensington Gardens. Unpleasant though it is, the story is not wholly surprising to anyone who has read Kipling's 'The Cat Who Walked by Himself' in *Just So Stories*.

J M Barrie (1860–1937) frequently walked in Kensington Gardens with his Newfoundland dog, Luath, the inspiration for Nana in Peter Pan. *Barrie moved to 100 Bayswater Road, near the Gardens in 1902.*

Peter Pan story. In it, 'all children in our part of London were once birds in the Kensington Gardens'. One such child, Peter Pan, has 'escaped from being human when he was seven years old' and returns to the gardens, where he plays a reed pipe on an island in the Serpentine. Barrie's play *Peter Pan* introduced the characters of Captain Hook, the Lost Boys and the Darling children, Wendy, John and Michael. When the play was performed at the Duke of York's Theatre at Christmas 1904, it was a phenomenal success, though one member of the original audience, Anthony Hope Hawkins, the author of *The Prisoner of Zenda*, was heard to mutter, 'Oh, for an hour of Herod!' In 1912, Barrie arranged for a statue of Peter Pan to be erected in Kensington Gardens. The figure was carved in secret by the sculptor Sir George Frampton and put in the gardens overnight, so that children would think it had appeared by magic.

Arthur Llewelyn Davies seems to have had mixed feelings about Barrie's role as a surrogate father to his children. Barrie, in turn,

Kipling's own illustration for 'The Cat Who Walked by Himself', one of his Just So Stories.

SirThomas More lived in Chelsea with his family until his execution. 'There is not any living man as affectionate as he,' declared his friend Erasmus who visited his house, which he described as 'neither mean nor subject to envy, yet magnificent and commodious enough'.

St Luke's Church, where Dickens and Catherine Hogarth were married.

CHELSEA

Chelsea's evolution from modest fishing village to fashionable riverside demesne dates from the 1520s, when Sir Thomas More built himself a house near Cheyne Walk and later reconstructed the south chapel of Chelsea Old Church for his private use. He was living in retirement in the house when Henry VIII sent him to the Tower, enraged by More's refusal to recognize either his divorce from Catherine of Aragon, or his supremacy over the Church in England. In 1627, John Donne preached in the church, at the funeral of Magdalen Herbert, mother of the poet George Herbert. Izaak Walton, the author of *The Compleat Angler*, was in the congregation.

By the turn of the century, the Duke of Norfolk, the Earl of Shrewsbury and Henry VIII had all built private residences in Chelsea, giving the area an ambience of quiet exclusivity which it has enjoyed ever since. Samuel Pepys visited 'Chelsey' in

April 1666, during the plague, 'thinking to have been merry', but the waterfront tavern which he had earmarked as the scene of merriment turned out to be 'shut up of the sickness'. The diarist beat a hasty retreat 'in great disorder.' In his *London Journal*, James Boswell relates a more successful excursion. On 10 June 1763, he 'went to Chelsea and saw Johnson ride, standing upon one and then two horses at full gallop' – the Johnson on this occasion being not the great lexicographer but a famous trick horseman.

Don Saltero's Coffee House, which stood on the site of 18 Cheyne Walk, opened around 1715. Its customers included Addison, Steele, Goldsmith and Dr Johnson. As well as serving them coffee, the owner, John Salter, also cut their hair, played them tunes on his violin and performed elementary dentistry. His nickname was probably invented by Vice-Admiral Munden, who had a liking for all things Spanish, or possibly by Sir Richard Steele. He referred frequently to Don Saltero's in the *Tatler*, as did Fanny Burney in her novel *Evelina*.

In 1835, Charles Dickens moved to Selwood Terrace, to be close to his fiancée, Catherine Hogarth, who lived with her parents at 18 York Place, off Fulham Road. The following year the couple were married at St Luke's Church, the ceremony later described by the best man, Thomas Beard, as 'altogether a very quiet piece of business'. The rector of St Luke's was the Reverend Charles Kingsley, whose son, also named Charles, attended a grammar school in Cornwall run by Coleridge's son Derwent and

256

who went on to write the novels *Westward Ho!* and *The Water-Babies*. Dickens and his new wife honeymooned in Kent, then moved into accommodation at Furnival's Inn (see Holborn). Long after Dickens's death, Ellen Ternan, the companion of the last dozen years of his life, was still living in nearby King's Road, in a secluded house opposite the junction with Sydney Street.

The pinkish-coloured, perfect little town house at 22 Upper Cheyne Row (formerly number 4) is just the sort of dwelling where one might expect to find Harold Skimpole, the indolent, loquacious dilettante who occasionally enlivens the pages of Dickens's gloomy masterpiece *Bleak House*. Leigh Hunt, the inspiration for Skimpole, lived here from 1833 to 1840, though his life here was anything but lazy. Despite producing a steady stream of articles, poetry and plays, he frequently had no money and no food in the house with which to feed his large family. In 1847, Dickens decided to help him out by organizing two benefit performances of Ben Jonson's *Every Man in his Humour*, to be performed by himself, his friends John Forster and Douglas Jerrold and others. Shortly before the first performance, the Prime Minister, Lord Russell, granted Hunt a state pension of £200 a year, so Dickens diverted his charity to another struggling writer, a dramatist named John Poole. Why Dickens turned against Hunt six years later, with the caricature in *Bleak House*, is not clear. Hunt did not recognize the portrait until it was pointed out to him by friends. He later challenged Dickens about it

SIR,
Monsters of all sorts
   here are seen,
Strange things in
   nature as they grew so,
Some relicks of the
   Sheba queen,
And fragments of the
   famed Bob Crusoe.

Knicknacks, too, dangle
   round the wall,
Some in glass cases,
   some on shelf;
But what's the rarest
   sight of all,
Your humble servant
   shows himself.

On this my chiefest hope
   depends—
Now if you will my
   cause espouse,
In journals pray direct
   your friends
To my Museum coffee-
   house...

A poetic announce-ment by the proprietor of the treasures at Don Saltero's that appeared in the *Weekly Journal*.

*E*llen *Ternan, the companion of Dickens in his later years, lived in King's Road.*

The poet and essayist Leigh Hunt who edited the Examiner *and was 'one of those invaluable people who introduce authors to each other.'*

Hunt's house in Upper Cheyne Row until 1840, when he moved to nearby Kensington.

recognizable, if not exactly approachable, figure.

A stonemason's son from Ecclefechan, near Dumfries, Carlyle contemplated, then rejected, the ministry and worked for a time as a schoolteacher – an unwise choice of career, as his pupils found him impatient and sarcastic. Carlyle then began to study German literature, publishing translations of Goethe which earned him praise from the author himself.

Carlyle's wife, Jane, whom he married in 1823, had a similarly impressive intellect. As a small child she insisted on learning Latin (usually only taught to boys), and on her tenth birthday she re-enacted a scene in Virgil's *Aeneid* by burning her new doll on a funeral pyre. Her marriage to Carlyle was at best a qualified success. Carlyle's in-laws considered him a social inferior and unworthy of their daughter, who had been a local beauty in her home town of Kirkcaldy. The marriage lasted 43 years, until Jane's death, but was marked by innumerable rows and separations, usually when Carlyle was immersed in a new book. Chronic financial problems didn't help.

It was due to such financial problems that the Carlyles initially came to Chelsea. Hoping to find employment writing articles, Thomas travelled alone to London in May 1834. He wrote to his wife after coming across the house at 5 (now 24) Cheyne Row: 'Chelsea is unfashionable; it was once the resort of the Court and the great, however; hence numerous old houses in it, at once cheap and

during a dinner at Dickens's home in Tavistock Square, when Dickens argued that Skimpole was an amalgam of various people and was not intended to cause offence. When Hunt died in 1859, Dickens composed a fulsome tribute. 'In the midst of the sorest temptations,' he wrote, 'he maintained his honesty unblemished by a single stain.'

Hunt's next-door neighbour, Thomas Carlyle, was a man of a very different cast. Where Hunt was cheerful, gossipy and noisy, Carlyle was serious-minded, moralistic and irritable – the latter trait exacerbated by a lifetime's martyrdom to dyspepsia. The English stereotype of the curmudgeonly Scot probably has something to do with Carlyle, whose lengthy residence in Chelsea made him an instantly excellent. ...The House itself is eminent antique; wainscotted to the very ceiling, and has been all new-painted and repaired.' They moved in the following month.

At Cheyne Row, Carlyle lived frugally and entertained sparingly. He liked his bohemian neighbour Leigh Hunt, and received visits from, among others, Charles Dickens, John Ruskin and Charles Kingsley; Carlyle and Tennyson used to smoke at the basement fireplace in order not to annoy Jane Carlyle with the fumes. Soon after moving in, Carlyle began his *History of the French Revolution*. His financial position, however, remained critical. In February 1835 he was complaining to a friend that it was 'some twenty-three months since I have earned one penny by the craft of literature'. The following month, disaster struck. After finishing the first volume of *The French Revolution*, he lent the only copy to John Stuart Mill, whose maidservant assumed it was worthless and used it to light the fire. Carlyle, who hadn't kept his original notes, had no option but to start again from scratch, though Mill did give him £100 as compensation. Eventually published in three volumes in 1837, the book established Carlyle's reputation, and was used and gracefully acknowledged by Dickens as source material for *A Tale of Two Cities*.

Always sensitive to the slightest noise, Carlyle had his top-floor study soundproofed (not wholly successfully – he was driven to distraction by the noise from Leigh Hunt's chickens). He came to spend most of his time there, seeing his wife only at mealtimes. He did, however, become a somewhat more attentive husband after Jane was knocked down and

injured by a cab in 1863. After years of relying on public transport and an occasional hired carriage, he agreed to buy a brougham.

In 1866, Jane Carlyle was found dead in her carriage, during a drive while she was on holiday in Scotland. Her lengthy correspondence with a friend, Geraldine Jewsbury, in which she wrote frankly about Carlyle's deficiencies as a husband, were published in 1883, not long after Thomas Carlyle's death. The letters were edited by James Froude, to whom Carlyle had entrusted them with permission to publish, but the frankness of the letters, and of Froude's subsequent biography of Carlyle, caused great controversy. Carlyle's house at 24 Cheyne Row was later turned into a museum, and remains almost exactly as he left it.

Chelsea's literary heavyweights have tended to gather in Cheyne Walk, which follows the Thames between Lots Road and Flood Street. Elizabeth Gaskell was born near Battersea Bridge, at 93 Cheyne Walk in 1810. Her mother died from childbirth complications, and Elizabeth was brought up by an aunt in Knutsford, Cheshire. Most of her novels were published by Dickens in his publications *Household Words* and *All the Year Round*. In 1862, Dante Gabriel Rossetti, Algernon Swinburne and George Meredith took out a joint lease at 16 Cheyne Walk. Rossetti turned the house into a menagerie, including a wombat and a number of peacocks. The birds were so noisy that for decades afterwards the lease at 16 Cheyne Walk

The austere figure of Thomas Carlyle, historian and essayist who lived in Chelsea from 1834. He retained his affection for his native Scotland and refused a grave in Westminster Abbey, choosing instead to be buried in Ecclefechan.

Rossetti moved to Chelsea after the death of his wife, Elizabeth Siddall. He buried some manuscripts with her in her grave at Highgate cemetery but then later had her exhumed to retrieve them.

George Meredith was famous for novels such as The Egoist *and* The Amazing Marriage *which were concerned with the difficulty of relations between the sexes – something which he had personal experience of after a disastrous marriage to Mary Ellen Nicolls.*

expressly forbade residents from keeping them.

The bachelor establishment suited all three men, particularly Rossetti and Meredith, who had recently lost their wives. Rossetti's wife Elizabeth Siddall had died earlier that year from a laudanum overdose. Meredith's wife had left him for the painter Henry Wallis, for whose best-known painting *The Death of Chatterton* Meredith had posed. While he was living at Hobury Street and writing his novel *The Ordeal of Richard Feverel*, Meredith often used to see Thomas Carlyle, who lived nearby, but was too shy to introduce himself. Carlyle, however, read and admired the novel and wrote to Meredith via his publisher, inviting him to his home in Cheyne Row.

In December 1880, the novelist George Eliot moved into 4 Cheyne Walk. The previous May, she had surprised her friends and family by marrying John Cross, a long-standing friend of Eliot and her former partner George Henry Lewes, who had died in 1878. At 40, he was 21 years her junior,

though it was Cross who confided to Henry James that he felt 'a carthorse yoked to a racer'. It is possible that he had doubts about the wisdom of the marriage: while on honeymoon in Venice, he jumped from the window of their hotel room into the Grand Canal, where he was rescued by gondoliers.

Seven months later, and within weeks of moving into their new home, Eliot was dead at 61, from kidney disease and heart failure. Her young widower was heard to say, 'And I am left alone in this new house we meant to be so happy in.' He remained celibate until his death in 1924.

In August 1911, Henry James wrote to a friend from Lamb House, his home in Rye: 'I can't stand lonely hibernations here, where for several years I have had too much of it. Miles of pavement and lamp light are good for me.'

Now 68, James usually stayed at the Reform Club when he was in London, but this arrangement had a serious drawback. For some years James had dictated all his novels and stories to his secretary, the faithful Theodora Bosanquet, who typed as James paced ruminatively about the room. However, women were banned from members' bedrooms at the Reform Club. For a while, James stayed at the Reform Club and took a taxi every morning to

10 Lawrence Street, where Theodora was living with a friend.

In January 1913 James moved in to 21 Carlyle Mansions, in Cheyne Walk, describing them in his inimitable prose to his friend Edward Warren:

This Chelsea perch, the haunt of the sage and the seagull, as you so happily term it (though I feel scarcely more like one of these, than like the other), proves, even after brief experiment, just the right thing for me; and though I have but a couple of ample rooms straight on the River, which I pay for by a much dimmer rearward residuum, such a fine scrap of a front, given what it is on fine days or on almost any days, very decently suffices and makes me more than content.

That spring, James sat for his portrait at John Singer Sargent's studio in Tite Street. Unlike so many sitters, he was delighted by the result, pronouncing it 'nothing less, evidently, than a very fine thing indeed, Sargent at his very best and poor old HJ not at his worst; in short, a living breathing likeness and a masterpiece of painting'. Less impressed was an elderly suffragette named Mary Wood, who attacked the portrait with a chopper when it was displayed at the Royal Academy. When she appeared in court, Mrs Wood explained that she didn't have anything against James personally (he was, in fact, cautiously supportive of women's rights) but 'because I wish to show the public that they have no security for their property nor for their art treasures until women are given political freedom'.

The outbreak of the First World War affected James deeply, and prompted him finally to become a British citizen – almost half a century after his arrival in London (see Mayfair). The last piece he ever wrote was an introduction to *Letters from America* by the war poet Rupert Brooke. A few days later James suffered a stroke at Carlyle Mansions. He recovered sufficiently to describe the curious sensation of hearing another voice in the room saying, 'So here it is at last, the distinguished thing!'

Another stroke followed, and when it became clear that he would not live much longer, the editor of *Letters from America*, Edward Marsh, made 'a cogent plea' to 10 Downing Street that he be awarded the Order of Merit. On New Year's Day 1916, one of James's closest friends, Edmund Gosse, called early in the morning at 21 Carlyle Mansions. James was lying in bed with his eyes closed, the sick room lit by a single candle. Leaning over the bed, Gosse whispered, 'Henry, they've given you the OM.' James did not respond and Gosse tiptoed out of the room, leaving James to the care of the maid. As soon as he

Lord Lundy, 'who was too freely moved to tears and thereby ruined his political career', an illustration by Lord Basil Blackwood (known as B.T.B.) from Hilaire Belloc's Cautionary Tales. *Hilaire Belloc (1870–1953) spent five years at 104 Cheyne Walk from 1900 to 1905, during which time he considered a career in politics and became a liberal MP in 1906. He later abandoned politics disillusioned with the compromise necessary for political success.*

George Eliot's home at 4 Cheyne Walk, which she shared with her husband John Cross for only a few weeks.

Statue of Sir Thomas More at Chelsea Old Church, where he regularly worshipped.

had closed the door, James opened his eyes and told the maid, 'Turn off the light to spare my blushes.'

James's funeral service the following March was held in Sir Thomas More's chapel at Chelsea Old Church. His commemorative plaque, erected by his brother William and sister Alice, pays tribute to him as a 'lover and interpreter of the fine amenities of brave decisions and generous loyalties: a resident of this parish who renounced a cherished citizenship to give his allegiance to England in the first year of the Great War'.

The future creator of James Bond, Ian Fleming, was still at Eton when his mother Eve moved to 119 Cheyne Walk, determined to transform herself from an upper-class widowed mother of four to a fully-fledged Chelsea bohemian. Deliberately choosing the unfashionable end of Cheyne Walk, near Lots Road power station, she bought three workers' cottages, one of which had belonged to the painter Turner, and knocked them into one. She was soon having an affair with a Chelsea neighbour, the portrait painter Augustus John, who years later would paint (and frequently subsidize) Dylan Thomas. Although John was a notorious womanizer, Eve Fleming was determined to bear his child, which she duly did in 1925. Ian Fleming was irritated and embarrassed by his mother's activities. But the house at 119 Cheyne Walk had the advantages of being both central and luxurious and Fleming was still living there with his mother in his late twenties, when he was working as a stockbroker in the City. Eventually, however, he moved into a former home of Oswald Mosley in Belgravia, where he could more conveniently entertain girlfriends and add to his growing collection of pornography. After the Second World War, Fleming moved to Carlyle Mansions, half a mile away from his mother's former home. (Eve was by now living as a tax exile in the south of France.)

Living two floors below was TS Eliot, who shared a flat with the editor and book collector John Hayward. Fleming had known Hayward since the 1930s, when he had started a journal called the *Book Collector*, which Hayward edited. Confined to a wheelchair through muscular dystrophy, Hayward was known, and somewhat feared, in literary circles for his scabrous wit and forthright opinions. The latter were usually heeded by his writer friends – Graham Greene was reassured by his praise for *The Heart of the Matter*, and Eliot deferred to his comments on his plays, especially on the occasions when they betrayed an incomplete knowledge of English social mores. Eliot and Hayward shared a passion for Sherlock Holmes, which in Eliot's case amounted almost to an obsession.

The pair moved into Carlyle Mansions in 1946, their third-floor flat directly under the one occupied by Henry James 30 years before. At weekends Eliot would push Hayward in his wheelchair across Albert Bridge to Battersea Park, or along Chelsea Embankment to the Royal Hospital. A friend, Christopher Sykes, who sometimes accompanied them, retained the image of Eliot, in pouring rain, watching a football match there between dustmen from Marylebone council and maintenance staff from Chelsea.

Ascetic as ever, Eliot spurned the river view from the front of Carlyle Mansions, selecting for his quarters the small, dark rooms at the back of the building which looked out on to a brick wall. Ezra Pound's daughter, who paid him a visit at Carlyle Mansions, was struck by the loneliness of his life.

Eliot's weekdays followed a set routine: up at 6.30a.m. for mass at St Stephen's Church in Gloucester Road, followed by breakfast at Carlyle Mansions, with a couple of games of patience and *The Times* crossword to get his creative juices flowing. Eliot would spend the rest of the morning on his own work (usually a play or a work of philosophy or literary criticism – he wrote little poetry after the early 1940s). He would leave for his job at Faber and Faber around

12 o'clock, catching a bus to Piccadilly Circus and completing the journey to Russell Square by tube. Usually he travelled anonymously, though on one occasion he was approached at his usual seat on the top deck by a young Indian student, who asked him if he was TS Eliot. He admitted to her that he was and got off at the next stop.

Eliot's monk-like existence was transformed in the mid-1950s, when he proposed to Valerie Fletcher, his secretary at Faber and Faber. Although he suffered continual ill health in his final years, this second marriage was exceptionally happy, despite their difference in age (when they married in 1957 he was 68, she 30). Eliot was to say that there were only two periods in his life when he had been happy: his childhood, and his second marriage. Left behind in Carlyle Mansions was John Hayward, who had only learnt of Eliot's impending marriage at the last moment and felt, under-standably, abandoned by his friend. He continued to live in the flat, latterly attended by a nurse, until his death in September 1965.

In 1897, Mark Twain was living at 23 Tedworth Square, a neat, red-brick building in a quiet, rather dull little square

Mark Twain was a frequent visitor to London between 1872 and 1907. It was during his lengthy stay in 1897 that he famously advised an American journalist who called on him to describe reports of his death as 'exaggerated'.

which must have had Twain feeling a long, long way from the Mississippi life he had described in *Tom Sawyer* and *Huckleberry Finn*. Twain spent an anxious winter there, trying to pay off the debts he had incurred when his New York publishing business, Wesbter and Co, had collapsed. The proceeds of a round-the-world lecture tour (he visited Australia, New Zealand, India and South Africa in 1895–6), and a book, *Following the Equator*, enabled him to pay off his creditors by 1899.

Meanwhile, Bram Stoker, the Dublin-born author of *Dracula*, was living at 18 St Leonard's Terrace – a tall white house, with a distinctive balcony overlooking playing fields and the Royal Hospital beyond. Stoker's novels were written mainly as a hobby, during the snatched periods of leisure time allowed by Stoker's demanding job as right-hand man to the actor-manager Sir Henry Irving. Stoker's duties involved the administration of the Lyceum Theatre, where Irving enjoyed a glittering career as the most famous Shakespearian actor of his generation. Irving also played the lead in the first dramatized version of *Dracula*.

Unlike his other novels, which were usually dashed off in months, *Dracula* was written painstakingly over five years, mainly during summer holidays in Whitby, where part of the novel is set. It's possible to read almost anything into Stoker's most famous tale – critics have identified, among other things, sexual guilt, closet homosexuality, oral sex and menstruation. It

*O*scar Wilde (right) *and the painter Whistler were Chelsea neighbours and verbal sparring partners: 'Mr Whistler has always spelled art with a capital "I".'*

seems likely Stoker's demanding, charismatic employer had something to do with the seductive, blood-sucking Count.

According to one story, Queen Victoria was so enthralled by *Dracula* that she asked her courtiers to bring her everything else the author had published – only to be presented with Stoker's first literary effort, *The Duties of Clerks of Petty Session in Ireland*. His post-*Dracula* output was undistinguished – *The Lair of the White Worm* has to be read to be believed – and after his death in 1912, his widow Florence devoted much of her energy to a Canute-like battle against the numerous unauthorized film versions of her husband's only enduring work.

In her youth in Dublin, Florence Balcombe had been the girlfriend of Oscar Wilde. Stoker had secured her affections while Oscar was being treated for syphilis and

under medical orders to abstain from sexual activity for two years. After graduating from Oxford University, Wilde moved to London and re-established contact with the Stokers, now becoming friends. Wilde did, however, retain his feelings for Florence. Confiding in Ellen Terry, Irving's principal leading lady at the Lyceum, he wailed, 'She thinks I never loved her, thinks I forget. My God, how could I?' He had yet to discover 'the love that dare not speak its name'.

Meanwhile, Wilde's mother and his brother Willie had also arrived in Chelsea. From her new residence at 146 Oakley Street, Lady Jane Wilde revived the literary salons for which she had been famous in Dublin. Self-conscious about her advancing years and her lack of servants, her Wednesday afternoon gatherings were conducted by candlelight, with the curtains drawn.

Wilde soon followed her to Chelsea. In 1881 he moved into 44 Tite Street, employing the artist Edward Godwin to repaint the bricks in red and yellow and the roof slates a demanding shade of green. Wilde shared the house with an Oxford friend, Frank Miles. Although Wilde had yet to prove himself as a writer, his legend was already growing: shortly after the move to Tite Street, Wilde heard that the Prince of Wales wanted to meet him ('I do not know Mr Wilde, and not to know Mr Wilde is not to be known'). Wilde and Miles invited him to Tite Street, where he arrived with Lillie Langtry and took part in a séance.

Among their Tite Street neighbours was the painter James Abbott McNeill Whistler, who was an acquaintance of Wilde's. Wilde and Whistler were at a party in Beaufort Street in 1883 when Wilde overheard a witty remark by a woman guest. 'How I wish I had said that,' Wilde said. 'You will, Oscar, you will,' Whistler replied.

Bram Stoker lived in Chelsea, writing as a hobby while working at the Lyceum Theatre under Henry Irving. The tyrannical actor-manager is thought to have partially inspired Stoker's Count Dracula.

Wilde and Miles's bachelor life at 44 Tite Street came to an abrupt halt when Miles' father, an Oxford canon, came across a copy of Wilde's *Poems* and was appalled by their erotic content. In an ultimatum which had ominous overtones for the future, he offered his son a choice between leaving Wilde and losing his inheritance. When Frank told his friend he was choosing the latter option, Wilde marched upstairs, packed a trunk and hurled it downstairs, destroying an antique table in the hall. He then stormed off into the night and out of Miles's life.

For the time being, Wilde moved in with his mother, who was now living at 1 Ovington Square. Miles, who was later revealed to have a penchant for sex with under-age girls, was eventually confined to a mental hospital, where he died in 1891.

When he married Constance Lloyd in May 1884, Wilde returned to Tite Street, leasing number 16 (now number 34). Edward Godwin again supplied the decor. In a letter, Wilde boasted of his dining room, 'done in different shades of white, with white curtains embroidered in yellow silk: the effect is absolutely delightful and the room beautiful'. His study, painted in red and yellow, was remembered by his son Vyvyan as 'a Holy of Holies': 'It was a place of awe, and it was sacrosanct; a place in the vicinity of which no noise was to be made, and which must only be passed on tiptoe.' Wilde also liked to work in the library, which was decorated in dark blue and gold. Instead of chairs, there was a divan around two sides of the room. Among the guests at Tite Street was WB Yeats, who tried to entertain Wilde's other son, Cyril, with a story about a giant. Instead, the child burst into tears.

London Society mourned Wilde's transformation into a respectable, married citizen. One magazine, the *Bat*, lamented:

> *At last he went and cut his*
> *   hair –*
> *The soil proved poor and arid.*
> *And things are much as they*
> *   once were –*
> *He's settled down and*
> *   married!*

Married Wilde may have been, but he had no intention of settling down. Three years into his marriage he had his first homo-sexual affair, with a 17-year-old Cambridge undergraduate named Robert Ross, whom Wilde nick-

*W*ilde's house in Tite Street, which he occupied with his wife Constance Lloyd.

named 'St Robert of Phillimore' after his parental home in Phillimore Gardens. Over the next few years, there were many more young men. As his biographer Richard Ellmann put it: 'Wilde prided himself on leading a life not double but multiple. He could be with Parnell and Gladstone one night, with Wilson Barrett and Ellen Terry the next, with young men the next. And Constance, with his children, was always there, to neglect or not.'

By the early 1890s he was actively courting disaster, openly sharing a room – and a bed – at the Savoy with Lord Alfred Douglas, the son of the Marquess of Queensberry. One night in June 1894, the Marquess turned up on the doorstep of 16 Tite Street. In *De Profundis*, written to Douglas from his prison cell, Wilde described the scene which followed, with Queensberry 'in my library in Tite Street, waving his small hands in the air in epileptic fury…uttering every foul word his foul mind could think of, and screaming the loathsome threats he afterwards with such cunning carried out'.

When the diatribe finally subsided, Wilde followed Queensberry into the hall and pointed him out to his servant, Arthur. 'This is the Marquess of Queensberry, the most infamous brute in London. You are never to allow him to enter my house again.'

The only possible outcome of Wilde's failed 1895 libel action against Queensberry was arrest and a criminal trial. In a bedroom at the Cadogan Hotel in Cadogan Gardens, Wilde waited stoically for the inevitable knock on the door as his friends vainly urged him to catch the boat train to Dover. When two detectives arrived at the

hotel, a waiter brought them to his room, where Wilde was charged with committing indecent acts. He was then driven to Bow Street police station. Queensberry was already demanding payment of his legal costs, and while Wilde was held in custody some of his most treasured possessions, including his writing desk, which had belonged to Carlyle, and his presentation books from Hugo, Whitman, Swinburne and others, were sold off. Later, with Wilde in prison and his wife and sons in hiding, Queensberry's supporters plundered the house in Tite Street.

While he was at boarding school during the First World War, John Betjeman's parents moved from Highgate to 53 Church Street in Chelsea. In *Summoned by Bells*, Betjeman remembered the house as 'poky, dark and cramped /

John Betjeman retained a lifelong affection for his teddy bear Archibald. He even used to take it on tube journeys with him into central London. The poet's relationship with the bear was probably the inspiration for Sebastian Flyte's affection for Aloysius in Brideshead Revisited *by Evelyn Waugh.*

Haunted by quarrels and the ground-floor ghost'. He missed Highgate, with its 'smell of trodden leaves and grass'. One compensation was the excitement of exploring London, accompanied by his friend Ronald Hughes Wright, who lived in Upper Cheyne Row.

*Great was my joy with
London at my feet –
All London mine, five
shillings in my hand
And not expected back till
after tea!*

Towards the end of his life, Betjeman returned to Chelsea, living at 29 Radnor Walk. A journalist, Graham Lord, came to interview him: 'As he pottered beside me down the Kings Rd, near his Chelsea home – with tie awry and a battered green felt hat plonked low about his ears – it looked as if Paddington Bear had escaped from a British Railways Left Luggage Office.'

Jerome K Jerome (1859–1927) was brought up in relative poverty in the East End before turning to writing. His sequel to Three Men in a Boat, Three Men on the Bummel, *was less successful, but he returned to public favour with the play* The Passing of the Third Floor Back, *about a Christ-like figure who comes to live in a London boarding house.*

Jerome K Jerome was living in the top-floor flat at 91–104 Chelsea Gardens, on the corner of Chelsea Bridge Road and Ebury Bridge Road, when he wrote *Three Men in a Boat*, about three young men and a dog who take a boating holiday on the Thames. Jerome recalled his flat as 'nearly all windows, suggestive of a lighthouse' and wrote nostalgically of the few months in 1889 when he wrote the novel:

*It was summer time,
and London is so beautiful in summer. It lay beneath my window, a fairy city veiled in golden mist, for I worked in a room high above the chimney-pots; and at night the lights shone far beneath me, so that I looked down as into an Aladdin's cave of jewels.'*

Jerome's turret-shaped flat is still visible from the pavement, though today the 'golden mist' is provided by the exhaust fumes from the incessant traffic on Chelsea Bridge Road.

In 1952, PG Wodehouse replied to a letter from a fan who wanted to know more about Ukridge, the amoral rogue whose adventures he had first chronicled in his 1906 novel *Love among the Chickens*. 'Ukridge is a real character,' Wodehouse wrote. 'He was drawn from a man with whom I used to run about London from about 1903 onwards.' This was Herbert Westbrook, who first came to Wodehouse's attention when he called at his then home at 23 Walpole Street, near King's Road, to seek advice on a career in literature. Westbrook, who was once described as having all the egotistical temperament of the true artist but none of the talent, was heroically lazy and permanently broke, perpetually tapping Wodehouse and other friends for loans which he never repaid. His fictional alter ego Ukridge was

268

never the most popular of Wodehouse's characters, probably because he lacks the innocence of a Bertie Wooster or a Lord Emsworth. Wodehouse, however, was fond of Ukridge and enjoyed writing about his antics, though he found it necessary to dispense with the wife with whom he endowed him in his first adventure.

In his autobiography *Over the Bridge* (1955) Richard Church describes his London childhood in the 1900s. As a Post Office worker covering the southwest district, Church's father seemed to know the names of every householder in the southwest district of London. More surprisingly, they also seemed to know him: when father and son walked through Chelsea together, Church Senior would be 'greeted with a nod and smile by strangers, whose names he would reel off to us when they were out of earshot; and it was exactly as though he were reading an address on an envelope'.

Church's father liked to tell the story of a chance encounter in Chelsea when he was a boy and living in one of the working-class backwaters of Chelsea. One day he was on his way home carrying a basin of pickled onions and accompanied by a couple of small friends. Near Cheyne Row they encountered a fierce-looking old man, dressed in black, wearing a black hat with a wide brim and carrying a walking stick, striding along the pavement, muttering to himself. The irascibility of the figure made him an obvious target for the three boys, who proceeded to pelt him with pickled onions. During the fusillade he retaliated by roaring at them and menacing them with his upraised walking stick. When the basin was empty

the engagement broke off, and Thomas Carlyle was able to continue his journey home.

In August 1919, AA Milne and his wife Daphne moved into 13 Mallord Street, Chelsea. A few years later, when Milne was enjoying the success of *When We Were Very Young*, he was visited by an American editor, Clara Hawkins, who went there to try to persuade him to write a story for her *Christmas Annual*:

Percy Bysshe Shelley's house on the Chelsea Embankment contained a private theatre where his play The Cenci *was performed.*

AA Milne lives in Chelsea, and there I went upon appointment. The houses of Chelsea are old and gracious of manner; with the classic red brick and white paint austerity of their Georgian origin relieved by brilliant doors of primary reds or blues or yellows – the happy inspiration of their present-day bohemian owners. Mr Milne's doorway was a brilliant blue ...There was a bluish haze of nice-smelling pipe smoke, and inside the smoke there was a lean, pleasant young man. He got up lazily as if he were a little tired after a long tramp on the moors. That was my impression of him – tweeds, dogs, gorse, and a pipe. As a matter of fact I don't believe he is especially any of these things; I just thought of them as he stood up to shake my hand.

The rotunda of Ranelagh Gardens, which were laid out near Chelsea Hospital in 1742. Edward Gibbon called Ranelagh 'the most convenient place for courtships of every kind – the best market we have in England'.

The Doors to be opened at nine

Dylan Thomas lived intermittently in Chelsea from 1934, when he and a friend, Fred Janes, a student at the Royal College of Art, moved into a lodging house at 5 Redcliffe Street, near Brompton Cemetery. In years to come, Thomas would be seen as aggressively, definitively Welsh, but in 1934 he was anxious to put it behind him. 'Land of my fathers,' he scoffed to his then girlfriend Pamela Hansford Johnson. 'My fathers can keep it.' Thomas launched himself wholeheartedly into the bohemian life, turning his rooms into a squalid battlefield, sleeping in whatever clothes he had happened to pass out in the night before, and distressing his flatmate with vigorous hawking every morning in the hope of finding evidence, *à la* Keats, of tubercular blood. At the time, and for some years afterwards, Thomas had a peculiar fascination for the disease, once announcing to Pamela Hansford Johnson that a poet had three duties: drinking heavily, getting fat and having TB. He succeeded with the first two.

In January 1935, Thomas, Janes and another painter, Thomas's former schoolmate Mervyn Levy, moved to another lodging house close by, at 21 Coleherne Road. From 1942–4 he was living with his wife Caitlin in a one-room flat, 8 Wentworth Studios,

EH Shepard's inimitable illustrations did much to define the Pooh stories in the public imagination. Shepard always drew from life, so Milne invited him to Mallord Street 'to get Pooh's and Piglet's likeness'. Milne's American publisher John Macrae later described how he 'happened to be present at one of the meetings of Milne and Shepard – Milne sitting on the sofa reading the story, Christopher Robin sitting on the floor playing with the characters, which are now famous in Winnie-the-Pooh, and, by his side, on the floor, sat EH Shepard making sketches for the illustrations which finally went into the book'.

A A Milne was assistant editor at Punch *and became well known for his light essays and comedies before achieving worldwide fame with his book of verse* When We Were Very Young.

in Manresa Road (since demolished).

As a freelance writer whose only regular income was £1 a week sent by his mother in Swansea, Thomas's finances began shakily and remained so for the rest of his life, through his chronic inability to manage his affairs. As a writer, he was the despair of his editors, from whom he would extract large advances, often in cash, which he would invariably spend before making any attempt to begin the project for which he had been commissioned. He would then send increasingly agonized letters, begging for further sums of money without which, he would argue, he could not possibly start work. More often than not the book or article in question never saw the light of day. Friends were treated in an equally cavalier fashion. Theodora FitzGibbon, who had been naïve enough to entrust Dylan with her keys, caught him in King's Road, with her sewing machine in his hands, on his way to a pawn shop. Another friend who let him stay in her flat when he had no money found him urinating against the living room wall. Bernard Spencer came up with a fitting nickname for Thomas, 'the Ugly Suckling', though the capriciousness was invariably leavened with charm. Geoffrey Grigson, who liked to call him 'the Changeling', conceded that 'When he disappeared, it was a relief; when he reappeared, a pleasure.'

I n the summer of 1940, Quentin Crisp, who had recently been rejected from military service on the grounds that he was 'suffering from sexual perversion', moved into the first-floor front bedsit at 129 Beaufort Street. He remained at 129

Beaufort Street for nearly 40 years, never once doing any cleaning or dusting. 'It is simply a question of keeping one's nerve,' he would tell appalled visitors. 'After the first four years the dirt doesn't get any worse.'

During the forties and fifties, Crisp scratched a living as a model, specializing in life-drawing classes in art schools, with one or two forays into writing. His wartime poem *All This and Bevin Too* was illustrated by Mervyn Peake, the creator of *Gormenghast*, after they had shared a table in a café. Following the success of his autobiography *The Naked Civil Servant* (1968) and its sequel *How to Become a Virgin* (1981), Crisp left London for Manhattan.

D espite his long residence, Crisp was never wholly enamoured of Chelsea; in *The Naked Civil Servant* he complains that, far from being the home of the broad-minded, it was 'merely lousy with people who lacked the nerve or the energy to give positive expression to moral judgement'. Others, too, have

The King's Head and Eight Bells became a fashionable meeting place for artists in the mid-nineteenth century and was frequented by Whistler, Carlyle and Augustus John. Later on it was to be Dylan Thomas's favourite Chelsea pub and a hangout for Chelsea's bohmeians whom Thomas called 'The Cheyne Gang'.

Bywater Street – the home of the master spy George Smiley in John Le Carré's Tinker Tailor Soldier Spy.

grimy trivia that underlie the glossy images of "smart" West London'. More disturbing still is Pamela Hansford Johnson's 1947 short story 'Sloane Square', about a dream-like late-night journey on the Underground by a possibly shell-shocked serviceman. Despite its brevity, it is impossible to read the story without experiencing a mounting sense of panic.

In John Le Carré's *Tinker Tailor Soldier Spy* (1974), the brilliant, world-weary spy George Smiley is also disillusioned with Chelsea. Smiley's home is off the King's Road, in Bywater Street – 'a cul-de-sac exactly one hundred and seventeen of his own paces long. When he had first come to live here these Georgian cottages had a modest, down-at-heel charm, with young couples making do on fifteen pounds a week and a tax-free lodger hidden in the basement. Now steel screens protected their lower windows and for each house three cars jammed the kerb.' The novelist Laurie Lee witnessed a similar transformation in Elm Park Gardens, near Fulham Road, where he lived from 1964 to 1984. His autobiographical book *As I Walked Out One Midsummer Morning* (1969) described his departure from the Gloucestershire village of Slad, the scene of his best-known book *Cider with Rosie*, and his experiences in Spain shortly before the Civil War. Lee's local pub was the Queen's Elm, near Queen's Elm Square, where he would sit on the bench seat on the right of the door. Lee died in 1997 and the pub has recently closed, its doorway currently occupied by a flower stall.

seen the darker sides to Chelsea. Robin Maugham's 1948 novel *The Servant* is set in an uneasy post-war Chelsea, in which the old social certainties are rapidly breaking down. The narrator, Richard Merton, who lives in Oakley Street, tells the story of his old army friend Tony, who is allowing his life to be controlled by his insolent, malevolent manservant, Barrett. As the novelist Neil Bartlett says in his introduction to the novel, the story unfolds against a background of 'small streets, small pubs, small independent incomes – all the

More than any theatre in London, the Royal Court in Sloane Square enjoys a reputation for presenting – and often defending – groundbreaking plays by new authors. More than a dozen of Bernard Shaw's plays had their first performances here, including *Major Barbara* (1905), *The Doctor's Dilemma* (1906) and *Heartbreak House* (1921). In 1956 the English Stage company was established with a remit 'to stage and encourage new writing'. At their new home at the Royal Court, the Company, under the direction of George Devine, pioneered the 'kitchen-sink drama' – stark, contemporary plays, usually with a domestic setting, written in deliberate contrast to the light drawing room dramas of Noel Coward and Terence Rattigan and the contrived verse dramas of TS Eliot and Christopher Fry. The first of these plays, John Osborne's *Look Back in Anger*, proved a landmark in British drama, and was followed by Osborne's *The Entertainer* (1957) which revived the stage career of Laurence Olivier, *Luther* (1961), *Inadmissible Evidence* (1964) and *A Patriot for Me* (1965).

The most controversial play ever produced at the Royal Court was probably Edward Bond's *Saved* (1965), a study of urban violence which caused uproar with a scene in which a baby is stoned. Defended by Laurence Olivier as 'compulsory viewing for every adult in this country', the play was nevertheless banned by the Lord Chamberlain, who until 1968 had the power to suppress plays for breaches of taste. Other major plays since staged at the Royal Court include David Storey's *In Celebration* (1969) and *Home* (1970), Mary O'Malley's *Once a Catholic* (1975), Caryl Churchill's *Serious Money* (1987) and Conor McPherson's *The Weir* (1998).

Look Back in Anger by John Osborne, staged at the Royal Court Theatre in Chelsea, was said to change the face of British drama in the 1950s and was hailed by Kenneth Tynan as 'the best young play of the decade'. Kenneth Haigh (right) played the 'angry young man' Jimmy Porter.

EARLS COURT

'To those whom God has forsaken,' wrote Patrick Hamilton in *Hangover Square*, 'is given a gas-fire in Earls Court.' Hamilton's gloomy but brilliant 1941 novel is the story of the lonely, mentally unstable George Harvey Bone, who lives in

Patrick Hamilton's novel Hangover Square *is set on the 'hard frozen plains of Earl's Court'.*

Earls Court on four pounds a week and is hopelessly infatuated with the worthless, egotistical Netta, a putative actress who lives in Cromwell Road. On the eve of the Second World War, Hamilton's characters live out their lives in the furnished flats and boozy pubs in and around the Earls Court Road. The pub to which Bone takes his friend Johnnie is almost certainly the King's Head in Howarth Place, which Hamilton describes with the acuity of a gifted writer hovering on the cusp of alcoholism. Johnnie, who unlike most of the characters is not a heavy drinker, 'could not see what George could see – the wet winter nights when the door was closed; the smoke, the noise, the wet people: the agony of Netta under the electric light: Mickey drunk and Peter arguing: mornings-after on dark November days: the dart-playing and boredom: the lunch-time drunks, the lunch-time snacks, the lunch-room upstairs: the whole poisoned nightmarish circle of the idle tippler's existence'.

Born in Hassocks, West Sussex, in 1904, Hamilton had lived in the White House Hotel in Earls Court in the early 1920s, when he was studying for the London Matriculation exam. As the 'Fauconberg', the White House appeared in Hamilton's cheerful first novel, *Monday Morning*, published in 1925, as well as in *Hangover Square*, where it is Bone's home. It was a hotel until the late 1990s, when it was converted into flats.

In January 1932, Hamilton and his wife Lois were staying with his sister Lalla in her flat at 134 Earls Court Road. One evening, the three of them were walking along Logan Place, a narrow street which then had no pavements, when a car suddenly shot out from Lexham Gardens, on the other side of Earls Court Road, and, as an eye witness later put it, 'leapt into the street like a slap in the face'. Hamilton was hit by the car and thrown into the road, receiving multiple fractures and lacerations; his face, particularly his nose, was permanently disfigured. Eventually, Hamilton put the accident to some use, in the appallingly realistic scene in *Twenty Thousand Streets under the Sky* in which a cyclist is hit by a car in the Great West Road.

In Iris Murdoch's picaresque novel *Under the Net* (1954), Jake Donaghue's friend and reluctant landlady Magdalen lives in 'one of those repulsive heavy-weight houses in Earls Court Road'. Jake reflects that 'There are some parts of London which are necessary and others which are contingent. Everywhere west of Earls Court is contingent, except for a few places along the river.' In the 1950s, Earls Court was colonized by expatriate Australians, who would drive camper vans overland through Asia and Europe, park them in Earls Court and put a For Sale sign on the windscreen to raise some cash. The world of 'Kangaroo Valley' was gleefully sent up by Barry Humphries in his *Private Eye* comic strip, 'The Wonderful World of Barry McKenzie'.

However, Earls Court first came to international attention in the 1880s, when the Exhibition Hall was opened in Warwick Road. Not long after it opened, Henry James treated the French

writer Guy de Maupassant to a trip to the hall. Surveying the scene, Maupassant told James: 'There's a woman sitting over there whom I would like to have. Go over and get her for me.'

James was polite but firm. 'My dear friend, I cannot possibly do that. She may be perfectly respectable. In England you have to be careful.'

Maupassant spotted another woman. 'Surely you know her at least! I could do quite well with her, if you would get her for me. If only I knew English!'

James stuck to his guns. Finally, Maupassant gave up in disgust. 'Really, Henry,' he exclaimed, 'you don't seem to know anybody in London!'

Patrick Hamilton (1904–1962). JB Priestley described Hamilton's fictional London as 'a kind of No-Man's-Land of shabby hotels, dingy boarding houses and those saloon bars where the homeless can meet'.

GAZETTEER

The gazetteer lists places of literary interest. They are arranged alphabetically under each district following the order of the book. Those buildings marked with a '**O**' have plaques marking them. Most of these are private residences that are not open to the public. Some streets have been re-numbered since the authors lived there: current street numbers are used in the gazetteer which may differ from addresses in the text.

CENTRAL LONDON

MAYFAIR AND PICCADILLY
Browns Hotel
Albemarle Street, W1
020 7493 6020
Agatha Christie
Rudyard Kipling
AA Milne

Hatchard's Bookshop
187 Piccadilly, W1
020 7439 9921
Oscar Wilde

ONancy Mitford
Heywood Hill Bookshop
10 Curzon Street, W1
020 7629 0647

OSomerset Maugham
6 Chesterfield Street, W1

ORichard Brinsley Sheridan
14 Savile Row, W1

ST JAMES'S
The Athenaeum
Pall Mall, SW1
Charles Dickens
Henry James
William Thackeray et al.

White's Club
37/38 St James's Street, SW1
Alexander Pope
Horace Walpole

WESTMINSTER
St Margaret's Church
Parliament Square, SW1
Samuel Pepys
John Milton
Winston Churchill
Frederick Farrar

Westminster Abbey
Parliament Square, SW1
020 7222 5152
Poets' Corner

BLOOMSBURY
British Museum
Great Russell Street, WC1
020 7636 1555
John Keats
Virginia Woolf
George Gissing
Max Beerbohm et al.

Coram Fields
93 Guildford Street, WC1
020 7837 6138
Charles Dickens

Dickens' House Museum
48 Doughty Street, WC1
020 7405 2127
Charles Dickens

OTS Eliot
The old Faber and
Faber Address
24 Russell Square, WC1

Church of St Giles in the Fields
St Giles High Street, WC2
James Shirley
Andrew Marvell

OLady Ottoline Morrell
10 Gower Street, WC1

Museum Tavern
49 Great Russell Street, WC1
020 7242 8987
Louis MacNeice
Karl Marx
Angus Wilson

Queen's Larder pub
1 Queen Square, WC1
020 7837 5627
Alan Bennett

OLytton Strachey
51 Gordon Square, WC1

OVirginia Woolf
29 Fitzroy Square, W1
46 Gordon Square, WC1

OWB Yeats
5 Woburn Walk, WC1

FITZROVIA
OJames Boswell
122 Great Portland Street W1

Fitzroy Tavern
16 Charlotte Street, W1
020 7580 3714
Patrick Hamilton
Dylan Thomas

The Green Man pub
383 Euston Road, NW1
020 7387 6977
Patrick Hamilton

OGeorge Bernard Shaw
29 Fitzroy Square, W1

SOHO
St Anne's Church
55 Dean Street, W1
John Betjeman
Dorothy L. Sayers

Coach and Horses pub
29 Greek Street, W1
020 7437 5920
Jeffrey Bernard

◑John Dryden
43 Gerrard Street, W1

W & G Foyle Ltd Bookshop
113–119 Charing Cross Rd
WC2
020 7440 3224

The French House pub
49 Dean Street, W1
020 7437 2799
Dylan Thomas
Brendan Behan
Colin Wilson

◑William Hazlitt
6 Frith Street, W1

◑Karl Marx
28, Dean Street, W1

◑Thomas De Quincey
36 Tavistock Street
WC2

◑Percy Bysshe Shelley
15 Poland Street, W1

OXFORD STREET AND MARYLEBONE
◑Elizabeth Barrett Browning
50 Wimpole Street, W1

◑Elizabeth Barrett Browning
99 Gloucester Place, W1

◑Wilkie Collins
65 Gloucester Place, W1

◑Sir Arthur Conan Doyle
2 Upper Wimpole Street
W1

Sherlock Holmes Museum
221B Baker Street
(actually at 239)
London, NW1
020 7935 8866

◑Rose Macaulay
Hinde House
11–14 Hinde Street, W1

◑Edward Lear
30 Seymour Street, W1

◑Anthony Trollope
39 Montagu Street, W1

◑HG Wells
13 Hanover Terrace, NW1

COVENT GARDEN
◑Jane Austen
10 Henrietta Street, WC2

The Devereux pub
(formerly the Grecian Coffee
House)
20 Devereux Court,
Essex Street, WC2
Joseph Addison
Richard Steele

◑Dr Johnson
& James Boswell
8 Russell Street
Covent Garden, WC2

Lamb and Flag Tavern
33 Rose Street, WC2
John Dryden

St Paul's Church
Covent Garden
George Bernard Shaw
Samuel Pepys

The Salisbury pub
90 Martin's Lane, WC2
020 7836 5863
H. E. Bates
Graham Greene
Julian Symons
Ross Macdonald
Margaret Millar

Theatre Royal
Drury Lane, WC2
020 78363687
Richard Brinsley Sheridan
David Garrick
John Gay

THEATRELAND
Albery Theatre
85 St Martin's Lane, WC2
020 7369 1730
TS Eliot

Aldwych Theatre
Aldwych, WC2
020 7416 6003
Tennessee Williams

Fortune Theatre
Russell Street, WC2
020 7836 2238
Sean O'Casey
Alan Bennett

Garrick Theatre
2 Charing Cross Road
WC2
020 7494 5085
JB Priestley

Theatre Museum
Russell Street
London, WC2
020 7836 7891
Agatha Christie
Noel Coward

◑Oscar Wilde
Theatre Royal
Haymarket, SW1
Henry Fielding

HOLBORN
◑Thomas Chatterton
39 Brooke Street, EC1

Old Curiosity Shop
13-14 Portsmouth Street
WC2
020 7405 9891
Charles Dickens

Prudential Building
High Holborn, WC1
Charles Dickens

BELGRAVIA
○Matthew Arnold
2 Chester Square, SW1

○Ian Fleming
Ebury Street, SW1

VICTORIA
○Joseph Conrad
17 Gillingham Street, SW1

PIMLICO
Dolphin Square
Pimlico, SW1
CP Snow
Radclyffe Hall
Angus Wilson

STRAND AND TRAFALGAR SQUARE
Clement Danes Church
The Strand, WC2
020 7242 8282
Dr Johnson
James Boswell

Sherlock Holmes pub
10 Northumberland Street
WC2
020 7930 2644
Sir Arthur Conan Doyle

○Rudyard Kipling
43 Villiers Street, WC2

National Gallery
Trafalgar Square, WC2
020 7747 2885
Siegfried Sassoon
Iris Murdoch
Julian Barnes

National Portrait Gallery
2 St Martin's Place, WC2
Various writers' portraits

○Samuel Pepys
12 Buckingham Street, WC2

Roman Baths
(National Trust)
Strand Lane
Surrey Street
Charles Dickens

Rule's Restaurant
35 Maiden Lane
Strand, WC2
020 7836 5314
Graham Greene

THE TEMPLE
○Charles Lamb
2 Crown Office Row, EC4

FLEET STREET
St Bride's Church
Fleet Street
EC4
020 7353 1301
Samuel Pepys
Edgar Wallace
John Dryden
John Milton

Ye Olde Cheshire Cheese
145 Fleet Street, EC4
020 7353 6170
Charles Dickens
Dr Johnson
Alfred Lord Tennyson
WB Yeats
GK Chesterton
Mark Twain

Cock Tavern
(formerly the Cock Alehouse)
22 Fleet Street, EC4
Samuel Pepys
Alfred Lord Tennyson

Church of St Dunstan
in the West
Fleet Street, EC4
020 7242 6027
John Donne
Izaak Walton
Samuel Pepys

○Dr Samuel Johnson
Dr Johnson's House
17 Gough Square, EC4
020 7353 3745

○Dr Samuel Johnson
Johnson's Court
Fleet Street
EC4

○Samuel Pepys
Westminster Bank
Salisbury Court
off Fleet Street, EC4

Pepys Exhibition
17 Fleet Street
EC4
020-7936 4004

Punch Tavern
99 Fleet Street, EC4
020 7353 6658

LONDON BRIDGE, BANK OF ENGLAND AND THE MONUMENT
Bank of England
Threadneedle Street
London, EC2
Kenneth Grahame

The Monument
Monument Street, EC3
020 7626 2717
Alexander Pope
James Boswell

○Alexander Pope
32 Lombard Street, EC3

CHRIST'S HOSPITAL, OLD BAILEY AND NEWGATE STREET
Viaduct Tavern
126 Newgate Street
EC1
020 7606 8476
Iris Murdoch

The Old Bailey
Corner of Newgate Street and
Old Bailey, EC4
Oscar Wilde
Norman Collins
D. H. Lawrence

ST PAUL'S AND CHEAPSIDE
St Paul's Cathedral
St Paul's Churchyard, EC4
020 7236 4128
John Donne
Sir Philip Sidney
Stephen Spender

BLACKFRIARS TO THE TOWER OF LONDON
St Magnus Martyr Church
Lower Thames Street, EC3
020 7236 4481
TS Eliot

◗Samuel Pepys
Site of the Navy Office
Seething Lane, EC3

Tower of London
Tower Hill, EC3
020 7709 0765
Samuel Pepys
Sir Walter Ralegh
Sir Thomas More
Thomas Wyatt

SMITHFIELD
Church of St Bartholomew
the Less
In the grounds of St Bart's
Hospital
West Smithfield, EC1
John Shirley

MOORGATE
Barbican Centre
Barbican
Silk Street, EC2
020 7638 4141

Bunhill Fields Burial Ground
38 City Road
Moorgate
EC1
Daniel Defoe
William and
Catherine Blake
John Bunyan

◗John Keats
The John Keats Pub
85 Moorgate
EC2

St Giles's Cripplegate
The Barbican
EC2
John Milton

NORTH LONDON

REGENT'S PARK AND PRIMROSE HILL
Ted Hughes & Sylvia Plath
3 Chalcot Square, NW1

◗George Grossmith
28 Dorset Square, NW1

London Zoo
Regent's Park
NW1
020 7722 3333
William Thackeray
Louis MacNeice
Ted Hughes
Angus Wilson

◗WB Yeats
29 Fitzroy Road
NW1
Sylvia Plath

SOMERS TOWN
British Library
96 Euston Road
NW1
020 7412 7514

CAMDEN TOWN
◗Charles Dickens
141 Bayham Street
Camden Town
NW1

◗Dylan Thomas
54 Delancey Street
NW1

HAMPSTEAD
Keats' House
Wentworth Place
Keat's Grove
NW3
020 7435 2062
John Keats

◗DH Lawrence
1 Byron Villas
Vale of Heath
Hampstead
NW3

The Load of Hay pub
94 Haverstock Hill, NW3
020 7485 3610
Joseph Addison
Richard Steele

◗Gerard Manley Hopkins
9 Oak Hill Park, NW3

Kenwood
Hampstead Lane
London, NW3
020 8248 1286
Charles Dickens

◗Katherine Mansfield &
John Middleton Murry
17 Heath Road, NW3

◗George Orwell
'Perfect Pizza'
South End Road, NW3

Jack Straw's Castle pub
North End Way, NW3
020 7435 8885
Charles Dickens
William Thackeray
Wilkie Collins

The Spaniards Inn
Spaniards Road, NW3
020 8731 6571
John Keats
Percy Shelley
Lord Byron
Charles Dickens

◐Evelyn Waugh
145 North End Road
Golders Green, NW11

HIGHGATE
Highgate Cemetery
Swains Lane, N6
020 8340 1834
John Betjeman
Charles Dickens
George Elliot
Karl Marx
James Thomson
Sir Leslie Stephen
Radclyffe Hall

◐Samuel Taylor Coleridge
3 The Grove, N6

◐AE Housman
17 North Road, N6

◐JB Priestley
3 The Grove, N6

ISLINGTON
Canonbury Square
Canonbury Place, N1
Francis Bacon
Oliver Goldsmith
Evelyn Waugh
George Orwell

◐Charles Lamb
64 Duncan Terrace, N1

◐George Orwell
27b Canonbury Square, N1

HOLLOWAY
Arsenal Stadium
Avenell Road
Highbury, N5
Nick Hornby

STOKE
NEWINGTON
◐Daniel Defoe
95 Stoke Newington Church
Street, N16

EAST LONDON

HACKNEY AND BETHNAL GREEN
◐Israel Zangwill
288 Old Ford Road, E2

SHOREDITCH AND HOXTON
St Leonard's Church
High Street
Shoreditch
James Burbage
Richard Burbage
Gabriel Spencer

The Eagle pub
2 Shepherdess Walk
N1
Charles Dickens

WAPPING, LIME-HOUSE AND THE ISLE OF DOGS
St Anne's Church
Commercial Road
Limehouse
Iain Sinclair
Peter Ackroyd

The Grapes pub
76 Narrow Street
E14
020 7987 4396
Charles Dickens
Angus Wilson

Prospect of Whitby pub
57 Wapping Wall
E1
Samuel Pepys
Charles Dickens
William Thackeray

WHITECHAPEL AND SPITALFIELDS
Christ Church
Commercial Street
Spitalfields, E1
Peter Ackroyd
Iain Sinclair

◐Isaac Rosenberg
Whitechapel Library
77 High Street, E1

SOUTH LONDON

RICHMOND AND BARNES
◐Henry Fielding
Milbourne House
Barnes Green, SW13

◐Virginia & Leonard Woolf
Hogarth House
Paradise Road, Richmond

BATTERSEA
St Mary's Church
Battersea Church Road
SW11
020 7228 9648
William Blake

DULWICH
Dulwich College
Dulwich Common, SE21
Raymond Chandler
PG Wodehouse

SYDENHAM AND CRYSTAL PALACE
◐Richard Jeffries
20 Sydenham Park Road
SE26

HERNE HILL
◐Sax Rohmer
51 Herne Hill
SE24

○John Ruskin
26 Herne Hill, SE24

THE BOROUGH
The George Inn
77 Borough High Street, SE1
020 7407 2056
William Shakespeare

Church of St George the
Martyr (Little Dorrit Church)
Southwark
Charles Dickens

○Dr Johnson
Anchor Brewery
Southwark Bridge Road, SE1

The Old Operating Theatre
Museum and Herb Garret
9a St Thomas Street, SE1
020 7955 4791
John Keats

Southwark Cathedral
Montague Close, SE1
020 7367 6712
John Fletcher
William Shakespeare
Sam Wanamaker
John Gower

BANKSIDE
New Globe Theatre
New Globe Walk
Bankside, SE1
020 7902 1500
Richard Burbage
William Shakespeare

Anchor Tavern
34 Park Street
Bankside, SE1
020 7407 1577
John Evelyn
Samuel Johnson

Tate Modern
(Bankside Power Station)
25 Sumner Street, SE1
020 7887 8000
Ian McKellen's *Richard III*

LAMBETH
Imperial War Museum
Lambeth Road
SE1
020 7416 5000
Tim Newark

DEPTFORD
St Nicholas' Church
Deptford Green
Christopher Marlowe

GREENWICH
Greenwich Observatory
Romney Road
SE10
020 8858 4422
(Recorded information 020
8312 6565)
Henry James
Joseph Conrad

Trafalgar Tavern
Park Row
SE10
020 8858 2437
Harrison Ainsworth
Charles Dickens
William Thackeray
Wilkie Collins
Henry James

BLACKHEATH AND SHOOTER'S HILL
○Nathaniel Hawthorne
4 Pond Street
SE3

WEST LONDON

TWICKENHAM
St Mary the Virgin
Church Street
Twickenham
020 8744 2693
Alexander Pope

HAMMERSMITH, CHISWICK AND SHEPHERD'S BUSH
The Dove pub
19 Upper Mall
Hammersmith
W6
AP Herbert

Kelmscott House
26 Upper Mall
London
W6 9TA
William Morris

Mawson Arms pub
110 Chiswick Lane South
W4
Alexander Pope

○'Ouida' (Maria Louisa de la
Ramée)
Bessborough House
11 Ravenscourt Square
Chiswick
W11

KENSAL GREEN
Kensal Green Cemetery
Harrow Road
W10
020 8969 0152
G. K. Chesterton
Arthur Machen
George Orwell
Iain Sinclair
Nicholas Royle
Harrison Ainsworth
John Forster
William Thackeray
Leigh Hunt
Anthony Trollope
Wilkie Collins

NOTTING HILL AND LADBROKE GROVE
○George Orwell
22 Portobello Road
Notting Hill, W11

PADDINGTON AND BAYSWATER

OThomas Hardy
16 Westbourne Park Villas
W2

Paddington Station
Paddington Bear (statue)

KENSINGTON AND HYDE PARK

OJM Barrie
100 Bayswater Road, W2

OGK Chesterton
11 Warwick Gardens
W14

OGK Chesterton
32 Sheffield Terrace
W8

OSamuel Taylor Coleridge
7 Addison Bridge Place
W14

OFord Madox Ford
80 Campden Hill Road
W8

OKenneth Grahame
16 Phillimore Place
W8

Kensington Gardens
JM Barrie

OMervyn Peake
1 Drayton Gardens
Kensington, SW10

OWilliam Makepeace
Thackeray
36 Onslow Square, SW7

OWilliam Makepeace
Thackeray
16 Young Street, W8

OWilliam Makepeace
Thackeray
2 Palace Green, W8

CHELSEA

OHilaire Belloc
104 Cheyne Walk
SW10

OThomas Carlyle
24 Cheyne Row, SW3
020 7352 7087

Chelsea Old Church
Old Church Street
Chelsea
Henry James
Sir Thomas More

OGeorge Eliot
4 Cheyne Walk, SW3

OElizabeth Gaskell
93 Cheyne Walk
SW10

OLeigh Hunt
22 Upper Cheyne Row
SW3

King's Head and Eight
Bells pub
50 Cheyne Walk
SW3
020 7352 1820
James McNeill Whistler
Thomas Carlyle
Augustus John
Dylan Thomas

OHenry James
34 De Vere Gardens
W8

OJerome K Jerome
91-94 Chelsea Gardens
Chelsea Bridge Road
SW1

OAA Milne
13 Mallord Street
SW3

ODante Gabriel Rossetti &
Algernon Swinburne
16 Cheyne Walk
SW3

Royal Court Theatre
Sloane Square
SW1
Box Office 020 7565 5000
George Bernard Shaw
John Osborne

OBram Stoker
18 St Leonard's Terrace
SW3

OMark Twain
23 Tedworth Square
SW3

OOscar Wilde
34 Tite Street
SW3

INDEX

Figures in italics refer to illustrations

PICTURE ACKNOWLEDGMENTS

Dickens House Museum 24, 27, 63, 147, 148

Hulton Archive 2, 12, 15 (bottom), 30, 32, 40, 41, 46, 48, 52, 54, 55, 56, 57, 64, 66, 67, 83, 96, 106, 120, 124, 133, 142, 146, 150, 158, 164 (both), 200, 207, 223, 246, 241, 253, 257, 270

The Illustrated London Evening News 275

John Murray Publishers 4 (top)

Mary Evans 4 (inset), 13 (bottom), 15 (top), 16, 26, 28, 29, 35, 39, 47, 59 (both), 60, 61, 62, 65, 70, 87, 93, 99, 102, 103, 128, 130, 138, 141, 143, 152, 157, 160, 169, 171, 197, 197, 202, 211, 219, 230, 232, 234, 241, 242, 245, 248, 250, 255, 256, 258, 259, 260 (both), 261, 263, 264, 270, 269. Mary Evans/The Coupland Collection 145. Mary Evans/Institute of Civil Engineers 231. Mary Evans/Jeffrey Morgan 267. Mary Evans/National Portrait Gallery 69, 86.

The Museum of London 25

The Ronald Grant Archive 11

THE PHOTOGRAPHER WOULD LIKE TO THANK THE FOLLOWING:

The Parish Church of St Giles-in-the-Fields, Curator and Staff of the Dickens House Museum, Dolphin Square Trust, Manager and Staff of Rules Restaurant – Covent Garden, City of Westminster Parks Department, Curator of Dr Johnson's House, Church of St Dunstan in the West – Fleet Street, St Brides Church – Fleet Street, Samuel Pepys Exhibition – Fleet Street, St Andrews Church – Holborn, Church of St Magnus the Martyr – City of London, Public Relations Office – Corporation of London, Curator and Staff of Keats House Museum – Hampstead, St Mary's Church – Battersea, Dean & Chapter of Southwark Cathedral, Royal Artillery Barracks – Woolwich, St Mary's University College – Twickenham, Railtrack Press Office, Godolphin Boy's School – Hammersmith.

The Managers and Staff of: Museum Tavern – Bloomsbury, The Salisbury – Covent Garden, Sherlock Holmes – Strand, Punch Tavern – Fleet Street, Ye Olde Cheshire Cheese – Fleet Street, The Grapes – Limehouse, The George Inn – Borough, Trafalgar Tavern – Greenwich.

TEXT ACKNOWLEDGMENTS

The publishers and author are grateful to the following for permission to publish extracts from copyright material:

Julian Barnes: *Metroland* © Julian Barnes 1980. Reprinted by permission of Peters Fraser and Dunlop Limited on behalf of Julian Barnes. **H E Bates:** *The Blossoming World* courtesy of Laurence Pollinger Limited and The Estate of H E Bates. **Alan Bennett:** *Writing Home* © Alan Bennett, 1994. Courtesy of Faber and Faber (publishers). **John Betjeman:** *Summoned by Bells*, 'Business Girls' from *Collected Poems* courtesy of John Murray Publishers. **E R Braithwaite:** *To Sir With Love* © E R Braithwaite. Reprinted by kind permission of E R Braithwaite. **Roy Campbell:** *Dylan Thomas* by kind permission of Teresa Campbell. **John le Carré:** *Tinker, Tailor, Soldier, Spy* published by Hodder & Stoughton, courtesy of John le Carré and David Higham Associates. **Richard Church:** *Over The Bridge*, © Richard Church, 1955. Courtesy of Laurence Pollinger Limited and the Estate of Richard Church. **Quentin Crisp:** *The Naked Civil Servant* © Quentin Crisp. Reproduced by kind permission of HarperCollins Publishers. **Richard Ellman:** *Oscar Wilde*, (Hamish Hamilton 1987) © The Estate of Richard Ellman, 1987. Reproduced by kind permission of Penguin Books Ltd. **T S Eliot:** *The Waste Land*, courtesy of Faber & Faber (publishers) and David Higham Associates. **Kenneth Grahame:** Extract from a letter to Theodore Roosevelt copyright © The University Chest, Oxford. **Grahame Greene:** courtesy of Random House Group Ltd and David Higham Associates. **Patrick Hamilton:** *The Slaves of Solitude* © Patrick Hamilton 1947. Reprinted by kind permission of Constable & Robinson Publishing Ltd. *Twenty Thousand Streets Under the Sky*, © Patrick Hamilton 1987 and *Hangover Square* © Patrick Hamilton 1942 by permission of A M Heath & Co. Ltd. on behalf of the estate of Patrick Hamilton. **John Heath-Stubbs:** *On the Demolition of the Odeon Cinema* from *Collected Poems 1943–1987*, © John Heath-Stubbs, published by Carcanet, courtesy of David Higham Associates. **Nick Hornby:** *High Fidelity* courtesy of Nick Hornby, Victor Gollancz Ltd (publishers) and Peters Fraser and Dunlop Group Limited. **Rudyard Kipling:** *Something of Myself* courtesy of A P Watt on behalf of The National Trust for Places of Historic Interest or Natural Beauty. **Emanuel Litvinoff** © Tribune Publications Ltd. Reprinted by kind permission of Tribune. **Compton Mackenzie:** *My Life and Times*. Reproduced by kind permission of the Society of Authors as the Literary Representative of the estate of Compton Mackenzie. **Julian Maclaren-Ross:** *Memoirs of the Forties*, by kind permission of Mr Alexander Maclaren-Ross. **Louis MacNeice:** *Collected Poems* courtesy of Faber & Faber (publishers) and David Higham Associates. **Iris Murdoch:** *Under the Net* by Iris Murdoch, published by Chatto & Windus. Reprinted by permission of the Random House Group Ltd. **Joe Orton:** *Diary of a Somebody*, courtesy of Methuen. **George Orwell:** *Down and Out in Paris and London* © George Orwell 1933, and an extract taken from a letter written by Orwell which appears in *George Orwell* by Bernard Crick (1980). Reprinted by kind permission of A.M. Heath on behalf of the Estate of George Orwell. **Sylvia Plath:** *Edge* courtesy of Faber & Faber (publishers) and David Higham Associates. **Nicholas Royle:** *The Director's Cut*, by kind permission of Nicholas Royle. **Siegfried Sassoon:** *In The National Gallery* © Siegfried Sassoon by kind permission of George Sassoon. **Will Self:** courtesy of Will Self and ES Magazine. **Iain Sinclair:** *Lights Out for the Territory* published by Granta, *Downriver* published by Vintage, by kind permission of Iain Sinclair. **Muriel Spark:** *The Ballad of Peckham Rye*, courtesy of Penguin (publishers) and David Higham Associates. **Stephen Spender:** *Epilogue to a Human Drama*, by kind permission of Lady Spender. **P G Wodehouse:** *Psmith in the City* courtesy of A P Watt on behalf of The Trustees of the Wodehouse Estate. **Virginia Woolf:** *Extract from The Diaries of Virginia Woolf* by Virginia Woolf, published by the Hogarth Press, by kind permission of the executors of the Virginia Woolf Estate and The Random House Group Ltd.

The author and publishers offer their apologies to any copyright holders not named above whom they were unable to identify or contact before publication; and we would be pleased to hear from them, in order to rectify any mistakes in subsequent editions.